AF579213

Taste of Home

PROTEIN-PACKED MEALS

TASTE OF HOME BOOKS • RDA ENTHUSIAST BRANDS, LLC • MILWAUKEE, WI

1610 N. 2nd St., Suite 102,
Milwaukee WI 53212-3906

Visit us at **tasteofhome.com** for other Taste of Home books and products.

International Standard Book Number:
Trade: 979-8-88977-180-7
Special Market: 979-8-88977-231-6

Content Directors: Ellie Martin Cliffe, Mark Hagen
Creative Director: Raeann Thompson
Associate Creative Director: Jami Geittmann
Deputy Editor: Adila Matra
Senior Editors: Simrran Gill, Christine Rukavena
Senior Art Director: Courtney Lovetere
Manager, Production Design: Satyandra Raghav
Assistant Art Director: Jogesh Antony
Senior Print Publication Designer: Bipin Balakrishnan
Print Production Artist: Nandini Mittal
Deputy Editor, Copy Desk: Ann M. Walter
Senior Copy Editor: Elizabeth Pollock Bruch
Contributing Assistant Art Director: Julie Wagner
Contributing Recipe Editor: Julie Andrews, MS, RDN, FAND
Contributing Copy Editor: Sara Strauss

Cover Photography
Photographer: Mark Derse
Set Stylist: Melissa Franco
Food Stylists: Josh Rink, Allison Cebulla

Pictured on front cover:
Greek Grilled Chicken Pita Bowls, p. 50

Pictured on back cover:
Makeover Creamy Mac & Cheese, p. 239
Baked Pork Chops, p. 158
Easy Pepper Steak, p. 104
Shortcut Minestrone, p. 143
Protein Waffles, p. 264

Printed in China
1 3 5 7 9 10 8 6 4 2

P. 265

P. 88

P. 302

CONTENTS

HOW TO ...
CALCULATE YOUR PROTEIN NEEDS

When calculating how much protein you need, it helps to start with a few well-established guidelines and then adjust based on your lifestyle.

The Recommended Dietary Allowance (RDA) for protein is 0.8 grams per kilogram of body weight, which is the amount needed to support basic daily living—not performance or peak health. To determine your weight in kilograms, simply divide your weight in pounds by 2.2. For example, a 200-pound (90.9-kg) person would need about 72 grams of protein per day. If you're even moderately active, however, protein needs increase. **A more practical target for active individuals is about 1.0 to 1.2 grams per kilogram of body weight.** This translates to 91 to 109 grams of protein per day for a 200-pound person. For the purpose of this cookbook, aiming for **around 100 grams of protein per day** is a realistic, easy-to-follow goal.

Another helpful way to think about protein needs comes from the **Institute of Medicine's Acceptable Macronutrient Distribution Range (AMDR), which recommends that protein make up 10% to 35% of your total daily calories.** On a 2,000-calorie diet, that equals anywhere from 50 to 175 grams of protein per day.

These guidelines provide a helpful starting point for your protein journey. Use them as a framework and then adjust as needed to support your energy levels and muscle maintenance as well as your overall health.

P. 18

PROTEIN BOOST
PAGE 320

This highlights easy add-ins to amp up the protein in a recipe, helping you power up any dish with minimal effort.

LOOK FOR THESE ICONS:

Fast Fix: Dishes are table-ready in 30 minutes or less.

5-Ingredient: These dishes have five or fewer ingredients, excluding water, salt, pepper, oils and optional items.

Power-Packed/GLP-1 Friendly: Power-Packed recipes dish out comfort and nutrition, whether you're using GLP-1 medications or simply prioritizing nutrient-dense meals. Every serving delivers at least 14 grams of lean protein to support steady energy and help preserve muscle, plus a minimum of 4 grams of fiber for digestive and heart health. Paired with plenty of whole fruits and vegetables, these healthy recipes help support appetite regulation while providing great taste and nutrition.

SMART SWAPS

This table spotlights simple ingredient upgrades that can significantly increase the protein in everyday meals. Each swap indicates the amount of protein you'll gain, making it easy to make smarter choices at a glance.

INSTEAD OF ...	TRY THIS ...	PROTEIN GAIN
IN RECIPES		
1½ cups flour (for brownies)	15-oz. can black beans, rinsed, drained & pureed	5-6g
¼ cup panko bread crumbs (as a breading or binder)	¼ cup ground nuts	3-4g
Roux (4 Tbsp. butter + 4 Tbsp. flour), for thickening	1 cup mashed or pureed cooked beans	8-10g
½ cup heavy cream	½ cup evaporated milk OR ½ cup silken tofu, pureed	4.5-5.5g 5-6g
½ cup sour cream	½ cup Greek yogurt	8-10g
½ cup mayonnaise (as a recipe base)	½ cup blended cottage cheese	11-12g
1.75 oz. pectin (in jam)	¼ cup chia seeds	9-11g
Water or broth	1 cup bone broth	6-8g
BREAKFAST FOODS		
1 cup almond milk	1 cup soy or pea milk	7-8g
1 cup fruit juice in a smoothie	1 cup Greek yogurt in a smoothie	12-13g
½ cup traditional Cheerios cereal	½ cup high-protein Cheerios cereal	3-4g
¼ cup traditional granola	¼ cup chopped nuts, chia seeds or hemp seeds	3-10g
SIDE DISHES		
½ cup cooked orzo	½ cup cooked lentils	5-6g
½ cup cooked traditional pasta	½ cup cooked chickpea, lentil or other high-protein pasta	8-10g
2 oz. potato chips	2 oz. roasted edamame beans	11-12g
½ cup cooked white rice	½ cup cooked quinoa	2-3g
½ cup croutons	½ cup crispy roasted chickpeas OR ¼ cup nuts or seeds	5-6g 4-8g
CONDIMENTS		
2 tsp. butter	2 Tbsp. cream cheese	2g
2 Tbsp. chocolate hazelnut spread	2 Tbsp. nut butter	5-6g
2 Tbsp. fruit jam/jelly (as a spread)	2 Tbsp. jam prepared with chia seeds	3-4g

PROTEIN CHOICES

Choosing lean meats can help support fat loss and muscle gain while achieving an overall balance of macronutrients. They're great sources of protein, but their fat content varies by cut—some are lean or extra lean, others are higher in fat, and many are in between. This quick guide helps you make smarter protein choices for everyday meals.

CHOOSE THESE MEATS MORE OFTEN:

Fish and seafood:

- **Lean, mild choices:** Cod, tilapia, haddock, flounder, mahi mahi, halibut, Alaskan pollock, bass, shrimp, scallops, crab, clams, mussels, octopus
- **Fish rich in omega-3s:** Salmon, sardines, trout, mackerel, herring, anchovies. These are fattier, but much of that fat is heart-healthy omega-3s, making them a smart regular pick.

Poultry: Skinless breasts, wings, tenderloins and cutlets, skinless chicken thighs

Beef: Eye of round, round tip, top round and bottom round roast and steak; top sirloin and top loin steak; chuck shoulder and arm roasts

Pork: Pork tenderloin, boneless top loin chops and sirloin roasts

Ground meat: At least 90% lean

CHOOSE FATTY CUTS LESS OFTEN:

Poultry: Skin-on thighs and legs

Beef: Ribeye, porterhouse, T-bone, skirt steak, short ribs, brisket and chuck eye steak

Pork: Pork belly (bacon), pork shoulder, spareribs, sausage

Ground meat: Ground chuck (80% lean)

BUSTING PROTEIN MYTHS

1. IT'S HARD TO EAT ENOUGH PROTEIN ON A VEGAN OR VEGETARIAN DIET With thoughtful planning, it's entirely possible to meet protein needs on a plant-based diet. Foods like beans, lentils, tofu, edamame, nuts, seeds and whole grains can easily add up to adequate daily protein.

2. I DON'T NEED MUCH PROTEIN IF I'M NOT PHYSICALLY ACTIVE Protein is an important component of a healthy diet for all. It supports important functions in the body, including maintaining healthy organs, skin, hair and nails; produces and regulates essential enzymes and hormones; and transports nutrients in the blood, etc.

3. YOU NEED PROTEIN POWDER AND SHAKES TO HIT PROTEIN GOALS Protein powders and shakes can be convenient tools, especially for busy days, but they're not required. Most people can meet their protein goals through balanced meals built around whole-food sources.

4. MORE PROTEIN IS ALWAYS BETTER Your body can only use a certain amount of protein efficiently, and excess won't automatically translate to more muscle or better health. Balance and consistency matter just as much as total intake.

5. PLANT PROTEIN IS INFERIOR TO ANIMAL PROTEIN Plant proteins can, indeed, provide all essential amino acids when you eat a variety of sources throughout the day. A diverse, well-rounded plant-based diet can fully support muscle repair and overall health.

6. HIGH-PROTEIN DIETS CAUSE KIDNEY DAMAGE In healthy people, higher-protein diets have not been shown to cause kidney damage. Those with existing kidney disease should follow medical guidance, but protein itself isn't harmful for most individuals.

PROTEIN-POWERED MEALS FOR EVERY BUDGET

Our simple budget-friendly swaps and shopping tips help you eat more protein without spending more money.

PRIORITIZE INEXPENSIVE WHOLE-FOOD PROTEINS Some of the most affordable proteins are also the most nutritious, such as dry lentils, beans and chickpeas, peanut butter, store-brand Greek yogurt, canned tuna, salmon and sardines, and tofu.

PURCHASE DRY INSTEAD OF PRECOOKED WHEN POSSIBLE Dry beans, lentils, rice and oats cost significantly less than canned or prepackaged versions. If shopping for convenience items, like frozen, pouched or canned foods, choose the store brand and buy in bulk when they're on sale.

USE PROTEIN "BOOSTERS" IN REGULAR MEALS Simply add protein to what you already eat. Add lentils to pasta sauce, mix cottage cheese into scrambled eggs, add beans to salads or soups, and add lean meat to casseroles, stews, soups and pastas.

BUY LARGER QUANTITIES STRATEGICALLY Bigger tubs of yogurt are cheaper than single cups; large bags of rice, oats and beans are much cheaper per pound than smaller packages; and family packs of chicken can be portioned and frozen. Only bulk-buy foods you know you'll use in a reasonable amount of time.

REPLACE SOME MEAT WITH PLANT PROTEINS Meat is often the most expensive protein source. Try half ground beef, half beans or lentils in tacos; half chickpeas, half chicken in curry; and beans instead of extra meat in chili.

CHOOSE MEAT WITH A BUDGET IN MIND Chicken thighs are cheaper than chicken breasts (with similar amounts of protein), whole chickens are cheaper than precut pieces, pork shoulder or loin is often cheaper than beef, and frozen fish is usually more affordable than fresh.

MAKE YOUR OWN BROTH With our *Homemade Bone Broth recipe (p. 301),* you can use up bones, meat and vegetables that you have on hand. Packaged and canned broths and stocks are often expensive.

USE PROTEIN POWDERS AND PROTEIN PRODUCTS WISELY Whey protein in large tubs can sometimes be one of the cheapest cost-per-gram protein options. Use the powder in oatmeal, smoothies and shakes. Supplement with protein bars and snacks when convenient and in budget (but they are not necessary to hit your goals).

7-DAY MEAL PLAN

This 7-day meal plan is designed to help you reach approximately 100 grams of protein each day. Balanced across meals and snacks or desserts, it makes hitting your daily protein goal simple and achievable.

DAY 1: 106G	DAY 2: 106G	DAY 3: 101G	DAY 4: 101G	DAY 5: 105G	DAY 6: 102G	DAY 7: 106G
25G PRO Quinoa Breakfast Bowl, p. 258 1 oz. cheese	**27G PRO** Hash Brown Breakfast Casserole, p. 284	**17G PRO** Protein Pancakes, p. 281	**38G PRO** Powerhouse Protein Parfaits, p. 278 1 boiled egg	**31G PRO** French Omelet, p. 273 1 vegetarian sausage patty	**8G PRO** Italian Cloud Eggs, p. 258	**13G PRO** Mixed Berry French Toast Bake, p. 277
36G PRO Greek Grilled Chicken Pita Bowls, p. 50	**35G PRO** Pork Chop Cacciatore, p. 129	**30G PRO** Barley Beef Skillet, p. 103	**26G PRO** Italian Herb-Lentil Patties with Mozzarella, p. 231	**20G PRO** Spicy Tuna Crunch Wraps, p. 192	**43G PRO** Pork Souvlaki, p. 148	**38G PRO** All-Day Brisket with Potatoes, p. 123
40G PRO Garlic Herbed Grilled Tuna Steaks, p. 177	**34G PRO** Tuna Artichoke Melts, p. 188	**40G PRO** Tuna with Citrus Ponzu Sauce, p. 201	**22G PRO** Curry Pomegranate Protein Bowl, p. 242	**37G PRO** Crispy Buffalo Chicken Rolls-Ups for Two, p. 83	**40G PRO** Easy & Elegant Tenderloin Roast, p. 119	**40G PRO** Spicy Oven-Fried Chicken, p. 72
5G PRO Oatmeal Cookie Treats, p. 289	**10G PRO** Bananas Foster Frozen Protein Dessert, p. 289	**14G PRO** Open-Faced Roast Beef Sandwiches, p. 294	**15G PRO** Vegetarian Pea Soup, p. 221	**17G PRO** Teriyaki Beef Jerky, p. 305	**11G PRO** Protein Ice Cream, p. 313	**15G PRO** Vegetarian Pea Soup, p. 221

CHICKEN & TURKEY

26g Pro

MANGO CHICKEN WRAPS

These easy wraps are my go-to recipe when I want to make an exciting sandwich. The spiced chicken strips taste amazing with a tangy mango sauce.
—Jan Warren-Rucker, Clemmons, NC

TAKES: 30 MIN. • **MAKES:** 5 SERVINGS

- 1½ cups chopped peeled mangoes
- ¼ cup chopped red onion
- 1 jalapeno pepper, seeded and chopped
- 2 Tbsp. lime juice
- 1 tsp. honey
- ¼ cup fresh cilantro leaves
- 2 pkg. (6 oz. each) ready-to-use grilled chicken breast strips
- 1½ tsp. ground cumin
- ¾ tsp. garlic powder
- ¾ tsp. chili powder
- ⅛ tsp. cayenne pepper
- Dash dried oregano
- 4 tsp. olive oil
- 5 whole wheat tortillas (8 in.)
- ¾ cup shredded Monterey Jack cheese
- 1 small sweet red pepper, julienned
- ¾ cup chopped tomatoes
- 1 cup torn leaf lettuce

1. In a food processor, combine the mangoes, onion, jalapeno, lime juice and honey. Cover and process until pureed. Stir in cilantro; set aside.
2. In a large skillet, saute the chicken, cumin, garlic powder, chili powder, cayenne and oregano in oil until heated through. Spread the mango sauce over tortillas. Layer with chicken, cheese, red pepper, tomatoes and lettuce; roll up.
NOTE Wear disposable gloves when cutting hot peppers; the oils can burn skin. Avoid touching your face.
1 WRAP 340 cal., 12g fat (4g sat. fat), 56mg chol., 619mg sod., 36g carb. (10g sugars, 5g fiber), 26g pro.

34g Pro

TURKEY FAJITAS

I prepare these quick and easy fajitas about once a week, and my family never gets tired of them. I like serving them with salsa and light sour cream on the side.
—Bonnie Basinger, Lees Summit, MO

TAKES: 30 MIN. • **MAKES:** 4 SERVINGS

- 1 Tbsp. canola oil
- 1 lb. boneless turkey breast tenderloins, cut into thin strips
- 1 each medium green, sweet red and yellow peppers, cut into ¼-in. strips
- 1 medium onion, thinly sliced
- 1 garlic clove, minced
- ½ tsp. salt
- ½ tsp. ground cumin
- ½ tsp. pepper
- ¼ tsp. cayenne pepper
- ½ cup minced fresh cilantro
- ¼ cup lime juice
- 8 flour tortillas (6 in.), warmed

In a large nonstick skillet, heat oil over medium-high heat. Add turkey; cook and stir 2 minutes. Add peppers, onion, garlic, salt, cumin, pepper and cayenne. Cook and stir 5 minutes or until turkey is no longer pink and peppers are crisp-tender. Stir in cilantro and lime juice; cook 1 minute longer. Serve in tortillas.
2 FAJITAS 414 cal., 12g fat (3g sat. fat), 45mg chol., 766mg sod., 42g carb. (6g sugars, 5g fiber), 34g pro.

29g Pro

PANKO CHICKEN TENDERS

Crispy, savory and simple—what's not to like about these chicken tenders? This lightened-up version is baked, not fried.
—Margaret Knoebel, Milwaukee, WI

TAKES: 30 MIN. • **MAKES:** 4 SERVINGS

- ¾ cup panko bread crumbs
- 2 large eggs
- 1 Tbsp. prepared mustard
- ½ tsp. garlic powder
- ½ tsp. dried oregano
- ½ tsp. salt
- ¼ tsp. pepper
- 1 lb. chicken tenderloins

1. In a small skillet, heat panko over medium heat. Stir constantly, until crumbs are toasted, about 3 minutes. Remove from pan and cool completely.
2. Preheat oven to 400°. In a shallow bowl, whisk eggs and mustard. In another shallow bowl, toss toasted panko with garlic powder, oregano, salt and pepper. Dip chicken in egg mixture, then coat with crumb mixture.
3. Place on a baking sheet coated with cooking spray. Bake until coating is golden brown and chicken is no longer pink, 10-13 minutes.
3 OZ. COOKED CHICKEN 159 cal., 2g fat (0 sat. fat), 83mg chol., 495mg sod., 7g carb. (0 sugars, 0 fiber), 29g pro.

26g Pro

NECTARINE CHICKEN SALAD

When guests are coming for lunch or dinner in the warm summer months, I like to serve this attractive, colorful salad. The dressing is refreshingly tart. A neighbor shared the recipe with me years ago and I've passed it on many times.
—Cathy Ross, Van Nuys, CA

TAKES: 15 MIN. • **MAKES:** 4 SERVINGS

- ¼ cup lime juice
- 1 Tbsp. sugar
- 1 Tbsp. minced fresh thyme or 1 tsp. dried thyme
- 1 Tbsp. olive oil
- 1 garlic clove, minced
- 6 cups torn mixed salad greens
- 1 lb. boneless skinless chicken breasts, cooked and sliced
- 5 medium ripe nectarines, thinly sliced

1. In a jar with a tight-fitting lid, combine lime juice, sugar, thyme, oil and garlic; shake well.
2. On a serving platter, arrange salad greens, chicken and nectarines. Drizzle with dressing. Serve immediately.
1½ CUPS 266 cal., 7g fat (1g sat. fat), 63mg chol., 76mg sod., 27g carb. (21g sugars, 5g fiber), 26g pro.

25g Pro

LASAGNA DELIZIOSA

Everyone loves this lasagna. It's often served as a birthday treat for guests. I've lightened it up a lot from the original, but no one can tell the difference!
—Heather O'Neill, Troy, OH

PREP: 45 MIN.
BAKE: 50 MIN. + STANDING
MAKES: 12 SERVINGS

- 9 uncooked lasagna noodles
- 1 pkg. (19½ oz.) Italian turkey sausage links, casings removed
- ½ lb. lean ground beef (90% lean)
- 1 large onion, chopped
- 2 garlic cloves, minced
- 1 can (28 oz.) diced tomatoes, undrained
- 1 can (12 oz.) tomato paste
- ¼ cup water
- 2 tsp. sugar
- 1 tsp. dried basil
- ½ tsp. fennel seed
- ¼ tsp. pepper
- 1 large egg, lightly beaten
- 1 carton (15 oz.) reduced-fat ricotta cheese
- 1 Tbsp. minced fresh parsley
- ½ tsp. salt
- 2 cups shredded part-skim mozzarella cheese
- ¾ cup grated Parmesan cheese
- Torn fresh basil leaves, optional

1. Cook noodles according to package directions. Meanwhile, in a Dutch oven, cook and crumble sausage and beef with onion over medium heat until meat is no longer pink. Add garlic; cook 1 minute longer. Drain.

2. Stir in tomatoes, tomato paste, water, sugar, basil, fennel and pepper. Bring to a boil. Reduce heat; cover and simmer 15-20 minutes, stirring occasionally.

3. Meanwhile, preheat oven to 375°. In a small bowl, combine egg, ricotta cheese, parsley and salt. Drain noodles and rinse in cold water. Spread 1 cup meat sauce into a 13x9-in. baking dish coated with cooking spray. Top with 3 noodles, 2 cups meat sauce, ⅔ cup ricotta mixture, ⅔ cup mozzarella and ¼ cup Parmesan cheese. Repeat layers twice.

4. Cover and bake 40 minutes. Uncover; bake 10-15 minutes longer or until bubbly. Let stand for 10 minutes before cutting. If desired, top with fresh basil leaves and sprinkle with additional Parmesan.

1 PIECE 323 cal., 12g fat (5g sat. fat), 79mg chol., 701mg sod., 28g carb. (11g sugars, 4g fiber), 25g pro.

NOTES

HEALTH TIP

Cut the sodium in this lasagna by omitting the salt and using no-salt-added diced tomatoes and tomato paste.

25g Pro

ITALIAN MUSHROOM MEAT LOAF

Healthful oats and flaxseed amp up the nutrition in this tasty Italian meat loaf.
—Kylie (Petrulia) Werning, Candler, NC

PREP: 30 MIN. • **BAKE:** 1 HOUR
MAKES: 8 SERVINGS

- 1 large egg, lightly beaten
- ¼ lb. fresh mushrooms, chopped
- ½ cup old-fashioned oats
- ½ cup chopped red onion
- ¼ cup ground flaxseed
- ½ tsp. pepper
- 1 pkg. (19½ oz.) Italian turkey sausage links, casings removed, crumbled
- 1 lb. ground beef (90% lean)
- 1 cup marinara or spaghetti sauce
- Shredded Parmesan cheese, optional

1. Preheat oven to 350°. In a large bowl, combine the egg, mushrooms, oats, onion, flaxseed and pepper. Crumble turkey and beef over mixture; mix lightly but thoroughly.
2. Shape into a 10x4-in. loaf. Place in a 13x9-in. baking dish coated with cooking spray. Bake, uncovered, for 50 minutes; drain. Top with marinara sauce. Bake until no pink remains and a thermometer inserted in center of meat loaf reads 160°, 10-15 minutes longer. If desired, top with Parmesan cheese.
1 PIECE 261 cal., 14g fat (3g sat. fat), 103mg chol., 509mg sod., 10g carb. (3g sugars, 2g fiber), 25g pro.

37g Pro

SLOW-COOKED CURRY CHICKEN

Our three children love the spicy flavors found in this dish. Add more or less curry depending on your taste preferences.
—Helen Toulantis, Wantagh, NY

PREP: 25 MIN. • **COOK:** 4½ HOURS
MAKES: 6 SERVINGS

- 6 boneless skinless chicken breast halves (6 oz. each)
- 1¼ tsp. salt
- 1 can (13.66 oz.) light coconut milk
- 1 tsp. curry powder
- ½ tsp. ground turmeric
- ½ tsp. cayenne pepper
- 3 green onions, sliced, divided
- 2 Tbsp. cornstarch
- 2 Tbsp. cold water
- 1 to 2 Tbsp. lime juice
- 3 cups hot cooked rice

1. Sprinkle chicken with salt. In a large skillet coated with cooking spray, brown chicken on both sides. Place in a 5-qt. slow cooker.
2. Combine the coconut milk, curry, turmeric and cayenne; pour over chicken. Sprinkle with half the onions. Cover and cook on low for 4-5 hours or until chicken is tender.
3. Combine cornstarch and water until smooth; stir into slow cooker. Cover and cook on high for 30 minutes or until sauce is thickened. Stir in the lime juice. Serve chicken with rice and sauce; sprinkle with remaining onions.
1 SERVING 353 cal., 9g fat (5g sat. fat), 94mg chol., 576mg sod., 27g carb. (2g sugars, 1g fiber), 37g pro.

PROTEIN BOOST
PAGE 320

23g Pro

SKINNY COBB SALAD

This skinny version of Cobb salad has all the taste and creaminess with half the fat and calories. You can skip the coleslaw mix and use all lettuce, but I like the crunch you get with cabbage.
—Taylor Kiser, Brandon, FL

TAKES: 25 MIN. • **MAKES:** 4 SERVINGS

- ¼ cup fat-free plain Greek yogurt
- 2 Tbsp. reduced-fat ranch salad dressing
- 1 to 2 tsp. cold water

SALAD

- 3 cups coleslaw mix
- 3 cups chopped lettuce
- 1 large apple, chopped
- ½ cup crumbled reduced-fat feta or blue cheese
- 1 cup cubed cooked chicken breast
- 2 green onions, chopped
- 4 turkey bacon strips, chopped and cooked
- 1 can (15 oz.) garbanzo beans or chickpeas, rinsed and drained
- 1 small ripe avocado, peeled and cubed

1. Mix yogurt and dressing; thin with water as desired. Toss coleslaw mix with lettuce; divide among 4 plates.
2. Arrange remaining ingredients in rows over top. Drizzle with yogurt mixture.

1 SERVING 324 cal., 13g fat (3g sat. fat), 48mg chol., 646mg sod., 31g carb. (11g sugars, 9g fiber), 23g pro.

23g Pro

15-MINUTE MARINATED CHICKEN

Whenever I serve this grilled chicken to family and friends, which is quite often, I'm bound to be asked for the recipe. It's a fast and tasty meal that I'm happy to share with others.
—Pam Shinogle, Arlington, TX

PREP: 15 MIN. + MARINATING
GRILL: 10 MIN. • **MAKES:** 4 SERVINGS

- ¼ cup Dijon mustard
- 2 Tbsp. lemon juice
- 1½ tsp. Worcestershire sauce
- ½ tsp. dried tarragon
- ¼ tsp. pepper
- 4 boneless skinless chicken breast halves (4 oz. each)

1. In a shallow dish, combine the first 5 ingredients; add chicken and turn to coat. Marinate at room temperature for 15 minutes or refrigerate up to 4 hours.
2. Drain chicken, discarding marinade. Grill, uncovered, over medium heat for 8-12 minutes, turning once, or until a thermometer reads 170°.
1 CHICKEN BREAST HALF 141 cal., 3g fat (1g sat. fat), 63mg chol., 436mg sod., 1g carb. (0 sugars, 0 fiber), 23g pro.

15g Pro

TUSCAN TURKEY SOUP

Ladle up this quick creamy soup chock-full of turkey, pumpkin and cannellini beans for hungry family and friends. It's fabulous!
—Marie McConnell, Shelbyville, IL

TAKES: 30 MIN.
MAKES: 8 SERVINGS (2 QT.)

- 2 Tbsp. olive oil
- 1 cup chopped onion
- 1 cup chopped celery
- 2 garlic cloves, minced
- 2 cans (14½ oz. each) reduced-sodium chicken broth
- 1 can (15 oz.) pumpkin
- 1 can (15 oz.) cannellini beans, rinsed and drained
- 2 cups cubed cooked turkey
- ½ tsp. salt
- ½ tsp. dried basil
- ¼ tsp. pepper
- Grated Parmesan cheese, optional

1. In a large saucepan, heat oil over medium-high heat. Add onion and celery; cook and stir until tender. Add garlic; cook 1 minute longer.
2. Stir in broth, pumpkin, beans, turkey, salt, basil and pepper. Heat through, stirring occasionally. If desired, serve with cheese.
1 CUP 167 cal., 6g fat (1g sat. fat), 27mg chol., 549mg sod., 14g carb. (3g sugars, 5g fiber), 15g pro.

28g Pro

PAN-ROASTED CHICKEN & VEGETABLES

This one-dish meal tastes as if it took hours of hands-on time, but the simple ingredients can be prepped in minutes. The rosemary gives it a rich flavor, and the meat juices cook the veggies to perfection. So easy!
—Sherri Melotik, Oak Creek, WI

PREP: 15 MIN. • **BAKE:** 45 MIN.
MAKES: 6 SERVINGS

- 2 lbs. red potatoes (about 6 medium), cut into ¾-in. pieces
- 1 large onion, coarsely chopped
- 2 Tbsp. olive oil
- 3 garlic cloves, minced
- 1 Tbsp. minced fresh rosemary or 1 tsp. dried rosemary, crushed
- 1¼ tsp. salt, divided
- ¾ tsp. pepper, divided
- ½ tsp. paprika
- 6 bone-in chicken thighs (about 2¼ lbs.), skin removed
- 6 cups fresh baby spinach (about 6 oz.)
- Lemon wedges, optional

1. Preheat the oven to 425°. In a large bowl, combine potatoes, onion, oil, garlic, fresh or dried rosemary, ¾ tsp. salt and ½ tsp. pepper; toss to coat. Transfer to a 15x10x1-in. baking pan coated with cooking spray.
2. In a small bowl, mix paprika and the remaining ½ tsp. salt and ¼ tsp. pepper. Sprinkle chicken with paprika mixture; arrange over potatoes and onion. Roast until a thermometer inserted in chicken reads 170°-175° and potatoes and onion are just tender, 35-40 minutes.
3. Remove chicken to a serving platter; keep warm. Top potatoes and onion with spinach. Roast until potatoes and onion are tender and spinach is wilted, 8-10 minutes longer. Stir vegetables to combine; serve with chicken. If desired, serve with additional fresh rosemary and lemon wedges.

1 CHICKEN THIGH WITH 1 CUP VEGETABLES
357 cal., 14g fat (3g sat. fat), 87mg chol., 597mg sod., 28g carb. (3g sugars, 4g fiber), 28g pro.

PROTEIN PICK

If you want a richer dish, you can use skin-on chicken, and if you want a lighter dish, use bone-in chicken breasts. Be sure to cook bone-in breasts just to 165-170°, since leaner meat can become dry at higher temperatures.

41g Pro

TZATZIKI CHICKEN

I like to make classic chicken recipes for my family but the real fun is trying a fresh new twist.
—Kristen Heigl, Staten Island, NY

TAKES: 30 MIN. • **MAKES:** 4 SERVINGS

- 1½ cups finely chopped peeled English cucumber
- 1 cup plain Greek yogurt
- 2 garlic cloves, minced
- 1½ tsp. chopped fresh dill
- 1½ tsp. olive oil
- ⅛ tsp. salt

CHICKEN

- ⅔ cup all-purpose flour
- 1 tsp. salt
- 1 tsp. pepper
- ¼ tsp. baking powder
- 1 large egg
- ⅓ cup 2% milk
- 4 boneless skinless chicken breast halves (6 oz. each)
- ¼ cup canola oil
- ¼ cup crumbled feta cheese
- Lemon wedges, optional

1. For sauce, mix the first 6 ingredients; refrigerate until serving.

2. In a shallow bowl, whisk together flour, salt, pepper and baking powder. In another bowl, whisk together egg and milk. Pound chicken breasts with a meat mallet to ½-in. thickness. Dip in flour mixture to coat both sides; shake off excess. Dip in egg mixture, then again in flour mixture.

3. In a large skillet, heat oil over medium heat. Cook chicken until golden brown and juices run clear, 5-7 minutes per side. Top with cheese. Serve with sauce and, if desired, additional fresh dill and lemon wedges.

1 CHICKEN BREAST HALF WITH ⅓ CUP SAUCE 482 cal., 27g fat (7g sat. fat), 133mg chol., 737mg sod., 17g carb. (4g sugars, 1g fiber), 41g pro.

CUCUMBER SWAP

An English cucumber works well in this recipe because it's seedless and doesn't thin out the sauce. But a regular cucumber can be used too—just seed before chopping.

33g Pro

TURKEY GINGER NOODLE SOUP

I wanted something comforting yet healthy. Ginger is my favorite spice, so this recipe was a must-try—and it didn't disappoint.
—Adina Monson, Nanaimo, BC

PREP: 20 MIN. • **COOK:** 4¼ HOURS
MAKES: 8 SERVINGS (3 QT.)

- 2 medium carrots, sliced
- 2 cans (8 oz. each) sliced water chestnuts, drained
- 3 to 4 Tbsp. minced fresh gingerroot
- 2 Tbsp. minced fresh parsley
- 2 tsp. chili powder
- 4 cups chicken stock
- 1 can (11.8 oz.) coconut water
- 3 Tbsp. lemon juice
- 2 lbs. boneless skinless turkey breast, cut into 1-in. cubes
- 2 tsp. pepper
- ½ tsp. salt
- 2 Tbsp. canola oil
- 1 cup frozen corn (about 5 oz.), thawed
- 1 cup frozen peas (about 4 oz.), thawed
- 8 oz. rice noodles or thin spaghetti

1. Place the first 8 ingredients in a 4- or 5-qt. slow cooker.
2. Toss turkey with pepper and salt. In a large skillet, heat oil over medium-high heat; brown turkey in batches. Add to slow cooker.
3. Cook, covered, on low 4-5 hours, until carrots are tender. Stir in corn and peas; heat through.
4. Cook noodles according to package directions; drain. Add to soup just before serving.

1½ CUPS 351 cal., 6g fat (1g sat. fat), 65mg chol., 672mg sod., 41g carb. (5g sugars, 4g fiber), 33g pro.

VEGGIE YOUR WAY

Switch up your veggies by using whatever you have on hand in place of the corn and peas. However, the more you add, the less stock remains at the end. So if you wish to load the soup with vegetables, add more stock or less noodles.

33g Pro

ITALIAN TURKEY SLOPPY JOES

Everyone seems to love my take on sloppy joes. For a change, I often fix them with ground chicken instead of ground turkey and use fresh parsley and oregano.
—Charlene Chambers, Ormond Beach, FL

PREP: 15 MIN. • **COOK:** 45 MIN.
MAKES: 8 SERVINGS

- 1 pkg. (19½ oz.) hot Italian turkey sausage links, casings removed
- 1 lb. extra-lean ground turkey
- 1 medium green pepper, chopped
- 1 small onion, chopped
- 4 garlic cloves, minced
- 2 cans (8 oz. each) no-salt-added tomato sauce
- 2 Tbsp. no-salt-added tomato paste
- 1 Tbsp. chili powder
- 2 tsp. dried parsley flakes
- 1 tsp. dried oregano
- 8 whole wheat hamburger buns, split
- ¾ cup shredded part-skim mozzarella cheese
- ¼ cup shredded Parmesan cheese

1. In a Dutch oven, cook the sausage, turkey, pepper and onion over medium heat until the meat is no longer pink, breaking it into crumbles. Add garlic; cook 1 minute longer. Drain. Stir in the tomato sauce, tomato paste and seasonings. Bring to a boil. Reduce heat; cover and simmer for 30 minutes.
2. Spoon ¾ cup turkey mixture onto each bun; sprinkle with cheeses.

1 SANDWICH 348 cal., 12g fat (3g sat. fat), 72mg chol., 775mg sod., 30g carb. (8g sugars, 5g fiber), 33g pro.

34g Pro 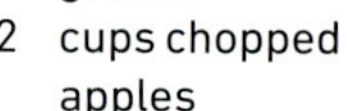

APPLE ORCHARD CHICKEN SALAD

My husband and I love salads, and we especially love this one! The apple flavor really compliments the tender chicken and rich cheese. You'll love how quickly this elegant medley comes together!
—Deborah Purdue, Westland, MI

TAKES: 20 MIN. • **MAKES:** 4 SERVINGS

- 4 boneless skinless chicken breast halves (5 oz. each)
- 6 Tbsp. thawed apple juice concentrate
- ¼ cup canola oil
- 2 Tbsp. vanilla yogurt
- 8 cups torn mixed salad greens
- 2 cups chopped apples
- 1 small red onion, cut into rings
- ½ cup chopped pecans
- ¼ cup crumbled Gorgonzola cheese
- 1 pkg. (2½ oz.) dried apple chips

1. Grill chicken on an indoor grill coated with cooking spray for 5-7 minutes or until a thermometer reads 165°. Meanwhile, for dressing, combine the apple juice concentrate, oil and yogurt in a jar with a tight-fitting lid; shake well.
2. On 4 plates, arrange the salad greens, apples, onion rings, pecans and cheese. Slice chicken; place over salads. Drizzle with dressing. Sprinkle with apple chips.

1 SERVING 588 cal., 34g fat (5g sat. fat), 85mg chol., 256mg sod., 41g carb. (26g sugars, 7g fiber), 34g pro.

24g Pro

CHICKEN TIKKA

Chicken tikka skewers make an easy and delectable party food. Though this recipe is mild, you can dial up the spice by increasing the amount of chili powder.
—Aleni Salcedo, East Elmhurst, NY

PREP: 15 MIN. + MARINATING
COOK: 25 MIN. • **MAKES:** 8 SERVINGS

- 1 cup plain Greek yogurt
- 2 Tbsp. lemon juice
- 2 Tbsp. garam masala
- 1 Tbsp. minced garlic
- 1 Tbsp. minced fresh gingerroot
- 1 Tbsp. paprika
- 1 tsp. salt
- 1 tsp. ground turmeric
- 1 tsp. chili powder
- 1 tsp. ground cumin
- 1 tsp. ground coriander
- ½ tsp. pepper
- 2 lbs. boneless skinless chicken breasts, cubed
- Metal or wooden skewers

1. In a large bowl, whisk together first 12 ingredients. Add chicken, tossing to coat. Cover; refrigerate 2 hours.
2. Preheat oven to 350°. On metal or soaked wooden skewers, thread chicken. Place on a parchment or foil-lined rimmed baking sheet; bake until chicken is cooked through, 25-30 minutes.
1 SKEWER 163 cal., 6g fat (3g sat. fat), 70mg chol., 378mg sod., 3g carb. (1g sugars, 1g fiber), 24g pro.

30g Pro

CRISPY ASIAN CHICKEN SALAD

Asian flavor, crunchy almonds and crispy chicken make this salad special.
—Beth Dauenhauer, Pueblo, CO

TAKES: 30 MIN. • **MAKES:** 2 SERVINGS

- 2 boneless skinless chicken breast halves (4 oz. each)
- 2 tsp. hoisin sauce
- 1 tsp. sesame oil
- ½ cup panko bread crumbs
- 4 tsp. sesame seeds
- 2 tsp. canola oil
- 4 cups spring mix salad greens
- 1 small green pepper, julienned
- 1 small sweet red pepper, julienned
- 1 medium carrot, julienned
- ½ cup sliced fresh mushrooms
- 2 Tbsp. thinly sliced onion
- 2 Tbsp. sliced almonds, toasted
- ¼ cup reduced-fat sesame ginger salad dressing

1. Flatten chicken breasts to ½-in. thickness. Combine hoisin sauce and sesame oil; brush over chicken. In a shallow bowl, combine bread crumbs and sesame seeds; dip chicken into mixture.

2. In a large nonstick skillet, cook chicken in oil until no longer pink, 5-6 minutes on each side.

3. Meanwhile, divide salad greens between 2 plates. Top with peppers, carrot, mushrooms and onion. Slice chicken; place on top. Sprinkle with almonds and drizzle with dressing.

1 SERVING 386 cal., 17g fat (2g sat. fat), 63mg chol., 620mg sod., 29g carb. (11g sugars, 6g fiber), 30g pro.

NOTES

35g Pro

CARIBBEAN CHICKEN STEW

I lived with a West Indian family for a while and enjoyed watching them cook. I lightened up this recipe by leaving out the oil and sugar, removing the skin from the chicken and using chicken sausage.
—Joanne Iovino, Kings Park, NY

PREP: 25 MIN. + MARINATING
COOK: 6 HOURS • **MAKES:** 8 SERVINGS

- ¼ cup ketchup
- 3 garlic cloves, minced
- 1 Tbsp. sugar
- 1 Tbsp. hot pepper sauce
- 1 tsp. browning sauce, optional
- 1 tsp. dried basil
- 1 tsp. dried thyme
- 1 tsp. paprika
- ½ tsp. salt
- ½ tsp. dried oregano
- ½ tsp. ground allspice
- ½ tsp. pepper
- 8 bone-in chicken thighs (about 3 lbs.), skin removed
- 1 lb. fully cooked andouille chicken sausage links, sliced
- 1 medium onion, finely chopped
- 2 medium carrots, finely chopped
- 2 celery ribs, finely chopped
- Hot cooked rice, optional

1. In a bowl, combine ketchup, garlic, sugar, pepper sauce and, if desired, browning sauce; stir in seasonings. Add chicken thighs, sausage and vegetables. Cover; refrigerate 8 hours or overnight.
2. Transfer chicken mixture to a 4- or 5-qt. slow cooker. Cook, covered, on low until chicken is tender, 6-8 hours. If desired, serve with rice.

1 SERVING 309 cal., 14g fat (4g sat. fat), 131mg chol., 666mg sod., 9g carb. (6g sugars, 1g fiber), 35g pro.

CARIBBEAN CHICKEN STEW TIPS

What is browning sauce? Browning sauce is an ingredient used to add flavor and brown color to recipes. It's used in this Caribbean chicken stew to enhance the color traditionally provided by brown sugar. You can find the sauce in the grocery store near the broth and gravy.

How can you make Caribbean chicken stew your own? To make this a more traditional Caribbean-inspired recipe, leave the skin on the chicken thighs, use traditional andouille sausage and brown the chicken in oil and brown sugar.

Easy, tasty and quick! It will make my rotation menu.
—LADENE, TASTEOFHOME.COM

31g Pro

AIR-FRYER COCONUT-CRUSTED TURKEY STRIPS

My granddaughter shared these turkey strips with me. With a plum dipping sauce, they're just the thing for a light supper.
—Agnes Ward, Stratford, ON

PREP: 20 MIN. • **COOK:** 10 MIN./BATCH
MAKES: 6 SERVINGS

- 2 large egg whites
- 2 tsp. sesame oil
- ½ cup sweetened shredded coconut, lightly toasted
- ½ cup dry bread crumbs
- 2 Tbsp. sesame seeds, toasted
- ½ tsp. salt
- 1½ lbs. turkey breast tenderloins, cut into ½-in. strips
- Cooking spray

DIPPING SAUCE

- ½ cup plum sauce
- ⅓ cup unsweetened pineapple juice
- 1½ tsp. prepared mustard
- 1 tsp. cornstarch
- Optional: Grated lime zest and lime wedges

1. Preheat air fryer to 400°. In a shallow bowl, whisk egg whites and oil. In another shallow bowl, mix coconut, bread crumbs, sesame seeds and salt. Dip turkey into egg mixture, then into coconut mixture, patting to help coating adhere.

2. Working in batches, place turkey in a single layer on a greased tray in air-fryer basket; spritz with cooking spray. Cook until golden brown, 3-4 minutes. Turn; spritz with cooking spray. Cook until golden brown and turkey is no longer pink, 3-4 minutes longer.

3. Meanwhile, in a small saucepan, mix 4 sauce ingredients. Bring to a boil; cook and stir until thickened, 1-2 minutes. Serve turkey with sauce. If desired, top turkey strips with grated lime zest and serve with lime wedges.

3 OZ. COOKED TURKEY WITH 2 TBSP. SAUCE 292 cal., 9g fat (3g sat. fat), 45mg chol., 517mg sod., 24g carb. (5g sugars, 1g fiber), 31g pro.

NOTES

24g Pro

CHICKEN VERONIQUE

I found this recipe in a gardening book. My family just loves it, and it's super easy! We think it's excellent served with rice pilaf on the side.
—Anita Dudiwka, Akron, OH

PREP: 15 MIN. • **COOK:** 20 MIN.
MAKES: 6 SERVINGS

- 6 boneless skinless chicken breast halves (4 oz. each)
- ¼ tsp. salt
- ⅛ tsp. ground nutmeg
- 4 tsp. butter
- ⅔ cup white wine or reduced-sodium chicken broth
- 2 Tbsp. orange marmalade spreadable fruit
- ¾ tsp. dried tarragon
- 2 tsp. all-purpose flour
- ½ cup half-and-half cream
- 1½ cups green grapes, halved

1. Sprinkle chicken with salt and nutmeg. In a large nonstick skillet, cook chicken in butter over medium heat for 3-5 minutes on each side or until lightly browned.
2. In a small bowl, combine the wine, marmalade and tarragon. Add to skillet; bring to a boil. Reduce heat; cover and simmer chicken for 4-6 minutes on each side or until a thermometer reads 170°. Remove chicken and keep warm.
3. Combine flour and cream until smooth. Gradually stir into skillet. Bring to a boil; cook 2 minutes longer or until thickened. Stir in grapes; heat through. Serve with chicken.

1 SERVING 226 cal., 7g fat (4g sat. fat), 79mg chol., 191mg sod., 13g carb. (10g sugars, 1g fiber), 24g pro.

31g Pro

EASY MEDITERRANEAN CHICKEN

Everyone I know loves this special chicken recipe. I changed a few things to make it healthier, but it tastes just as good.
—Kara Zilis, Oak Forest, IL

TAKES: 30 MIN. • **MAKES:** 4 SERVINGS

- 4 boneless skinless chicken breast halves (4 oz. each)
- 1 Tbsp. olive oil
- 1 can (14½ oz.) no-salt-added stewed tomatoes
- 1 cup water
- 1 tsp. dried oregano
- ¼ tsp. garlic powder
- 1½ cups instant brown rice
- 1 pkg. (12 oz.) frozen cut green beans
- 12 pitted Greek olives, halved
- ½ cup crumbled feta cheese

1. In a large nonstick skillet, brown chicken in oil on each side. Stir in the tomatoes, water, oregano and garlic powder. Bring to a boil; reduce heat. Cover and simmer 10 minutes.
2. Stir in rice and green beans. Return to a boil. Cover and simmer until a thermometer reads 165° and rice is tender, 8-10 minutes longer. Stir in olives; sprinkle with cheese.

1 SERVING 417 cal., 12g fat (3g sat. fat), 70mg chol., 386mg sod., 44g carb. (6g sugars, 6g fiber), 31g pro.

32g Pro

CHICKEN PESTO MEATBALLS

These tender pesto-stuffed meatballs get gobbled up in our house. They're short on ingredients but packed with flavor. I always make a double batch, freezing the other half for a busy night.
—Ally Billhorn, Wilton, IA

TAKES: 30 MIN. • **MAKES:** 4 SERVINGS

- 6 oz. uncooked whole grain spaghetti
- ¼ cup dry bread crumbs
- 2 Tbsp. prepared pesto
- 2 Tbsp. grated Parmesan cheese
- 1 tsp. garlic powder
- 1 lb. lean ground chicken
- 1½ cups marinara sauce
- ¼ cup water
- Optional: Torn fresh basil and additional Parmesan cheese

1. Cook spaghetti according to package directions; drain.
2. In a large bowl, combine bread crumbs, pesto, cheese and garlic powder. Add chicken; mix lightly but thoroughly. Shape into 1-in. balls.
3. In a large skillet, brown meatballs over medium heat, turning occasionally. Add sauce and water; bring to a boil. Reduce heat; simmer, covered, until meatballs are cooked through, about 5 minutes. Serve with spaghetti. If desired, top with basil and additional cheese.

FREEZE OPTION Freeze cooled meatball mixture in freezer containers. To use, partially thaw in refrigerator overnight. Heat through in a covered saucepan over low heat, stirring gently; add water if necessary.

¾ CUP MEATBALL MIXTURE WITH 1 CUP SPAGHETTI 422 cal., 12g fat (3g sat. fat), 85mg chol., 706mg sod., 45g carb. (7g sugars, 7g fiber), 32g pro.

35g Pro

STRAWBERRY MINT CHICKEN

I handpick wild strawberries for this saucy chicken dish. We love it with fresh spring greens and a sweet white wine.
—Alicia Duerst, River Falls, WI

TAKES: 30 MIN. • **MAKES:** 4 SERVINGS

- 1 Tbsp. cornstarch
- 1 Tbsp. sugar
- ⅛ tsp. ground nutmeg
- ⅛ tsp. pepper
- ½ cup water
- 1 cup fresh strawberries, coarsely chopped
- ½ cup white wine or white grape juice
- 2 tsp. minced fresh mint

CHICKEN

- 4 boneless skinless chicken breast halves (6 oz. each)
- ½ tsp. salt
- ¼ tsp. pepper
- Sliced green onion

1. In a small saucepan, mix the first 5 ingredients until smooth; stir in strawberries and wine. Bring to a boil. Reduce heat; simmer, uncovered, 3-5 minutes or until thickened and strawberries are softened, stirring occasionally. Remove from heat; stir in mint.
2. Sprinkle chicken with salt and pepper. On a lightly oiled grill rack, grill chicken, covered, over medium heat 5-7 minutes on each side or until a thermometer reads 165°; brush occasionally with ¼ cup sauce during the last 4 minutes. Serve with remaining sauce. Sprinkle with green onion.

1 CHICKEN BREAST HALF WITH ¼ CUP SAUCE 224 cal., 4g fat (1g sat. fat), 94mg chol., 378mg sod., 8g carb. (5g sugars, 1g fiber), 35g pro.

30g Pro

GINGER-CURRY CHICKEN TACOS

I love tacos (who doesn't?), but I wanted to put my own unique twist on them by incorporating some Indian flavors. This ginger-curry version hit the spot!
—Michael Cohen, Los Angeles, CA

PREP: 25 MIN. • **COOK:** 10 MIN.
MAKES: 4 SERVINGS

- ⅔ cup chopped cucumber
- ⅔ cup chopped peeled mango
- ⅓ cup chopped red onion
- ½ serrano pepper, seeded and sliced
- 3 Tbsp. lime juice, divided
- ¼ tsp. salt, divided
- ⅛ tsp. pepper, divided
- ⅓ cup fat-free plain Greek yogurt
- ½ tsp. minced fresh gingerroot
- ⅛ tsp. curry powder

TACOS

- 1 tsp. canola oil
- 1 lb. boneless skinless chicken breasts, cut into ½-in. cubes
- 1 tsp. curry powder
- ⅛ tsp. salt
- ⅛ tsp. pepper
- 4 naan flatbreads, halved, or 8 corn tortillas (6 in.), warmed
- 1½ tsp. minced fresh mint
- Lime wedges

1. In a small bowl, combine the cucumber, mango, red onion, serrano pepper, 2 Tbsp. lime juice, ⅛ tsp. salt and dash of pepper. In another small bowl, combine the yogurt, ginger, curry powder, remaining lime juice, and remaining salt and pepper.

2. For the tacos, in a large nonstick skillet, heat oil over medium-high heat. Sprinkle chicken with curry, salt and pepper. Cook chicken until no longer pink, 6-8 minutes. Serve in naan halves with mango slaw, yogurt sauce and mint. Garnish with lime wedges.

NOTE Wear disposable gloves when cutting hot peppers; the oils can burn skin. Avoid touching your face.

2 TACOS 335 cal., 8g fat (2g sat. fat), 68mg chol., 768mg sod., 36g carb. (9g sugars, 2g fiber), 30g pro.

ZERO-WASTE GINGER

Seal fresh gingerroot in an airtight container in the freezer. That way, when you need just a little bit, you can grate the frozen chunk directly into your dish. Then just put it back into the freezer for the next time you need a bright pop of flavor.

> This is delicious! I threw in another half cup of noodles to bulk it up a bit and there was still enough broth, even after reheating leftovers. Great recipe!
>
> —REBECCA967, TASTEOFHOME.COM

18g Pro

AMISH CHICKEN CORN SOUP

Creamed corn and butter make my chicken noodle soup homey and rich. This recipe makes a big batch, but the soup freezes well for future meals.
—Beverly Hoffman, Sandy Lake, PA

PREP: 15 MIN. • **COOK:** 50 MIN.
MAKES: 12 SERVINGS (4 QT.)

- 1 medium onion, chopped
- 2 celery ribs, chopped
- 1 cup shredded carrots
- 2 lbs. boneless skinless chicken breasts, cubed
- 3 chicken bouillon cubes
- 1 tsp. salt
- ¼ tsp. pepper
- 12 cups water
- 2 cups uncooked egg noodles
- 2 cans (14¾ oz. each) cream-style corn
- ¼ cup butter
- Optional: Celery leaves and coarsely ground pepper

1. Place first 8 ingredients in a Dutch oven; bring slowly to a boil. Reduce heat; simmer, uncovered, until chicken is no longer pink and vegetables are tender, about 30 minutes.
2. Stir in noodles, corn and butter. Cook, uncovered, until noodles are tender, about 10 minutes, stirring occasionally. If desired, top with celery leaves and pepper.

1⅓ CUPS 201 cal., 6g fat (3g sat. fat), 57mg chol., 697mg sod., 19g carb. (3g sugars, 2g fiber), 18g pro.

33g Pro

HERBED SLOW-COOKER CHICKEN

I use my slow cooker to prepare these well-seasoned chicken breasts that cook up moist and tender. My daughter, who has two young sons to keep up with, shared this great recipe with me several years ago. I've made it repeatedly ever since.
—Sundra Hauck, Bogalusa, LA

PREP: 5 MIN. • **COOK:** 4 HOURS
MAKES: 4 SERVINGS

- 1 Tbsp. olive oil
- 1 tsp. paprika
- ½ tsp. garlic powder
- ½ tsp. seasoned salt
- ½ tsp. dried thyme
- ½ tsp. dried basil
- ½ tsp. pepper
- ½ tsp. browning sauce, optional
- 4 bone-in chicken breast halves (8 oz. each)
- ½ cup chicken broth

In a small bowl, combine the first 7 ingredients and, if desired, browning sauce; rub over chicken. Place in a 5-qt. slow cooker; add broth. Cook, covered, on low until chicken is tender, 4-5 hours.

1 CHICKEN BREAST HALF 211 cal., 7g fat (2g sat. fat), 91mg chol., 392mg sod., 1g carb. (0 sugars, 0 fiber), 33g pro.

30g Pro

HEARTY CHICKEN GYROS

I love reinventing classic recipes to fit our taste and healthy living lifestyle. This recipe is quick to prepare and can be made ahead to be served on the go. You can add Greek olives, omit the onion or even use cubed pork tenderloin for a new taste.
—Kayla Douthitt, Elizabethtown, KY

PREP: 30 MIN. + MARINATING
COOK: 5 MIN. • **MAKES:** 6 SERVINGS

- 1½ lbs. boneless skinless chicken breasts, cut into ½-in. cubes
- ½ cup salt-free lemon-pepper marinade
- 3 Tbsp. minced fresh mint

SAUCE

- ½ cup fat-free plain Greek yogurt
- 2 Tbsp. lemon juice
- 1 tsp. dill weed
- ½ tsp. garlic powder

ASSEMBLY

- 1 medium cucumber, seeded and chopped
- 1 medium tomato, chopped
- ¼ cup finely chopped onion
- 6 whole wheat pita pocket halves, warmed
- ⅓ cup crumbled feta cheese

1. Place chicken, marinade and mint in a shallow dish and turn the chicken to coat. Cover and refrigerate up to 6 hours.
2. Drain chicken, discarding marinade. Place a large nonstick skillet over medium-high heat. Add chicken; cook and stir until no longer pink, 4-6 minutes.
3. In a small bowl, mix sauce ingredients. In another bowl, combine cucumber, tomato and onion. Serve chicken in pita pockets with sauce, vegetable mixture and cheese.

1 GYRO 248 cal., 4g fat (2g sat. fat), 66mg chol., 251mg sod., 22g carb. (4g sugars, 3g fiber), 30g pro.

NOTES

PROTEIN
BOOST
PAGE 320

PROTEIN BOOST
PAGE 320

18g Pro

CONFETTI KIELBASA SKILLET

Here's one of my husband's favorite dishes. When fresh corn is in season, substitute fresh for frozen. Add a dash of cayenne pepper if you like a little heat.
—Sheila Gomez, Shawnee, KS

TAKES: 30 MIN. • **MAKES:** 4 SERVINGS

- 1 Tbsp. canola oil
- 7 oz. smoked turkey kielbasa, cut into ¼-in. slices
- 1 medium onion, halved and sliced
- ½ cup sliced baby portobello mushrooms
- 2 garlic cloves, minced
- ½ cup reduced-sodium chicken broth
- ¾ tsp. Mrs. Dash Garlic & Herb Seasoning Blend
- 1 can (15 oz.) no-salt-added black beans, rinsed and drained
- 1 pkg. (8.8 oz.) ready-to-serve brown rice
- 1 cup frozen corn
- ½ cup chopped roasted sweet red peppers
- 4 tsp. minced fresh cilantro

1. In a large skillet, heat oil over medium-high heat. Add kielbasa, onion and mushrooms; cook and stir 4-6 minutes or until vegetables are tender. Add garlic; cook 1 minute longer.
2. Add broth and seasoning blend, stirring to loosen browned bits from pan. Bring to a boil; cook 2-3 minutes or until liquid is almost evaporated. Stir in remaining ingredients; heat through.
1¼ CUPS 347 cal., 9g fat (1g sat. fat), 31mg chol., 692mg sod., 45g carb. (4g sugars, 7g fiber), 18g pro.

35g Pro

GARLIC-GINGER TURKEY TENDERLOINS

This good-for-you entree can be on your dinner plates quicker than Chinese takeout—and for a lot less money! Ginger and brown sugar flavor the sauce that spices up the turkey as it bakes.
—Taste of Home *Test Kitchen*

TAKES: 30 MIN. • **MAKES:** 4 SERVINGS

- 3 Tbsp. brown sugar, divided
- 2 Tbsp. plus 2 tsp. reduced-sodium soy sauce, divided
- 2 Tbsp. minced fresh gingerroot
- 6 garlic cloves, minced
- ½ tsp. pepper
- 1 pkg. (20 oz.) turkey breast tenderloins
- 1 Tbsp. cornstarch
- 1 cup reduced-sodium chicken broth

1. Preheat oven to 375°. In a small saucepan, mix 2 Tbsp. brown sugar, 2 Tbsp. soy sauce, ginger, garlic and pepper.
2. Place turkey in a 13x9-in. baking dish coated with cooking spray; drizzle with half the soy sauce mixture. Bake, uncovered, until a thermometer reads 165°, 25-30 minutes.
3. Meanwhile, add cornstarch and the remaining brown sugar and soy sauce to the remaining mixture in saucepan; stir until smooth. Stir in broth. Bring to a boil; cook and stir until thickened, 1-2 minutes. Cut turkey into slices; serve with sauce.
4 OZ. COOKED TURKEY WITH 2 TBSP. SAUCE 212 cal., 2g fat (1g sat. fat), 69mg chol., 639mg sod., 14g carb. (10g sugars, 0 fiber), 35g pro.

33g Pro

THAI CHICKEN PASTA

I try to buy fresh chicken when it's on sale. I cook a big batch in the slow cooker, then cut it up and package it in small amounts suitable for recipes like this. When I want it, I just need to pull it out of the freezer and let it thaw.
—Jeni Pittard, Statham, GA

TAKES: 25 MIN. • **MAKES:** 2 SERVINGS

- 3 oz. uncooked whole wheat linguine
- ½ cup salsa
- 2 Tbsp. reduced-fat creamy peanut butter
- 1 Tbsp. orange juice
- 1½ tsp. honey
- 1 tsp. reduced-sodium soy sauce
- 1 cup cubed cooked chicken breast
- 1 Tbsp. chopped unsalted peanuts
- 1 Tbsp. minced fresh cilantro

1. Cook linguine according to package directions.
2. Meanwhile, in a microwave-safe dish, combine salsa, peanut butter, orange juice, honey and soy sauce. Cover and microwave on high for 1 minute; stir. Add chicken; heat through.
3. Drain linguine. Serve with chicken mixture. Garnish with peanuts and cilantro.

1 SERVING 409 cal., 10g fat (2g sat. fat), 54mg chol., 474mg sod., 46g carb. (10g sugars, 6g fiber), 33g pro.

NOTES

20g Pro

LEMON CHICKEN & RICE SOUP

Years ago, I fell hard for a lemony Greek soup at one of my favorite restaurants. I re-created it at home so we could eat it whenever a craving hit!
—*Kristin Cherry, Bothell, WA*

PREP: 35 MIN. • **COOK:** 4¼ HOURS
MAKES: 12 SERVINGS (4 QT.)

- 2 Tbsp. olive oil
- 2 lbs. boneless skinless chicken breasts, cut into ½-in. pieces
- 5 cans (14½ oz. each) reduced-sodium chicken broth
- 8 cups coarsely chopped Swiss chard, kale or spinach
- 2 large carrots, finely chopped
- 1 small onion, chopped
- 1 medium lemon, halved and thinly sliced
- ¼ cup lemon juice
- 4 tsp. grated lemon zest
- ½ tsp. pepper
- 4 cups cooked brown rice

1. In a large skillet, heat 1 Tbsp. oil over medium-high heat. Add half the chicken; cook and stir until browned. Transfer to a 6-qt. slow cooker. Repeat with remaining oil and chicken.
2. Stir broth, vegetables, lemon slices, lemon juice and zest, and pepper into slow cooker with chicken. Cook, covered, on low 4-5 hours or until chicken is tender. Stir in rice; heat through.

1⅓ CUPS 203 cal., 5g fat (1g sat. fat), 42mg chol., 612mg sod., 20g carb. (3g sugars, 2g fiber), 20g pro.

12g Pro

SESAME CHICKEN VEGGIE WRAPS

I'm always on the lookout for fast, nutritious recipes that will appeal to my three little kids. They happen to love edamame, so this is a smart choice for those on-the-go days. *—Elisabeth Larsen, Pleasant Grove, UT*

TAKES: 30 MIN. • **MAKES:** 8 SERVINGS

- 1 cup frozen shelled edamame

DRESSING

- 2 Tbsp. orange juice
- 2 Tbsp. olive oil
- 1 tsp. sesame oil
- ½ tsp. ground ginger
- ¼ tsp. salt
- ⅛ tsp. pepper

WRAPS

- 2 cups fresh baby spinach
- 1 cup thinly sliced cucumber
- 1 cup fresh sugar snap peas, chopped
- ½ cup shredded carrots
- ½ cup thinly sliced sweet red pepper
- 1 cup chopped cooked chicken breast
- 8 whole wheat tortillas (8 in.), warmed

1. Cook edamame according to package directions. Drain; rinse with cold water and drain well. Whisk together dressing ingredients.

2. In a large bowl, combine the next 6 ingredients and edamame; toss with dressing. Place about ½ cup mixture on each tortilla. Fold bottom and sides of each tortilla over filling and roll up.

1 WRAP 214 cal., 7g fat (1g sat. fat), 13mg chol., 229mg sod., 28g carb. (2g sugars, 5g fiber), 12g pro.

PROTEIN BOOST
PAGE 320

26g Pro

CALIFORNIA BURGER BOWLS

Burgers are a weekly staple at our house year-round. Skip the fries, chips and bun—you won't need them with these loaded veggie and fruit burgers. To spice up the mayo, add 1/2 tsp. of chipotle powder.
—Courtney Stultz, Weir, KS

TAKES: 25 MIN. • **MAKES:** 4 SERVINGS

- 3 Tbsp. fat-free milk
- 2 Tbsp. quick-cooking oats
- ¾ tsp. salt
- ½ tsp. ground cumin
- ½ tsp. chili powder
- ½ tsp. pepper
- 1 lb. lean ground turkey
- 4 cups baby kale salad blend
- 1½ cups cubed fresh pineapple (½ in.)
- 1 medium mango, peeled and thinly sliced
- 1 medium ripe avocado, peeled and thinly sliced
- 1 medium sweet red pepper, cut into strips
- 4 tomatillos, husks removed, thinly sliced
- ¼ cup reduced-fat chipotle mayonnaise

1. In a large bowl, mix milk, oats and seasonings. Add turkey; mix lightly but thoroughly. Shape into four ½-in.-thick patties.
2. Place burgers on an oiled grill rack over medium heat. Grill, covered, until a thermometer reads 165°, 4-5 minutes per side. Serve over salad blend, along with remaining ingredients.
1 SERVING 390 cal., 19g fat (4g sat. fat), 83mg chol., 666mg sod., 33g carb. (22g sugars, 7g fiber), 26g pro.

26g Pro

30-MINUTE COQ AU VIN

I love being able to fix a fancy gourmet dish in such a short amount of time and still have it turn out so delicious. To reduce fat, use chicken tenderloin pieces or skinless chicken breasts. This recipe is really fabulous served with rice.
—Judy VanCoetsem, Cortland, NY

TAKES: 30 MIN. • **MAKES:** 6 SERVINGS

- ¼ cup all-purpose flour
- 1 tsp. dried thyme
- 1 tsp. salt, divided
- 6 boneless skinless chicken thighs (4 oz. each)
- 1 Tbsp. olive oil
- 6 cups quartered baby portobello mushrooms
- 2 cups sliced fresh carrots
- 3 pieces Canadian bacon, chopped
- 1 Tbsp. tomato paste
- 1 cup chicken broth
- 1 cup dry red wine
- Chopped fresh thyme, optional

1. In a shallow dish, combine flour, thyme and ½ tsp. salt. Dip chicken in flour mixture to coat both sides; shake off excess.
2. In a Dutch oven or high-sided skillet, heat oil over medium-high heat. Cook chicken until golden brown, 3-4 minutes per side. Remove from pan; keep warm.
3. In same pan, cook mushrooms, carrots, bacon, tomato paste and remaining ½ tsp. salt for 2 minutes. Add broth and wine; bring to a boil. Return chicken to pan; reduce heat. Cook until chicken reaches 170° and carrots are just tender, 8-10 minutes. If desired, top with chopped fresh thyme.
1 SERVING 255 cal., 11g fat (3g sat. fat), 80mg chol., 648mg sod., 9g carb. (4g sugars, 2g fiber), 26g pro.

STAUB

Wonderful and light meal. I replaced the chicken with vegan "chicken" but otherwise made the recipe as directed. I highly recommend this as a lunch or dinner staple!

—DARLYN29, TASTEOFHOME.COM

32g Pro

ASIAN CHICKEN RICE BOWL

This super flavorful, nutrient-packed dish makes use of supermarket conveniences like coleslaw mix and rotisserie chicken. This recipe is easily doubled or tripled for large families.
—Christianna Gozzi, Astoria, NY

TAKES: 20 MIN. • **MAKES:** 4 SERVINGS

- ¼ cup rice vinegar
- 1 green onion, minced
- 2 Tbsp. reduced-sodium soy sauce
- 1 Tbsp. toasted sesame seeds
- 1 Tbsp. sesame oil
- 1 Tbsp. honey
- 1 tsp. minced fresh gingerroot
- 1 pkg. (8.8 oz.) ready-to-serve brown rice
- 4 cups coleslaw mix (about 9 oz.)
- 2 cups shredded rotisserie chicken, chilled
- 2 cups frozen shelled edamame, thawed

1. For dressing, whisk together first 7 ingredients. Cook rice according to package directions. Divide among 4 bowls.
2. In a large bowl, toss coleslaw mix and chicken with half the dressing. Serve edamame and slaw mixture over rice; drizzle with remaining dressing.
1 SERVING 429 cal., 15g fat (2g sat. fat), 62mg chol., 616mg sod., 38g carb. (13g sugars, 5g fiber), 32g pro.

PROTEIN BOOST
PAGE 320

19g Pro

GREEK PASTA TOSS

My husband and I developed this bright pasta dish by tossing in our favorite Greek ingredients, such as olives, feta cheese and sun-dried tomatoes. Try it with shrimp or chicken too!
—Terri Gilson, Calgary, AB

TAKES: 30 MIN. • **MAKES:** 4 SERVINGS

- 3 cups uncooked whole wheat spiral pasta (about 7 oz.)
- ¾ lb. Italian turkey sausage links, casings removed
- 2 garlic cloves, minced
- 4 oz. fresh baby spinach (about 5 cups)
- ½ cup Greek olives, halved
- ⅓ cup julienned oil-packed sun-dried tomatoes, drained and chopped
- ¼ cup crumbled feta cheese
- Lemon wedges, optional

1. In a 6-qt. stockpot, cook the pasta according to package directions; drain and return to pot.
2. Meanwhile, in a large skillet, cook and coarsely crumble sausage over medium-high heat until no longer pink, 4-6 minutes. Add garlic; cook and stir 1 minute. Add to pasta.
3. Stir in spinach, olives and tomatoes; heat through, allowing spinach to wilt slightly. Stir in cheese. If desired, serve with lemon wedges.
2 CUPS 335 cal., 13g fat (3g sat. fat), 35mg chol., 742mg sod., 36g carb. (1g sugars, 6g fiber), 19g pro.

36g Pro

GREEK GRILLED CHICKEN PITA BOWLS

I switched up my mom's recipe to create this tasty variation. It's delicious and perfect for warm days. The creamy cucumber sauce goes great with fresh, crunchy veggies.
—Blair Lonergan, Rochelle, VA

PREP: 20 MIN. + MARINATING
GRILL: 10 MIN. • **MAKES:** 4 SERVINGS

- ¾ cup plain Greek yogurt
- 1 Tbsp. lemon juice
- 1 Tbsp. olive oil
- 1 tsp. poultry seasoning
- 1 tsp. dried oregano
- ½ tsp. grated lemon zest
- ¼ tsp. salt
- ¼ tsp. onion powder
- ¼ tsp. pepper
- 1 lb. boneless skinless chicken breasts

CUCUMBER SAUCE

- 1 cup plain Greek yogurt
- ½ cup finely chopped cucumber
- ¼ cup finely chopped red onion
- 1 Tbsp. minced fresh parsley
- 1 Tbsp. snipped fresh dill
- 1 Tbsp. lemon juice
- 1 garlic clove, minced
- ⅛ tsp. salt
- ⅛ tsp. pepper

BOWLS

- 2 cups cooked brown rice
- 1 cup hummus
- ½ cup sliced cucumber
- ½ cup grape tomatoes, quartered
- ½ cup sliced red onion
- ½ cup shrededed romaine
- ¼ cup crumbled feta cheese
- ¼ cup Greek olives
- Pita bread
- Lemon wedges, optional

1. In a large bowl, combine the yogurt, lemon juice, olive oil, poultry seasoning, oregano, lemon zest, salt, onion powder and pepper. Add chicken breasts; toss lightly. Cover; refrigerate 10 minutes or up to 8 hours. In a small bowl, combine the sauce ingredients; refrigerate until serving.

2. Remove chicken from marinade, discarding marinade. On a lightly oiled grill rack, grill chicken, covered, over medium heat or broil 4 in. from the heat until a thermometer reads 165°, 4-7 minutes on each side.

3. Cut chicken into strips. Assemble bowls by layering cooked brown rice, hummus, chicken, cucumber, tomatoes, onion, romaine, feta cheese and olives; drizzle with sauce. Serve with pita bread; if desired, top with additional fresh dill and serve with lemon wedges.

1 SERVING 599 cal., 31g fat (10g sat. fat), 93mg chol., 807mg sod., 46g carb. (7g sugars, 7g fiber), 36g pro.

NOTES

21g Pro

CHICKEN FLORENTINE MEATBALLS

Served over spaghetti squash and a chunky mushroom-tomato sauce, these tender meatballs are tops when it comes to great flavor.
—Diane Nemitz, Ludington, MI

PREP: 40 MIN. • **COOK:** 20 MIN.
MAKES: 6 SERVINGS

- 2 large eggs, lightly beaten
- 1 pkg. (10 oz.) frozen chopped spinach, thawed and squeezed dry
- ½ cup dry bread crumbs
- ¼ cup grated Parmesan cheese
- 1 Tbsp. dried minced onion
- 1 garlic clove, minced
- ¼ tsp. salt
- ⅛ tsp. pepper
- 1 lb. ground chicken
- 1 medium spaghetti squash (about 4 lbs.)

SAUCE

- ½ lb. sliced fresh mushrooms
- 2 tsp. olive oil
- 1 can (14½ oz.) diced tomatoes, undrained
- 1 can (8 oz.) tomato sauce
- 2 Tbsp. minced fresh parsley
- 1 garlic clove, minced
- 1 tsp. dried oregano
- 1 tsp. dried basil
- Grated Parmesan cheese, optional

1. In a large bowl, combine the first 8 ingredients. Crumble chicken over mixture and mix well. Shape into 1½-in. balls.

2. Place the meatballs on a rack in a shallow baking pan. Bake, uncovered, at 400° for 20-25 minutes or until no longer pink. Meanwhile, cut squash in half lengthwise; discard seeds. Place squash cut side down on a microwave-safe plate. Microwave, uncovered, on high for 15-18 minutes or until tender.

3. For sauce, in a large nonstick skillet, saute mushrooms in oil until tender. Stir in the next 6 ingredients. Bring to a boil. Reduce the heat; simmer, uncovered, for 8-10 minutes or until slightly thickened. Add meatballs and heat through.

4. When the squash is cool enough to handle, use a fork to separate strands. Serve with meatballs and sauce, and if desired, garnish with Parmesan cheese.

FREEZE OPTION Place individual portions of the cooled meatballs and squash in freezer containers. To use, partially thaw in refrigerator overnight. Microwave, covered, on high in a microwave-safe dish until heated through, gently stirring and adding a little water to the sauce if necessary.

1 SERVING 272 cal., 12g fat (3g sat. fat), 115mg chol., 635mg sod., 25g carb. (8g sugars, 6g fiber), 21g pro.

20g Pro

TURKEY MEAT LOAF

I first made this recipe when my husband and I had to start watching our diets. Since then, I've been asked to make my turkey meat loaf many times.
—Ruby Rath, New Haven, IN

PREP: 15 MIN. • **BAKE:** 1 HOUR + STANDING
MAKES: 10 SERVINGS

- 1 cup quick-cooking oats
- 1 medium onion, chopped
- ½ cup shredded carrot
- ½ cup fat-free milk
- ¼ cup egg substitute
- 2 Tbsp. ketchup
- 1 tsp. garlic powder
- ¼ tsp. pepper
- 2 lbs. lean ground turkey

TOPPING

- ¼ cup ketchup
- ¼ cup quick-cooking oats

1. Preheat oven to 350°. Combine first 8 ingredients. Add turkey; mix lightly but thoroughly.
2. Transfer to a 9x5-in. loaf pan coated with cooking spray. Mix the topping ingredients; spread over loaf. Bake until a thermometer reads 165°, 60-65 minutes. Let stand 10 minutes before slicing.

1 PIECE 195 cal., 8g fat (2g sat. fat), 63mg chol., 188mg sod., 12g carb. (4g sugars, 1g fiber), 20g pro.

NOTES

> *I made this exactly as written. My husband, who usually is not thrilled with ground chicken, raved about it. There were no leftovers!*
>
> —ELAINE115, TASTEOFHOME.COM

22g Pro

EASY WHITE CHICKEN CHILI

Chili is one of our favorite cold-weather foods. We use chicken and white beans for a twist on the regular bowl of red. This is wonderful comfort food.
—Rachel Lewis, Danville, VA

TAKES: 30 MIN. • **MAKES:** 6 SERVINGS

- 1 Tbsp. vegetable oil
- 1 lb. lean ground chicken
- 1 medium onion, chopped
- 2 cans (15 oz. each) cannellini beans, rinsed and drained
- 1 can (4 oz.) chopped green chiles
- 1 tsp. ground cumin
- ½ tsp. dried oregano
- ¼ tsp. pepper
- 1 can (14½ oz.) reduced-sodium chicken broth
- Optional toppings: Sour cream, shredded cheddar cheese and chopped fresh cilantro

1. Heat oil in a large pan; add chicken and onion and cook over medium-high heat until chicken is no longer pink, 6-8 minutes, breaking chicken into crumbles.
2. Pour 1 can of beans in a small bowl; mash slightly. Stir mashed beans, remaining can of beans, chiles, seasonings and broth into chicken mixture; bring to a boil. Reduce heat; simmer, covered, until flavors are blended, 12-15 minutes. Serve with toppings as desired.
FREEZE OPTION Freeze cooled chili in freezer containers. To use, partially thaw in refrigerator overnight. Heat through in a saucepan, stirring occasionally; add broth if necessary.
1 CUP 228 cal., 5g fat (1g sat. fat), 54mg chol., 504mg sod., 23g carb. (1g sugars, 6g fiber), 22g pro.

24g Pro 5i

LEMON FETA CHICKEN

This bright Greek-inspired chicken has only five ingredients—it's a busy-day lifesaver! My husband and I prepare the dish often, and it's a hit every time.
—Ann Cain, Morrill, NE

TAKES: 25 MIN. • **MAKES:** 4 SERVINGS

- 4 boneless skinless chicken breast halves (4 oz. each)
- 2 to 3 Tbsp. lemon juice
- ¼ cup crumbled feta cheese
- 1 tsp. dried oregano
- ¼ to ½ tsp. pepper

1. Place chicken in a 13x9-in. baking dish coated with cooking spray. Pour lemon juice over chicken; sprinkle with feta cheese, oregano and pepper.
2. Bake, uncovered, at 400° for 20-25 minutes or until a thermometer reads 165°.
1 CHICKEN BREAST HALF 143 cal., 4g fat (1g sat. fat), 66mg chol., 122mg sod., 1g carb. (0 sugars, 0 fiber), 24g pro.

CHEESE SWAP

Crumbled goat cheese makes an easy, flavorful substitute for feta. You could also replace the crumbled feta with 4 ounces of cubed halloumi.

22g Pro

CHICKEN FAJITA SALAD

This recipe came from Texas, which is famous for its Tex-Mex food. I love to cook, even though it's just for me and my husband now. I invite our grown kids over a lot, and they just love this recipe. I'm happy to share it!
—Lois Proudfit, Eugene, OR

PREP: 15 MIN. + MARINATING
COOK: 15 MIN. • **MAKES:** 6 SERVINGS

- 4 Tbsp. canola oil, divided
- ½ cup lime juice
- 2 garlic cloves, minced
- 1 tsp. ground cumin
- 1 tsp. dried oregano
- 1 lb. boneless skinless chicken breasts, cut into thin strips
- 1 medium onion, cut into thin wedges
- 1 medium sweet red pepper, cut into thin strips
- 2 cans (4 oz. each) chopped green chiles
- 1 cup unblanched almonds, toasted
- 3 cups shredded lettuce
- 3 medium tomatoes, cut into wedges
- 1 medium ripe avocado, peeled and sliced

1. In a small bowl, combine 2 Tbsp. oil, lime juice, garlic, cumin and oregano. Pour half in a large bowl or dish; add chicken and turn to coat. Marinate for at least 30 minutes. Cover and refrigerate remaining marinade.
2. In a large skillet, heat remaining oil on medium-high. Saute onion for 2-3 minutes or until crisp-tender.
3. Drain chicken, discarding marinade. Add chicken to skillet; stir-fry until meat is no longer pink. Add the red pepper, chiles and reserved marinade; cook 2 minutes or until heated through. Stir in almonds. Serve immediately over shredded lettuce; top with tomatoes and avocado.

1½ CUPS 372 cal., 26g fat (3g sat. fat), 42mg chol., 203mg sod., 16g carb. (5g sugars, 6g fiber), 22g pro.

NOTES

PROTEIN
BOOST
PAGE 320

32g Pro 5i

GOLDEN APRICOT-GLAZED TURKEY BREAST

Basted with a simple glaze, this tender turkey bakes to a lovely golden brown. Make it the centerpiece of your holiday table; you'll be glad you did.
—Greg Fontenot, The Woodlands, TX

PREP: 10 MIN.
BAKE: 1½ HOURS + STANDING
MAKES: 15 SERVINGS

- ½ cup apricot preserves
- ¼ cup balsamic vinegar
- ¼ tsp. pepper
- Dash salt
- 1 bone-in turkey breast (5 lbs.)

1. Preheat oven to 325°. Combine apricot preserves, vinegar, pepper and salt. Place turkey breast on a rack in a large shallow roasting pan.
2. Bake, uncovered, 1½-2 hours or until a thermometer reads 170°, basting every 30 minutes with apricot mixture. (Cover loosely with foil if turkey browns too quickly.) Cover and let stand 15 minutes before slicing.
4 OZ. COOKED TURKEY 236 cal., 8g fat (2g sat. fat), 81mg chol., 84mg sod., 8g carb. (5g sugars, 0 fiber), 32g pro.

37g Pro

CHICKEN OLE FOIL SUPPER

These Mexi-style chicken packets can be assembled ahead of time and frozen if you like. Just thaw them overnight in the fridge, then grill as directed. I serve them with warm tortillas and fresh fruit on the side.
—Mary Peck, Salina, KS

TAKES: 30 MIN. • **MAKES:** 4 SERVINGS

- 1 can (15 oz.) black beans, rinsed and drained
- 2 cups fresh or frozen corn (about 10 oz.), thawed
- 1 cup salsa
- 4 boneless skinless chicken breast halves (4 oz. each)
- ¼ tsp. garlic powder
- ¼ tsp. pepper
- ⅛ tsp. salt
- 1 cup shredded cheddar cheese
- 2 green onions, chopped

1. Mix beans, corn and salsa; divide among four 18x12-in. pieces of heavy-duty foil. Top with chicken. Mix the 3 seasonings; sprinkle over chicken. Fold foil over chicken, sealing tightly.
2. Grill packets, covered, over medium heat until a thermometer inserted in chicken reads 165°, 15-20 minutes. Open foil carefully to allow steam to escape. Sprinkle with cheese and green onions.
1 SERVING 405 cal., 13g fat (6g sat. fat), 91mg chol., 766mg sod., 34g carb. (8g sugars, 6g fiber), 37g pro.

30g Pro

SOUTHWEST CHICKEN DINNER

My family loves to order gigantic takeout Tex-Mex burritos, but they can be expensive and we always have leftovers. I created a lighter, no-guilt alternative with the flavors they love that skips the tortilla.
—Marquisha Turner, Denver, CO

TAKES: 30 MIN. • **MAKES:** 4 SERVINGS

- 2 cups water
- 2 Tbsp. olive oil, divided
- ½ tsp. salt
- ¼ tsp. pepper
- 1 cup uncooked long grain rice
- 1 Tbsp. taco seasoning
- 4 boneless skinless chicken breast halves (4 oz. each)
- 1 cup canned black beans or pinto beans, rinsed and drained
- ¼ cup chopped fresh cilantro
- 1 tsp. grated lime zest
- 2 Tbsp. lime juice
- Optional: Pico de gallo, shredded Mexican cheese blend, sour cream, avocado, shredded lettuce and lime wedges

1. In a large saucepan, combine water, 1 Tbsp. oil, and the salt and pepper; bring to a boil. Stir in rice. Reduce heat; simmer, covered, 15-17 minutes or until liquid is absorbed and rice is tender.
2. Meanwhile, sprinkle taco seasoning over both sides of chicken. In a large skillet, heat remaining 1 Tbsp. oil over medium heat. Add the chicken; cook 4-5 minutes on each side or until a thermometer reads 165°.
3. In a microwave, heat beans until warmed. To serve, gently stir cilantro, lime zest and lime juice into rice; divide among 4 bowls. Cut chicken into slices. Place chicken and beans over rice; top as desired with optional ingredients.

1 SERVING 398 cal., 7g fat (1g sat. fat), 63mg chol., 678mg sod., 52g carb. (1g sugars, 3g fiber), 30g pro.

21g Pro

COLD-DAY CHICKEN NOODLE SOUP

When I was sick, my mom would make me this heartwarming chicken noodle soup. It was soothing when I had a cold, but this soup is a bowlful of comfort on any chilly day. *—Anthony Graham, Ottawa, IL*

PREP: 15 MIN. • **COOK:** 25 MIN.
MAKES: 8 SERVINGS (3 QT.)

- 1 Tbsp. canola oil
- 2 celery ribs, chopped
- 2 medium carrots, chopped
- 1 medium onion, chopped
- 8 cups reduced-sodium chicken broth
- ½ tsp. dried basil
- ¼ tsp. pepper
- 3 cups uncooked whole wheat egg noodles (about 4 oz.)
- 3 cups coarsely chopped rotisserie chicken
- 1 Tbsp. minced fresh parsley

1. In a 6-qt. stockpot, heat the oil over medium-high heat. Add celery, carrots and onion; cook and stir 5-7 minutes or until tender.

2. Add broth, basil and pepper; bring to a boil. Stir in noodles; cook 12-14 minutes or until al dente. Stir in the chicken and parsley; heat through.

1½ CUPS 195 cal., 6g fat (1g sat. fat), 47mg chol., 639mg sod., 16g carb. (2g sugars, 3g fiber), 21g pro.

23g Pro

STRAWBERRY TARRAGON CHICKEN SALAD

After thinking about creating this salad for some time, this past spring I used my homegrown strawberries and fresh tarragon to do a little experimenting. It didn't take me very long to come up with a winner! My husband enjoyed my creation as much as I did, and we can't wait for strawberry season to come around again!
—Sue Gronholz, Beaver Dam, WI

TAKES: 30 MIN. • **MAKES:** 5 SERVINGS

- ½ cup mayonnaise
- 2 tsp. sugar
- 2 tsp. minced fresh tarragon or 1 tsp. dried tarragon
- ¼ tsp. salt
- ⅛ tsp. pepper
- 2½ cups cubed cooked chicken breasts
- 2 cups quartered fresh strawberries
- 1 cup fresh shelled peas or frozen peas, thawed
- ½ cup chopped celery
- 2 Tbsp. chopped sweet onion
- Torn mixed salad greens
- ½ cup chopped pecans, toasted

In a large bowl, whisk the first 5 ingredients until blended. Stir in chicken, strawberries, peas, celery and onion. Serve over salad greens; sprinkle with pecans.

1 CUP 378 cal., 26g fat (4g sat. fat), 56mg chol., 285mg sod., 13g carb. (7g sugars, 4g fiber), 23g pro.

TEST KITCHEN TIP

This salad is better when made ahead of time so the flavors can blend. But don't add the strawberries until you're ready to serve, as they tend to turn the salad pink when they sit.

> *This recipe is excellent! It's different enough to create a unique chicken salad that is so delicious. I love the use of tarragon in this recipe, and the strawberries make it, oh, so good. This recipe is a winner!*
>
> —LVARNER, TASTEOFHOME.COM

PROTEIN BOOST
PAGE 320

19g Pro

SKILLET TACOS

If you enjoy Mexican food, you'll be whipping up these fast, healthy skillet tacos often.
—Maria Gobel, Greenfield, WI

TAKES: 30 MIN. • **MAKES:** 2 SERVINGS

- 1 Tbsp. olive oil
- ¼ lb. lean ground turkey
- 2 Tbsp. chopped onion
- 2 Tbsp. chopped green pepper
- 1 can (8 oz.) tomato sauce
- ½ cup uncooked elbow macaroni
- ½ cup water
- ¼ cup picante sauce
- 2 Tbsp. shredded reduced-fat cheddar cheese
- ¼ cup crushed baked tortilla chip scoops
- ¼ cup chopped avocado
- Optional: Iceberg lettuce wedges and sour cream

1. Heat the olive oil in a large nonstick skillet over medium-high heat; add turkey, onion and green pepper. Cook until vegetables are tender and turkey is no longer pink.
2. Stir in the tomato sauce, macaroni, water and picante sauce. Bring to a boil. Reduce heat; cover and simmer until macaroni is tender, 10-15 minutes.
3. Divide between 2 plates; top with cheese, tortilla chips and avocado. Serve with lettuce and sour cream if desired.
1 CUP 337 cal., 17g fat (4g sat. fat), 44mg chol., 861mg sod., 30g carb. (4g sugars, 5g fiber), 19g pro.

29g Pro

RASPBERRY PECAN CHICKEN SALAD

I gave this sweet-savory chicken salad a little zip with Chinese five-spice powder, which tastes a bit like pumpkin pie spice. Also sprinkle some on roasted carrots for an awesome meal.
—Lisa Renshaw, Kansas City, MO

TAKES: 15 MIN. • **MAKES:** 6 SANDWICHES

- 1 carton (6 oz.) orange yogurt
- ½ cup mayonnaise
- ¼ tsp. Chinese five-spice powder
- 3 cups cubed cooked chicken
- 2 green onions, chopped
- ¼ cup sliced celery
- ¼ cup chopped pecans, toasted
- 1 cup fresh raspberries
- 12 slices multigrain bread

In a large bowl, mix yogurt, mayonnaise and five-spice powder. Stir in chicken, green onions, celery and pecans. Gently stir in raspberries. Serve on bread.
1 SANDWICH 463 cal., 24g fat (4g sat. fat), 65mg chol., 371mg sod., 31g carb. (10g sugars, 6g fiber), 29g pro.

34g Pro

MUSHROOM TURKEY TETRAZZINI

This creamy, comforting casserole makes a fantastic way to use up any leftover Thanksgiving turkey. It's a real family-pleaser!
—Linda Howe, Lisle, IL

PREP: 35 MIN. • **BAKE:** 25 MIN.
MAKES: 8 SERVINGS

- 12 oz. uncooked multigrain spaghetti, broken into 2-in. pieces
- 2 tsp. chicken bouillon granules
- 2 Tbsp. butter
- ½ lb. sliced fresh mushrooms
- 2 Tbsp. all-purpose flour
- ¼ cup sherry or additional pasta water
- ¾ tsp. salt-free lemon-pepper seasoning
- ½ tsp. salt
- ⅛ tsp. ground nutmeg
- 1 cup fat-free evaporated milk
- ⅔ cup grated Parmesan cheese, divided
- 4 cups cubed cooked turkey breast
- ¼ tsp. paprika, optional

1. Preheat oven to 375°. Cook spaghetti according to package directions for al dente. Drain, reserving 2½ cups pasta water; transfer spaghetti to a 13x9-in. baking dish coated with cooking spray. Dissolve bouillon in the reserved pasta water.
2. In a large nonstick skillet, heat the butter over medium-high heat; saute mushrooms until tender. Stir in flour until blended. Gradually stir in sherry, reserved pasta water and seasonings. Bring to a boil; cook and stir until thickened, about 2 minutes.
3. Reduce heat to low; stir in milk and ⅓ cup cheese until blended. Add turkey; heat through, stirring constantly. Pour over spaghetti; toss to combine. Sprinkle with remaining cheese and, if desired, paprika.
4. Bake, covered, until bubbly, 25-30 minutes.
1 CUP 357 cal., 7g fat (3g sat. fat), 71mg chol., 717mg sod., 38g carb. (5g sugars, 3g fiber), 34g pro.

NOTES

35g Pro 5i

GRILLED BUTTERMILK CHICKEN

I created this recipe years ago after one of our farmers market customers, a chef, shared the idea of marinating chicken in buttermilk. The chicken is easy to prepare and always turns out moist and delicious! I bruise the thyme sprigs by twisting them before adding them to the buttermilk mixture; this releases the oils in the leaves and flavors the chicken better.
—Sue Gronholz, Beaver Dam, WI

PREP: 10 MIN. + MARINATING
GRILL: 10 MIN. • **MAKES:** 12 SERVINGS

- 1½ cups buttermilk
- 4 fresh thyme sprigs
- 4 garlic cloves, halved
- ½ tsp. salt
- 12 boneless skinless chicken breast halves (about 4½ lbs.)

1. Place buttermilk, thyme, garlic and salt in a large bowl or shallow dish. Add the chicken and turn to coat. Refrigerate 8 hours or overnight, turning chicken occasionally.

2. Drain chicken, discarding marinade. Grill, covered, over medium heat until a thermometer reads 165°, 5-7 minutes per side.

1 CHICKEN BREAST HALF 189 cal., 4g fat (1g sat. fat), 95mg chol., 168mg sod., 1g carb. (1g sugars, 0 fiber), 35g pro.

34g Pro

SIMPLE SALSA CHICKEN

My husband and I prefer our food a little spicier than our children like it, so one evening I baked plain chicken for the kids and created this dish for us. It's now a regular menu item at our house.
—Jan Cooper, Troy, AL

PREP: 10 MIN. • **BAKE:** 25 MIN.
MAKES: 2 SERVINGS

- 2 boneless skinless chicken breast halves (5 oz. each)
- 1/8 tsp. salt
- 1/3 cup salsa
- 2 Tbsp. taco sauce
- 1/3 cup shredded Mexican cheese blend
- Optional: Lime wedges and sliced avocado

1. Place chicken in a shallow 2-qt. baking dish coated with cooking spray. Sprinkle with salt. Combine salsa and taco sauce; drizzle over chicken. Sprinkle with the cheese.
2. Cover and bake at 350° for 25-30 minutes or until a thermometer reads 165°. If desired, serve with lime wedges and sliced avocado.
1 SERVING 226 cal., 7g fat (3g sat. fat), 92mg chol., 628mg sod., 3g carb. (2g sugars, 0 fiber), 34g pro.

36g Pro

MEATY SLOW-COOKED JAMBALAYA

This recipe makes a big batch of delicious, meaty gumbo. Stash some away in the freezer for days you don't feel like cooking.
—Diane Atherton, Pine Mountain, GA

PREP: 25 MIN. • **COOK:** 7¼ HOURS
MAKES: 12 SERVINGS (3 QT.)

- 1 can (28 oz.) diced tomatoes, undrained
- 1 cup reduced-sodium chicken broth
- 1 large green pepper, chopped
- 1 medium onion, chopped
- 2 celery ribs, sliced
- 1/2 cup white wine or additional reduced-sodium chicken broth
- 4 garlic cloves, minced
- 2 tsp. Cajun seasoning
- 2 tsp. dried parsley flakes
- 1 tsp. dried basil
- 1 tsp. dried oregano
- 3/4 tsp. salt
- 1/2 to 1 tsp. cayenne pepper
- 2 lbs. boneless skinless chicken thighs, cut into 1-in. pieces
- 1 pkg. (12 oz.) fully cooked andouille or other spicy chicken sausage links, sliced
- 2 lbs. uncooked shrimp (31-40 per lb.), peeled and deveined
- 8 cups hot cooked brown rice

1. In a large bowl, combine the first 13 ingredients. Place chicken and sausage in a 6-qt. slow cooker. Pour tomato mixture over top. Cook, covered, on low until chicken is tender, 7-9 hours.
2. Stir in shrimp. Cook, covered, until shrimp turn pink, 15-20 minutes longer. Serve with rice.
1 CUP JAMBALAYA WITH 2/3 CUP COOKED RICE 387 cal., 10g fat (3g sat. fat), 164mg chol., 674mg sod., 37g carb. (4g sugars, 4g fiber), 36g pro.

25g Pro

PIZZA SPAGHETTI

The idea for this recipe came to me when I saw someone dip a slice of pizza into a pasta dish. My wife and kids love it and so do my friends!
—Robert Smith, Las Vegas, NV

PREP: 10 MIN. • **COOK:** 30 MIN.
MAKES: 6 SERVINGS

- ½ lb. lean ground beef (90% lean)
- ½ lb. Italian turkey sausage links, casings removed, sliced
- ½ cup chopped sweet onion
- 4 cans (8 oz. each) no-salt-added tomato sauce
- 3 oz. sliced turkey pepperoni
- 1 Tbsp. sugar
- 2 tsp. minced fresh parsley or ½ tsp. dried parsley flakes
- 2 tsp. minced fresh basil or ½ tsp. dried basil
- 9 oz. uncooked whole wheat spaghetti
- 3 Tbsp. grated Parmesan cheese

1. In a large nonstick skillet, cook beef and sausage with onion over medium-high heat until no longer pink, 5-7 minutes, crumbling ground beef. Stir in the tomato sauce, pepperoni, sugar and herbs; bring to a boil. Reduce heat; simmer, uncovered, until thickened, 20-25 minutes.
2. Meanwhile, in a 6-qt. stockpot, cook spaghetti according to package directions; drain and return to pot. Toss with sauce. Sprinkle with cheese.
1⅓ CUPS 354 cal., 9g fat (3g sat. fat), 57mg chol., 512mg sod., 45g carb. (11g sugars, 7g fiber), 25g pro.

25g Pro

CASABLANCA CHICKEN COUSCOUS

Risotto has always been a favorite Italian comfort food. To give it an update, I use lively North African-inspired flavors that still pack all the comfort of the creamy classic.
—Roxanne Chan, Albany, CA

PREP: 20 MIN.
COOK: 15 MIN. + STANDING
MAKES: 6 SERVINGS

- 1 Tbsp. olive oil
- 1 medium onion, chopped
- 1 lb. boneless skinless chicken thighs, cut into 1-in. pieces
- 1 pkg. (8.8 oz.) uncooked Israeli couscous
- ½ tsp. salt
- ¼ tsp. pepper
- ¼ tsp. crushed red pepper flakes
- 2 cans (14½ oz. each) reduced-sodium chicken broth
- ⅔ cup dried tropical fruit
- 1 can (15 to 15½ oz.) garbanzo beans or chickpeas, rinsed and drained
- ½ cup plain yogurt
- 1 small carrot, grated
- ¼ cup minced fresh parsley
- 1 medium lemon

1. In a large skillet, heat olive oil over medium-high heat. Add onion; saute until softened, 3-4 minutes. Add chicken, couscous, salt, pepper and pepper flakes; cook and stir until the chicken begins to brown, 3-5 minutes. Add broth and dried fruit; cook, uncovered, until chicken and couscous are tender and fruit is moist, 8-10 minutes.
2. Stir in next 4 ingredients; heat through. Remove from heat. Let stand, covered, 10 minutes. Meanwhile, zest lemon peel into strips; cut lemon into 6 wedges. Top couscous with zest strips and serve with lemon wedges.
1⅓ CUPS 448 cal., 11g fat (3g sat. fat), 53mg chol., 715mg sod., 63g carb. (17g sugars, 4g fiber), 25g pro.

40g Pro

SPICY OVEN-FRIED CHICKEN

My family adores this chicken recipe. The coating keeps the chicken nice and moist. With the taste enhanced by marinating, the result is delicious.
—Stephanie Otten, Byron Center, MI

PREP: 25 MIN. + MARINATING
BAKE: 35 MIN. • **MAKES:** 8 SERVINGS

- 2 cups buttermilk
- 2 Tbsp. Dijon mustard
- 2 tsp. salt
- 2 tsp. hot pepper sauce
- 1½ tsp. garlic powder
- 8 bone-in chicken breast halves, skin removed (8 oz. each)
- 2 cups soft bread crumbs
- 1 cup cornmeal
- 2 Tbsp. canola oil
- ½ tsp. poultry seasoning
- ½ tsp. ground mustard
- ½ tsp. paprika
- ½ tsp. cayenne pepper
- ¼ tsp. dried oregano
- ¼ tsp. dried parsley flakes

1. Preheat oven to 400°. In a large bowl or dish, combine the first 5 ingredients. Add chicken and turn to coat. Refrigerate 1 hour or overnight.
2. Drain chicken, discarding marinade. In a large bowl, combine remaining ingredients. Add chicken, 1 piece at a time, and coat with crumb mixture. Place on a parchment-lined baking sheet. Bake 35-40 minutes or until a thermometer reads 170°.

NOTE To make soft bread crumbs, tear bread into pieces and place in a food processor or blender. Cover and pulse until crumbs form. One slice of bread yields ½ to ¾ cup crumbs. To substitute for each cup of buttermilk, use 1 Tbsp. white vinegar or lemon juice plus enough milk to measure 1 cup. Stir, then let stand 5 minutes. Or, use 1 cup plain yogurt or 1¾ tsp. cream of tartar plus 1 cup milk.

1 CHICKEN BREAST HALF 296 cal., 7g fat (2g sat. fat), 103mg chol., 523mg sod., 15g carb. (2g sugars, 1g fiber), 40g pro.

TEST KITCHEN TIP

To prepare the chicken in an air fryer, preheat the air fryer to 375°. Drain chicken, discarding marinade. Combine remaining ingredients in a shallow dish and stir to combine. Add chicken, 1 piece at a time, and turn to coat. Place in air-fryer basket sprayed with cooking spray in a single layer. Air-fry until a thermometer reads 170°, about 20 minutes, turning halfway. Repeat with remaining chicken. When the last batch of chicken is cooked, return all chicken to basket and air-fry 2-3 minutes longer to heat through.

38g Pro

TROPICAL CHICKEN CAULIFLOWER RICE BOWLS

This tropical favorite is a delicious and healthy dinner with tons of flavor. You can substitute regular rice for the cauliflower rice if desired.
—Bethany DiCarlo, Harleysville, PA

PREP: 40 MIN. + MARINATING
GRILL: 10 MIN. • **MAKES:** 4 SERVINGS

- 1 fresh pineapple, peeled, cored and cubed (about 3 cups), divided
- ½ cup plain or coconut Greek yogurt
- 2 Tbsp. plus ½ cup chopped fresh cilantro, divided
- 3 Tbsp. lime juice, divided
- ¾ tsp. salt, divided
- ¼ tsp. crushed red pepper flakes
- ⅛ tsp. chili powder
- 4 boneless skinless chicken breast halves (6 oz. each)
- 3 cups fresh cauliflower florets (about ½ small cauliflower)
- 1 Tbsp. canola oil
- 1 small red onion, finely chopped
- Optional: Toasted sweetened shredded coconut or lime wedges

1. For marinade, place 1 cup pineapple, yogurt, 2 Tbsp. each cilantro and lime juice, ¼ tsp. salt, pepper flakes and chili powder in a food processor; process until blended. In a large bowl, toss chicken with marinade; refrigerate, covered, 1-3 hours.

2. In a clean food processor, pulse the cauliflower until it resembles rice (do not overprocess). In a large skillet, heat oil over medium-high heat; saute onion until lightly browned, 3-5 minutes. Add cauliflower; cook and stir until lightly browned, 5-7 minutes. Stir in 1 cup pineapple and the remaining 1 Tbsp. lime juice and ½ tsp. salt; cook, covered, over medium heat until cauliflower is tender, 3-5 minutes. Stir in remaining ½ cup cilantro. Keep warm.

3. Preheat grill or broiler. Drain chicken, discarding marinade. Place chicken on an oiled grill rack over medium heat or in a greased foil-lined 15x10x1-in. pan. Grill, covered, or broil 4 in. from heat until a thermometer reads 165°, 4-6 minutes per side. Let stand 5 minutes before slicing.

4. To serve, divide cauliflower mixture among 4 bowls. Top with the chicken, remaining 1 cup pineapple and, if desired, coconut and lime wedges.

1 SERVING 325 cal., 10g fat (3g sat. fat), 100mg chol., 529mg sod., 22g carb. (15g sugars, 4g fiber), 38g pro.

TEST KITCHEN TIP

To save some time, buy cauliflower that's already been processed. Look for riced cauliflower in the refrigerated section of the produce department. You'll need 3 cups.

49g Pro

ITALIAN TURKEY SANDWICHES

I hope you enjoy these tasty turkey sandwiches as much as our family does. The recipe makes plenty, so it's great for potlucks. Plus, the leftovers are just as good.
—Carol Riley, Ossian, IN

PREP: 10 MIN. • **COOK:** 5 HOURS
MAKES: 12 SANDWICHES

- 1 bone-in turkey breast (6 lbs.), skin removed
- 1 medium onion, chopped
- 1 small green pepper, chopped
- ¼ cup chili sauce
- 3 Tbsp. white vinegar
- 2 Tbsp. dried oregano or Italian seasoning
- 4 tsp. beef bouillon granules
- 12 kaiser or hard rolls, split

1. Place turkey breast in a greased 5-qt. slow cooker. Add onion and green pepper.
2. Combine the chili sauce, vinegar, oregano and bouillon; pour over turkey and vegetables. Cover and cook on low until turkey is tender, 5-6 hours.
3. Shred the turkey with 2 forks and return to the slow cooker; heat through. Spoon ½ cup onto each roll.

FREEZE OPTION Place cooled meat and its juices in freezer containers. To use, partially thaw in refrigerator overnight. Microwave, covered, on high in a microwave-safe dish until heated through, stirring gently; add water if necessary.

1 SANDWICH 374 cal., 4g fat (1g sat. fat), 118mg chol., 724mg sod., 34g carb. (3g sugars, 2g fiber), 49g pro.

17g Pro

CHICKEN & APPLE SALAD WITH GREENS

My favorite memory of eating this dish was when my mom made it for lunch on weekends when we were home from school and we could have something other than brown-bag lunches. Happy memories of childhood days make this salad extra-special.
—Trisha Kruse, Eagle, ID

TAKES: 30 MIN. • **MAKES:** 6 SERVINGS

VINAIGRETTE
- ¼ cup balsamic vinegar
- ¼ cup orange juice
- ¼ cup olive oil
- 2 Tbsp. lemon juice
- 2 Tbsp. reduced-sodium soy sauce
- 1 Tbsp. brown sugar
- 1 Tbsp. Dijon mustard
- ½ tsp. curry powder, optional
- ½ tsp. salt
- ¼ tsp. pepper
- ¼ tsp. ground ginger

SALAD
- 2 cups shredded cooked chicken
- 2 medium apples, chopped
- ½ cup thinly sliced red onion
- 10 cups torn mixed salad greens
- ½ cup chopped walnuts, toasted

In a large bowl, whisk the vinaigrette ingredients until blended. Add chicken, apples and onion; toss to coat. Just before serving, place greens on a large serving plate; top with chicken mixture. Sprinkle with walnuts.
NOTE To toast nuts, bake in a shallow pan in a 350° oven for 5-10 minutes or cook in a skillet over low heat until lightly browned, stirring occasionally.
1 SERVING 306 cal., 19g fat (3g sat. fat), 42mg chol., 549mg sod., 20g carb. (12g sugars, 4g fiber), 17g pro.

40g Pro

SLOW-COOKER CASSOULET WITH CRUMB TOPPING

Classically inspired, this dish is loaded with chicken thighs, pork and smoked sausage. Tomatoes, beans and wine round out the hearty French stew, and bread crumbs thicken it slightly.
—Marie Rizzio, Interlochen, MI

PREP: 20 MIN. • **COOK:** 7 HOURS
MAKES: 8 SERVINGS

- 1 cup soft bread crumbs
- 2 lbs. boneless skinless chicken thighs
- 1 lb. boneless pork shoulder, trimmed and cut into 1-in. pieces
- 8 oz. kielbasa, halved lengthwise and cut into ½-in. thick slices
- 2 cans (15 oz. each) cannellini beans, rinsed and drained
- 1 can (14½ oz.) petite diced tomatoes, drained
- 1 cup chopped onion
- 1 cup chicken broth
- ¾ cup white wine
- 1 Tbsp. tomato paste
- ½ tsp. salt
- ½ tsp. pepper
- 2 garlic cloves, crushed
- 2 fresh thyme sprigs
- 1 bay leaf
- Minced fresh parsley, optional

1. Preheat oven to 350°. Place bread crumbs in a 15x10x1-in. baking pan. Bake, uncovered, until crumbs are lightly browned, stirring occasionally, 8-12 minutes. Set aside.
2. Combine the next 14 ingredients in a 5- or 6-qt. slow cooker. Cover and cook on low until meat is tender, about 7 hours. Remove and discard thyme sprigs and bay leaf. Stir in ¾ cup toasted bread crumbs. Top individual servings with remaining toasted bread crumbs. If desired, sprinkle with chopped parsley.
1¼ CUPS 482 cal., 22g fat (7g sat. fat), 129mg chol., 802mg sod., 24g carb. (4g sugars, 6g fiber), 40g pro.

23g Pro

TANDOORI CHICKEN THIGHS

I spent some time in India, and I love reminders of this vibrant culture, so serving this tandoori chicken makes me happy. Paired with warmed naan bread and a cool tomato and cucumber salad, it makes a whole meal.
—Claire Elston, Spokane, WA

TAKES: 30 MIN. • **MAKES:** 4 SERVINGS

- 1 cup reduced-fat plain yogurt
- 1 Tbsp. minced fresh gingerroot
- 1 tsp. ground cumin
- 1 garlic clove, minced
- ¾ tsp. kosher salt
- ½ tsp. curry powder
- ½ tsp. pepper
- ¼ tsp. cayenne pepper
- 4 boneless skinless chicken thighs (about 1 lb.)

1. In a small bowl, mix the first 8 ingredients until blended. Add chicken to marinade; turn to coat. Let stand 10 minutes.
2. Place the chicken on greased grill rack. Grill, covered, over medium heat 6-8 minutes on each side or until a thermometer reads 170°.
1 CHICKEN THIGH 193 cal., 9g fat (3g sat. fat), 78mg chol., 333mg sod., 4g carb. (3g sugars, 0 fiber), 23g pro.

> This recipe was so good. It is so easy to make but full of flavor! I think next time I will add some mushrooms, but overall, a great recipe.
>
> —LPHJKITCHEN, TASTEOFHOME.COM

23g Pro

CHICKEN THIGHS WITH SHALLOTS & SPINACH

What could be better than an entree that comes with its own creamy vegetable side? This healthy supper comes together in no time flat and makes an eye-catching presentation.
—Genna Johannes, Wrightstown, WI

TAKES: 30 MIN. • **MAKES:** 6 SERVINGS

- 6 boneless skinless chicken thighs (about 1½ lbs.)
- ½ tsp. seasoned salt
- ½ tsp. pepper
- 1½ tsp. olive oil
- 4 shallots, thinly sliced
- ⅓ cup white wine or reduced-sodium chicken broth
- 1 pkg. (10 oz.) fresh spinach, trimmed
- ¼ tsp. salt
- ¼ cup sour cream

1. Sprinkle chicken with seasoned salt and pepper. In a large nonstick skillet, heat oil over medium heat. Add chicken; cook until a thermometer reads 170°, about 6 minutes on each side. Remove from pan; keep warm.
2. In same pan, cook and stir shallots until tender. Add wine; bring to a boil. Cook until wine is reduced by half. Add spinach and salt; cook and stir just until spinach is wilted. Stir in sour cream; serve with chicken.

FREEZE OPTION Before adding the sour cream, cool chicken and spinach mixture. Freeze in freezer containers. To use, partially thaw in refrigerator overnight. Heat through slowly in a covered skillet, stirring occasionally, until a thermometer inserted in chicken reads 170°. Stir in sour cream.

1 CHICKEN THIGH WITH ¼ CUP SPINACH MIXTURE 223 cal., 10g fat (3g sat. fat), 77mg chol., 360mg sod., 7g carb. (2g sugars, 1g fiber), 23g pro.

NOTES

29g Pro

TANDOORI SPICED CHICKEN PITA PIZZA WITH GREEK YOGURT & CILANTRO

My family and I are big picnickers, and I'm always looking for new dishes to try in the great outdoors. The amazing flavors at our favorite Indian restaurant inspired these mini pizzas.
—Angela Spengler, Niceville, FL

TAKES: 25 MIN. • **MAKES:** 4 SERVINGS

- 1 cup plain Greek yogurt, divided
- 2 Tbsp. chopped fresh cilantro
- ½ tsp. ground coriander
- ½ tsp. ground cumin
- ½ tsp. ground ginger
- ½ tsp. ground turmeric
- ½ tsp. paprika
- ½ tsp. cayenne pepper
- ¾ lb. boneless skinless chicken breasts, cut into ½-in.-thick strips
- 4 whole wheat pita breads (6 in.)
- ⅔ cup crumbled feta cheese
- ⅓ cup chopped seeded tomato
- ⅓ cup chopped fresh Italian parsley

1. For sauce, mix ½ cup yogurt and cilantro. In a large bowl, mix spices and remaining yogurt; stir in chicken to coat.

2. Place chicken on an oiled grill rack over medium heat; grill, covered, until no longer pink, 2-3 minutes per side. Grill pita breads until warmed, about 1 minute per side.

3. Spread pitas with sauce. Top with chicken, cheese, tomato and parsley.

1 PIZZA 380 cal., 12g fat (6g sat. fat), 72mg chol., 598mg sod., 41g carb. (5g sugars, 5g fiber), 29g pro.

37g Pro 5i

CRISPY BUFFALO CHICKEN ROLL-UPS FOR TWO

These winning chicken rolls with a crispy crust are both impressive and easy to make. My family and friends absolutely love them!
—Lisa Keys, Kennett Square, PA

PREP: 15 MIN. • **BAKE:** 30 MIN.
MAKES: 2 SERVINGS

- 2 boneless skinless chicken breast halves (6 oz. each)
- ¼ tsp. salt
- ¼ tsp. pepper
- 2 Tbsp. crumbled blue cheese
- 2 Tbsp. hot pepper sauce
- 1 Tbsp. mayonnaise
- ½ cup crushed cornflakes

1. Preheat oven to 400°. Flatten chicken breasts to ¼-in. thickness. Season with salt and pepper; sprinkle with blue cheese. Roll up each chicken breast from a short side and secure with toothpicks.
2. In a shallow bowl, combine pepper sauce and mayonnaise. Place cornflakes in a separate shallow bowl. Dip chicken roll-ups in pepper sauce mixture, then coat with cornflakes. Place seam side down in a greased 11x7-in. baking dish.
3. Bake, uncovered, until chicken is no longer pink, 30-35 minutes. Discard toothpicks.
1 SERVING 270 cal., 8g fat (3g sat. fat), 101mg chol., 617mg sod., 10g carb. (1g sugars, 0 fiber), 37g pro.

31g Pro

TASTY TURKEY & MUSHROOMS

Fresh mushrooms star in this tender turkey entree that comes together in 15 minutes. Served with a side of brown rice, it makes a light but satisfying dinner.
—Nancy Zimmerman, Cape May Court House, NJ

TAKES: 15 MIN. • **MAKES:** 2 SERVINGS

- 1 garlic clove, minced
- 1 Tbsp. butter
- ½ lb. boneless skinless turkey breast, cut into 2-in. strips
- ¾ cup reduced-sodium beef broth
- 1 Tbsp. tomato paste
- 2 cups sliced fresh mushrooms
- ⅛ tsp. salt

In a large nonstick skillet, saute garlic in butter until tender. Add turkey; cook until juices run clear. Remove and keep warm. Add the broth, tomato paste, mushrooms and salt to skillet; cook for 3-5 minutes or until mushrooms are tender, stirring occasionally. Return turkey to the pan and heat through.
1 CUP 209 cal., 7g fat (4g sat. fat), 88mg chol., 435mg sod., 5g carb. (3g sugars, 1g fiber), 31g pro.

BEEF

35g Pro 5i

ITALIAN CRUMB-CRUSTED BEEF ROAST

Italian-style panko crumbs and seasoning give this roast beef a special touch. It's a nice, effortless weeknight meal that allows you to put your time and energy into relaxing.
—Maria Regakis, Saugus, MA

PREP: 10 MIN.
BAKE: 1¾ HOURS + STANDING
MAKES: 8 SERVINGS

- 1 beef sirloin tip roast (3 lbs.)
- ¼ tsp. salt
- ¾ cup Italian-style panko bread crumbs
- ¼ cup mayonnaise
- 3 Tbsp. dried minced onion
- ½ tsp. Italian seasoning
- ¼ tsp. pepper

1. Preheat oven to 325°. Place roast on a rack in a shallow roasting pan; sprinkle with salt. In a small bowl, mix remaining ingredients; press onto top and sides of roast.
2. Roast until meat reaches desired doneness (for medium-rare, a thermometer should read 135°; medium, 140°; medium well, 145°), 1¾-2¼ hours. Remove roast from oven; tent with foil. Let stand 10 minutes before slicing.
5 OZ. COOKED BEEF 319 cal., 15g fat (3g sat. fat), 111mg chol., 311mg sod., 7g carb. (0 sugars, 0 fiber), 35g pro.

27g Pro

SLOW-COOKED BEEF TIPS

These slow-cooked beef tips remind me of a childhood favorite. I cook them with mushrooms and serve over brown rice, noodles or mashed potatoes.
—Amy Lents, Grand Forks, ND

PREP: 25 MIN. • **COOK:** 6¼ HOURS
MAKES: 2 SERVINGS

- ¼ lb. sliced baby portobello mushrooms
- ½ small onion, sliced
- 1 beef top sirloin steak (½ lb.), cubed
- ¼ tsp. salt
- ⅛ tsp. pepper
- 1 tsp. olive oil
- 3 Tbsp. dry red wine or beef broth
- 1 cup beef broth
- 1½ tsp. Worcestershire sauce
- 1 Tbsp. cornstarch
- 2 Tbsp. water
- Hot cooked mashed potatoes

1. Place mushrooms and onion in a 3-qt. slow cooker. Sprinkle beef with salt and pepper. In a large skillet, heat oil over medium-high heat; brown meat. Transfer meat to slow cooker.
2. Add wine to skillet, stirring to loosen browned bits from pan. Stir in broth and Worcestershire sauce; pour over meat. Cook, covered, on low 6-8 hours or until meat is tender.
3. In a small bowl, mix cornstarch and water until smooth; gradually stir into slow cooker. Cook, covered, on high for 15-30 minutes or until gravy is thickened. Serve with mashed potatoes.
1 CUP 213 cal., 7g fat (2g sat. fat), 46mg chol., 836mg sod., 8g carb. (2g sugars, 1g fiber), 27g pro.

> *The entire family loves this dish. We make it nearly every month. It's got a great flavor and it's a fantastic way to sneak a few vegetables into the kids.*
>
> —ASPEAR, TASTEOFHOME.COM

20g Pro

CORNY CHILI

This southwestern chili full of corn is so delicious and fuss free, I love to share the recipe. Busy moms really appreciate its simplicity.
—Marlene Olson, Hoople, ND

PREP: 20 MIN. • **COOK:** 3 HOURS
MAKES: 6 SERVINGS

- 1 lb. ground beef
- 1 small onion, chopped
- 1 can (16 oz.) kidney beans, rinsed and drained
- 2 cans (14½ oz. each) diced tomatoes, undrained
- 1 can (11 oz.) whole kernel corn, drained
- ¾ cup picante sauce
- 1 Tbsp. chili powder
- ¼ to ½ tsp. garlic powder
- Optional: Corn chips, sour cream and shredded cheddar cheese

1. In a large skillet, cook beef and onion over medium heat until meat is no longer pink, breaking into crumbles; drain.
2. Transfer to a 3-qt. slow cooker. Stir in beans, tomatoes, corn, picante sauce, chili powder and garlic powder. Cover and cook on low for 3-4 hours or until heated through. If desired, serve with corn chips, sour cream and cheese.
1 CUP 274 cal., 9g fat (3g sat. fat), 47mg chol., 790mg sod., 27g carb. (10g sugars, 8g fiber), 20g pro.

15g Pro

MAKEOVER LI'L CHEDDAR MEAT LOAVES

My husband loves mini meat loaves, but this family-favorite recipe wasn't very healthy when I first received it. The Taste of Home Test Kitchen experts slashed the calories and fat while keeping the original's tender and delicious qualities.
—Jodie Mitchell, Denver, PA

PREP: 15 MIN. • **BAKE:** 25 MIN.
MAKES: 8 SERVINGS

- 2 large egg whites, beaten
- ¾ cup fat-free milk
- 1 cup shredded reduced-fat cheddar cheese
- ¾ cup quick-cooking oats
- 1 medium onion, chopped
- 1 medium carrot, shredded
- ½ tsp. salt
- ¾ lb. lean ground beef (90% lean)
- ⅔ cup ketchup
- 2 Tbsp. brown sugar
- 1½ tsp. prepared mustard

1. In a large bowl, whisk egg whites and milk. Stir in cheese, oats, onion, carrot and salt. Crumble beef over mixture and mix lightly but thoroughly.
2. Shape into 8 loaves; place in a 13x9-in. baking dish coated with cooking spray. In a small bowl, combine the ketchup, brown sugar and mustard; spoon over loaves.
3. Bake, uncovered, at 350° for 25-30 minutes or until a thermometer inserted in a loaf reads 160°.
1 MEAT LOAF 187 cal., 7g fat (3g sat. fat), 36mg chol., 550mg sod., 18g carb. (11g sugars, 1g fiber), 15g pro.

27g Pro

PRESSURE-COOKER SALSA LONDON BROIL

I love using my pressure cooker for this recipe because it comes together so quickly but still has that long, slow-cooked flavor. The veggies semi-melt into the sauce to give it an added savory taste, and the lime gives it a pleasant finish.
—Ann Sheehy, Londonderry, NH

PREP: 15 MIN.
COOK: 10 MIN. + RELEASING
MAKES: 4 SERVINGS

- 1 to 1½ lbs. beef top round steak
- 1 jar (16 oz.) salsa
- 1 medium sweet potato, peeled and chopped
- 1 large carrot, thinly sliced
- 1 garlic clove, minced
- Lime wedges
- Chopped fresh cilantro, optional

1. Cut steak into thirds; place in a 6-qt. electric pressure cooker. Add salsa, sweet potato, carrot and garlic. Lock lid; close pressure-release valve. Adjust to pressure-cook on high for 10 minutes. Let pressure release naturally.
2. Slice steak. Serve with vegetables. Garnish with lime wedges and, if desired, chopped cilantro.

1 SERVING 239 cal., 4g fat (1g sat. fat), 63mg chol., 503mg sod., 23g carb. (10g sugars, 2g fiber), 27g pro.

39g Pro

SLOW-COOKED COFFEE BEEF ROAST

Coffee is the key to a flavorful beef roast that simmers in the slow cooker until it's fall-apart tender. Try it once, and I'm sure you'll cook it again.
—Charles Trahan, San Dimas, CA

PREP: 15 MIN. • **COOK:** 8 HOURS
MAKES: 6 SERVINGS

- 1 beef sirloin tip roast (2½ lbs.), cut in half
- 2 tsp. canola oil
- 1½ cups sliced fresh mushrooms
- ⅓ cup sliced green onions
- 2 garlic cloves, minced
- 1½ cups brewed coffee
- 1 tsp. liquid smoke, optional
- ½ tsp. salt
- ½ tsp. chili powder
- ¼ tsp. pepper
- ¼ cup cornstarch
- ⅓ cup cold water

1. In a large nonstick skillet, brown roast on all sides in oil over medium-high heat. Place in a 5-qt. slow cooker. In the same skillet, saute mushrooms, onions and garlic until tender; stir in coffee, liquid smoke if desired, salt, chili powder and pepper. Pour over roast.
2. Cover and cook on low for 8-10 hours or until meat is tender. Remove roast and keep warm. Pour cooking juices into a 2-cup measuring cup; skim off fat.
3. In a small saucepan, combine cornstarch and water until smooth. Gradually stir in 2 cups cooking juices. Bring to a boil; cook and stir until thickened, about 2 minutes. Serve with beef.

5 OZ. COOKED BEEF 281 cal., 10g fat (3g sat. fat), 120mg chol., 261mg sod., 6g carb. (1g sugars, 0 fiber), 39g pro.

> Easy fix, easy cleanup, very delicious, and versatile as well. My family enjoyed the tender steak and flavorful veggies. This recipe was filed immediately in my recipe box after dinner!
>
> —LUA210, TASTEOFHOME.COM

40g Pro 5i

STEAK & POTATO FOIL PACKS

As a park ranger, I've cooked a lot of meals outdoors. I often assemble foil packs and toss them into my backpack with some ice. Then when I set up camp, it's easy to cook them over a campfire. If I'm at home, I use my grill, and the food is just as good.
—Ralph Jones, San Diego, CA

PREP: 20 MIN. • **GRILL:** 20 MIN.
MAKES: 8 SERVINGS

- 2 beef top sirloin steaks (1½ lbs. each)
- 3 lbs. red potatoes, cut into ½-in. cubes
- 1 medium onion, chopped
- 4 tsp. minced fresh rosemary
- 1 Tbsp. minced garlic
- 2 tsp. salt
- 1 tsp. pepper

1. Prepare grill for medium heat or preheat oven to 450°. Cut each steak into 4 pieces. In a large bowl, combine steak, potatoes, onion, rosemary, garlic, salt and pepper.
2. Divide mixture among eight 18x12-in. pieces of heavy-duty foil, placing food on dull side of foil. Fold foil around potato mixture, sealing tightly.
3. Place packets on grill or in oven; cook until potatoes are tender, 8-10 minutes on each side. Open packets carefully to allow steam to escape. If desired, sprinkle with additional rosemary.

1 PACKET 348 cal., 7g fat (3g sat. fat), 69mg chol., 677mg sod., 29g carb. (2g sugars, 3g fiber), 40g pro.

STEAK & POTATO FOIL PACK TIPS

Can you bake steak and potato foil packs in the oven? Absolutely! If it's a rainy day, or you simply don't want to fire up the grill, you can opt for the oven. Bake the steak and potato foil packs in a 450° oven for 20-25 minutes.

Can you cook the steak medium-rare in the foil packs? Although it's harder to monitor the steak as it cooks because it's wrapped up in foil, you can still cook it medium-rare when you're making this steak and potato foil pack recipe. Cut the steaks in half and prepare them in 4 foil packs instead of 8. The bigger pieces will result in meat that's more rare.

22g Pro

FREEZER BURRITOS

I love burritos, but the frozen ones are high in salt and chemicals. So I created these. They're wonderful to have on hand for quick dinners or late-night snacks—I've even had them for breakfast!
—Laura Winemiller, Delta, PA

PREP: 35 MIN. • **COOK:** 15 MIN.
MAKES: 12 SERVINGS

- 1¼ lbs. lean ground beef (90% lean)
- ¼ cup finely chopped onion
- 1¼ cups salsa
- 2 Tbsp. reduced-sodium taco seasoning
- 2 cans (15 oz. each) pinto beans, rinsed and drained
- ½ cup water
- 2 cups shredded reduced-fat cheddar cheese
- 12 flour tortillas (8 in.), warmed

1. In a large skillet, cook beef and onion over medium heat until meat is no longer pink, 5-7 minutes, breaking meat into crumbles; drain. Stir in salsa and taco seasoning. Bring to a boil. Reduce heat; simmer, uncovered, for 2-3 minutes. Transfer to a large bowl; set aside.
2. In a food processor, combine pinto beans and water. Cover and process until almost smooth. Add to beef mixture. Stir in cheese.
3. Spoon ½ cup beef mixture down the center of each tortilla. Fold ends and sides over filling; roll up. Wrap each burrito in waxed paper and foil. Freeze for up to 1 month.
4. To use frozen burritos: Remove foil and waxed paper. Place 1 burrito on a microwave-safe plate. Microwave on high until a thermometer reads 165°, 2½-2¾ minutes, turning burrito over once. Let stand for 20 seconds.
1 BURRITO 345 cal., 11g fat (4g sat. fat), 36mg chol., 677mg sod., 40g carb. (3g sugars, 3g fiber), 22g pro.

33g Pro

BRAISED HANUKKAH BRISKET

My mother, Enid, always used the most marbled cut of brisket she could find to make this recipe so she'd get the most flavor. When she added carrots to the pan, she threw in some potatoes too.
—Ellen Ruzinsky, Yorktown Heights, NY

PREP: 25 MIN. • **COOK:** 2¾ HOURS
MAKES: 12 SERVINGS (4 CUPS VEGETABLES)

- 2 Tbsp. canola oil
- 1 fresh beef brisket (4 to 5 lbs.)
- 3 celery ribs, cut into 1-in. pieces
- 3 large carrots, cut into ¼-in. slices
- 2 large onions, sliced
- 1 lb. medium fresh mushrooms
- ¾ cup cold water
- ¾ cup tomato sauce
- 3 Tbsp. Worcestershire sauce
- 1 Tbsp. prepared horseradish

1. In a Dutch oven, heat oil over medium heat. Brown the brisket on both sides. Remove from pan.

2. Add the celery, carrots, onions and mushrooms to same pan; cook and stir 4-6 minutes or until crisp-tender. Stir in remaining ingredients.

3. Return brisket to pan, fat side up. Bring mixture to a boil. Reduce heat; simmer, covered, 2½-3 hours or until meat is tender. Remove beef and vegetables; keep warm. Skim fat from pan juices. If desired, thicken juices.

4. Cut brisket diagonally across the grain into thin slices. Serve with vegetables and pan juices.

4 OZ. COOKED MEAT WITH ⅓ CUP VEGETABLES AND ½ CUP JUICES 247 cal., 9g fat (3g sat. fat), 64mg chol., 189mg sod., 8g carb. (3g sugars, 2g fiber), 33g pro.

SLOW-HEAT SECRET

The key to making a tender brisket is using low and slow heat. Don't try to rush it by boiling the brisket; it'll turn out chewy and dry. If you have time, the best way to keep the brisket moist is to make it a day in advance. Cool it whole in the cooking liquid overnight and reheat it the next day.

20g Pro

SPAGHETTI SQUASH BOATS

Made with a bounty of fresh ingredients, this recipe creates a refreshing summer dish. The spaghetti sauce has a texture that's delightfully different.
—Vickey Lorenger, Detroit, MI

PREP: 1 HOUR • **BAKE:** 20 MIN.
MAKES: 2 SERVINGS

- 1 medium spaghetti squash (about 4 lbs.)
- ¼ lb. ground beef
- ½ cup chopped onion
- ½ cup chopped green pepper
- ½ cup sliced fresh mushrooms
- 1 garlic clove, minced
- ½ tsp. dried basil
- ½ tsp. dried oregano
- ¼ tsp. salt
- ⅛ tsp. pepper
- 1 can (14½ oz.) diced tomatoes, drained
- ⅓ cup shredded part-skim mozzarella cheese
- Sliced fresh basil, optional

1. Preheat oven to 375°. Cut squash in half lengthwise; scoop out seeds. Place squash cut side down in a baking dish. Fill dish with ½ in. hot water. Bake, uncovered, until tender, 30-40 minutes. Reduce oven setting to 350°.
2. When cool enough to handle, scoop out flesh, separating strands with a fork; set squash shells and flesh aside.
3. In a large skillet, cook beef, onion and green pepper over medium-heat until meat is no longer pink, 3-4 minutes, breaking up beef into crumbles; drain. Add mushrooms, garlic, basil, oregano, salt and pepper; cook and stir 2 minutes. Add tomatoes; cook and stir 2 minutes longer. Stir in squash.
4. Cook, uncovered, until the liquid has evaporated, about 10 minutes. Fill shells; place in shallow baking dish.
5. Bake, uncovered, for 15 minutes. Sprinkle with cheese; bake until cheese is melted, about 5 minutes longer. If desired, top with basil.

1 STUFFED SQUASH HALF 335 cal., 12g fat (5g sat. fat), 47mg chol., 852mg sod., 43g carb. (20g sugars, 10g fiber), 20g pro.

SQUASH TWIST

The Italian flavors in this dish pair well with the squash strands since they make a great substitute for noodles, but you can fill your squash with many other flavors. Give it a taco twist with red peppers, tomatoes, and olives; make it work for meatless Monday with artichokes, spinach, and cheese; or give it an Asian flair by making spaghetti squash lo mein with soy sauce, julienned carrots and red cabbage.

30g Pro

EASY SLOW-COOKER POT ROAST

I love making this pot roast for a couple of reasons. First, it's delicious. Second, it's so easy! I can't describe the feeling of walking into my house after work and smelling this dish that's been simmering in the slow cooker all day. There's nothing better.
—James Schend, Pleasant Prairie, WI

PREP: 10 MIN. • **COOK:** 10 HOURS
MAKES: 10 SERVINGS

- 1 boneless beef rump or chuck roast (3 to 3½ lbs.)
- 1 Tbsp. canola oil
- 6 medium carrots, cut into thirds
- 6 medium potatoes, peeled and quartered
- 1 large onion, quartered
- 3 tsp. Montreal steak seasoning
- 1 carton (32 oz.) beef broth
- 3 Tbsp. cornstarch
- 3 Tbsp. water

1. In a large skillet over medium heat, brown roast in oil on all sides. Place carrots, potatoes and onion in a 6-qt. slow cooker. Place roast on top of vegetables; sprinkle with steak seasoning. Add broth. Cook, covered, on low 10-12 hours or until beef and vegetables are tender.
2. Remove roast and vegetables from slow cooker; keep warm.
3. Transfer cooking juices to a saucepan; skim off fat. Bring juices to a boil. In a small bowl, mix cornstarch and water until smooth; stir into juices. Return to a boil, stirring constantly; cook and stir until thickened, 1-2 minutes. Serve with roast and vegetables.

1 SERVING 354 cal., 15g fat (5g sat. fat), 88mg chol., 696mg sod., 24g carb. (4g sugars, 3g fiber), 30g pro.

28g Pro

FETA MUSHROOM BURGERS

My son-in-law gave me this recipe and I tweaked it to make it healthier. The burgers are so quick to whip up on the grill.
—Dolores Block, Frankenmuth, MI

TAKES: 25 MIN. • **MAKES:** 6 SERVINGS

- 1 lb. lean ground beef (90% lean)
- 3 Italian turkey sausage links (4 oz. each), casings removed
- 2 tsp. Worcestershire sauce
- ½ tsp. garlic powder
- 2 Tbsp. balsamic vinegar
- 1 Tbsp. olive oil
- 6 large portobello mushrooms, stems removed
- 1 large onion, cut into ½-in. slices
- 6 Tbsp. crumbled feta or blue cheese
- 6 whole wheat hamburger buns or sourdough rolls, split
- 10 fresh basil leaves, thinly sliced

1. Combine first 4 ingredients; mix lightly but thoroughly. Shape into six ½-in.-thick patties. Mix vinegar and oil; brush over mushrooms.
2. Place burgers, mushrooms and onion on an oiled grill rack over medium heat. Grill, covered, until a thermometer inserted in burgers reads 160° and mushrooms and onion are tender, 4-6 minutes per side.
3. Fill mushroom caps with cheese; grill, covered, until the cheese is melted, 1-2 minutes. Grill buns, cut side down, until toasted, 30-60 seconds. Serve burgers on buns; top with mushrooms, basil and onion.

1 BURGER 371 cal., 15g fat (5g sat. fat), 72mg chol., 590mg sod., 31g carb. (8g sugars, 5g fiber), 28g pro.

21g Pro

COLORFUL BEEF STIR-FRY

I really like this beef stir-fry recipe. Who wouldn't love the easy sesame-ginger marinade and the vibrant mix of vegetables?
—Deb Blendermann, Boulder, CO

PREP: 35 MIN. + MARINATING
COOK: 15 MIN. • **MAKES:** 4 CUPS

- ¼ cup reduced-sodium soy sauce
- 1 Tbsp. honey
- 2 tsp. sesame oil
- 3 garlic cloves, minced
- ⅛ tsp. ground ginger
- ½ lb. boneless beef sirloin steak, thinly sliced
- 4½ tsp. cornstarch
- ½ cup reduced-sodium beef broth
- 1½ tsp. canola oil, divided
- 1 small green pepper, cut into chunks
- 1 small onion, cut into chunks
- 1 medium carrot, julienned
- ¼ cup sliced celery
- 1 small zucchini, julienned
- ½ cup fresh snow peas
- ½ cup canned bean sprouts, rinsed and drained
- Optional: Hot cooked rice or linguine

1. In a small bowl, combine the first 5 ingredients. Place beef in a shallow dish; add half of the marinade. Turn to coat; cover and refrigerate for at least 2 hours. Cover and refrigerate remaining marinade.

2. In a small bowl, combine cornstarch and broth until smooth. Stir in reserved marinade; set aside. Drain the beef, discarding marinade. In a large nonstick skillet or in a wok, cook beef in 1 tsp. oil until no longer pink; drain. Remove and keep warm.

3. In the same pan, stir-fry green pepper and onion in remaining ½ tsp. oil for 2 minutes. Add carrot and celery; cook 2-3 minutes longer. Add zucchini and snow peas; stir-fry for 1 minute. Stir in bean sprouts and heat through.

4. Stir broth mixture and stir into vegetable mixture. Bring to a boil; cook and stir until thickened, 1-2 minutes. Return beef to the pan; heat through. If desired, serve over rice or linguine.

1 CUP 318 cal., 8g fat (2g sat. fat), 43mg chol., 542mg sod., 41g carb. (8g sugars, 4g fiber), 21g pro.

NOTES

PROTEIN
BOOST
PAGE 320

32g Pro

BEEF BURGUNDY OVER NOODLES

I got this delightful recipe from my sister-in-law many years ago. Whenever I serve it to guests, they always request the recipe. The tender beef, mushrooms and flavorful sauce are delicious over noodles.
—Margaret Welder, Madrid, IA

PREP: 10 MIN. • **COOK:** 1 HOUR 20 MIN.
MAKES: 2 SERVINGS

- 2 tsp. butter
- ½ lb. beef top sirloin steak, cut into ¼-in.-thick strips
- 2 Tbsp. diced onion
- 1½ cups quartered fresh mushrooms
- ¾ cup Burgundy wine or beef broth
- ¼ cup plus 2 Tbsp. water, divided
- 3 Tbsp. minced fresh parsley, divided
- 1 bay leaf
- 1 whole clove
- ¼ tsp. salt
- ⅛ tsp. pepper
- 2 cups uncooked medium egg noodles (about 4 oz.)
- 1 Tbsp. all-purpose flour
- ½ tsp. browning sauce, optional

1. In a Dutch oven or large nonstick skillet, heat butter over medium-high heat; saute beef and onion just until beef is lightly browned, 1-2 minutes. Stir in mushrooms, wine, ¼ cup water, 2 Tbsp. parsley and seasonings; bring to a boil. Reduce heat; simmer, covered, until beef is tender, about 1 hour.

2. Meanwhile, cook the egg noodles according to package directions. Drain.

3. In a small bowl, mix the flour and remaining water until smooth; stir into beef mixture. Bring to a boil; cook and stir until thickened, about 2 minutes. Discard bay leaf and clove. If desired, stir in browning sauce. Serve over noodles. Sprinkle with remaining parsley.

1½ CUPS 376 cal., 10g fat (5g sat. fat), 88mg chol., 391mg sod., 34g carb. (2g sugars, 2g fiber), 32g pro.

36g Pro

CURRIED BEEF PITAS WITH CUCUMBER SAUCE

A good friend gave me this recipe when I first got married. Because some of the ingredients weren't familiar to me, I was a bit apprehensive about trying it. But years later, it's a family favorite!
—Shannon Koene, Blacksburg, VA

TAKES: 25 MIN.
MAKES: 4 SERVINGS (1½ CUPS SAUCE)

- 1 cup fat-free plain Greek yogurt
- 1 cup finely chopped peeled cucumber
- 1 Tbsp. minced fresh mint
- 2 garlic cloves, minced
- 2 tsp. snipped fresh dill
- 2 tsp. lemon juice
- ¼ tsp. salt

PITAS

- 1 lb. lean ground beef (90% lean)
- 1 small onion, chopped
- 1 medium Golden Delicious apple, finely chopped
- ¼ cup raisins
- 2 tsp. curry powder
- ¼ tsp. salt
- 8 whole wheat pita pocket halves

1. In a small bowl, mix first 7 ingredients. Refrigerate until serving.

2. In a large skillet, cook beef and onion over medium heat 6-8 minutes or until beef is no longer pink, crumbling beef; drain. Add apple, raisins, curry powder and salt; cook until the apple is tender, stirring occasionally. Serve in pita halves with sauce.

2 FILLED PITA HALVES WITH ⅓ CUP SAUCE 429 cal., 11g fat (4g sat. fat), 71mg chol., 686mg sod., 50g carb. (13g sugars, 6g fiber), 36g pro.

STAUB

30g Pro

BARLEY BEEF SKILLET

Even my 3-year-old loves this family favorite. It's very filling, inexpensive and packed with veggies. It's also really good spiced up with chili powder, cayenne or a dash of hot pepper sauce.
—Kit Tunstall, Boise, ID

PREP: 20 MIN. • **COOK:** 20 MIN.
MAKES: 4 SERVINGS

- 1 lb. lean ground beef (90% lean)
- ¼ cup chopped onion
- 1 garlic clove, minced
- 1 can (14½ oz.) reduced-sodium beef broth
- 1 can (8 oz.) tomato sauce
- 1 cup water
- 2 small carrots, chopped
- 1 small tomato, seeded and chopped
- 1 small zucchini, chopped
- 1 cup medium pearl barley
- 2 tsp. Italian seasoning
- ¼ tsp. salt
- ⅛ tsp. pepper

In a large cast-iron or other heavy skillet, cook beef and onion over medium heat until meat is no longer pink. Add garlic; cook 1 minute longer. Drain. Add the broth, tomato sauce and water; bring to a boil. Stir in the remaining ingredients. Reduce heat; cover and simmer until barley is tender, 20-25 minutes.

1½ CUPS 400 cal., 10g fat (4g sat. fat), 73mg chol., 682mg sod., 48g carb. (4g sugars, 10g fiber), 30g pro.

37g Pro 5i

CHOCOLATE-CHIPOTLE SIRLOIN STEAK

Looking to do something a little different with grilled sirloin? Add smoky heat and chocolaty rich color with this easy five-ingredient rub.
—Taste of Home *Test Kitchen*

PREP: 10 MIN. + CHILLING
GRILL: 20 MIN. • **MAKES:** 4 SERVINGS

- 3 Tbsp. baking cocoa
- 2 Tbsp. chopped chipotle peppers in adobo sauce
- 4 tsp. Worcestershire sauce
- 2 tsp. brown sugar
- ½ tsp. salt
- 1½ lbs. beef top sirloin steak

1. Place the first 5 ingredients in a blender; cover and process until blended. Rub over beef. Cover and refrigerate for at least 2 hours.

2. Grill beef, covered, over medium heat or broil 4 in. from heat for 8-10 minutes on each side or until meat reaches desired doneness (for medium-rare, a thermometer should read 135°; medium, 140°; medium-well, 145°).

5 OZ. COOKED BEEF 246 cal., 7g fat (3g sat. fat), 69mg chol., 477mg sod., 6g carb. (3g sugars, 1g fiber), 37g pro.

34g Pro

APPLE & ONION BEEF POT ROAST

I thicken the cooking juices from this roast to make a pleasing apple gravy that's wonderful over the beef and onions.
—Rachel Koistinen, Hayti, SD

PREP: 30 MIN.
COOK: 5¼ HOURS + STANDING
MAKES: 8 SERVINGS

- 1 beef sirloin tip roast (3 lbs.), cut in half
- 1 cup water
- 1 tsp. seasoned salt
- ½ tsp. reduced-sodium soy sauce
- ½ tsp. Worcestershire sauce
- ¼ tsp. garlic powder
- 1 large tart apple, quartered
- 1 large onion, sliced
- 2 Tbsp. cornstarch
- 2 Tbsp. cold water
- ⅛ tsp. browning sauce

1. In a large skillet coated with cooking spray, brown the roast on all sides. Transfer to a 5-qt. slow cooker. Add water to the skillet, stirring to loosen any browned bits; pour over roast. Sprinkle with the seasoned salt, soy sauce, Worcestershire sauce and garlic powder. Top with apple and onion.
2. Cover and cook on low for 5-6 hours or until the meat is tender.
3. Remove roast and onion; let stand for 15 minutes before slicing. Strain cooking liquid into a saucepan, discarding apple. Bring liquid to a boil; cook until reduced to 2 cups, about 15 minutes. Combine cornstarch and cold water until smooth; stir in browning sauce. Stir into cooking liquid. Bring to a boil; cook and stir for 2 minutes or until thickened. Serve with beef and onion.
1 SERVING 242 cal., 8g fat (3g sat. fat), 108mg chol., 256mg sod., 7g carb. (3g sugars, 1g fiber), 34g pro.

32g Pro

EASY PEPPER STEAK

This popular beef dish is tasty as well as colorful.
—Carolyn Butterfield, Atkinson, NE

PREP: 10 MIN. • **COOK:** 55 MIN.
MAKES: 4 SERVINGS

- 1 lb. beef top round steak, cut into ¼x2-in. strips
- 1 Tbsp. paprika
- 2 Tbsp. butter
- 1 can (10½ oz.) beef broth
- 2 garlic cloves, minced
- 2 medium green peppers, cut into strips
- 1 cup thinly sliced onion
- 2 Tbsp. cornstarch
- 2 Tbsp. reduced-sodium soy sauce
- ⅓ cup cold water
- 2 fresh tomatoes, peeled and cut into wedges
- Cooked rice

1. Sprinkle meat with paprika. In a large skillet, melt butter over medium-high heat. Brown beef. Add broth and garlic. Simmer, covered, for 30 minutes.
2. Add green peppers and onion. Cover and continue to simmer for 5 minutes. Combine cornstarch, soy sauce and water; stir into meat mixture. Cook and stir until thickened. Gently stir in tomatoes and heat through. Serve over rice.
1 SERVING 365 cal., 4g fat (1g sat. fat), 65mg chol., 465mg sod., 48g carb. (5g sugars, 4g fiber), 32g pro.

POWER PLAY

To bump up the protein, add an extra handful of beef strips or stir in cooked chicken or turkey at the end. Three ounces (a serving the size of a deck of cards) of cooked sirloin steak, pork loin, tuna, chicken or turkey breast provides about 25 grams of protein.

"
This was excellent! I've made beef barbacoa before, but I will keep this as my favorite. The seasonings were just right and the meat very tender and tasty.
—BONNIETURNER, TASTEOFHOME.COM

38g Pro

SLOW-COOKER BEEF BARBACOA

I love this beef barbacoa because the meat is fall-apart tender and the sauce is smoky, slightly spicy and so flavorful. It's an amazing alternative to ground beef tacos or even pulled pork carnitas. It's also versatile. You can have a soft taco bar and let people make their own—or offer mouthwatering Mexican pizzas or rice bowls.
—Holly Sander, Lake Mary, FL

PREP: 20 MIN. • **COOK:** 6 HOURS
MAKES: 8 SERVINGS

- 1 beef rump or bottom round roast (3 lbs.)
- ½ cup minced fresh cilantro
- ⅓ cup tomato paste
- 8 garlic cloves, minced
- 2 Tbsp. chipotle peppers in adobo sauce plus 1 Tbsp. sauce
- 2 Tbsp. cider vinegar
- 4 tsp. ground cumin
- 1 Tbsp. brown sugar
- 1½ tsp. salt
- 1 tsp. pepper
- 1 cup beef stock
- 1 cup beer or additional stock
- 16 corn tortillas (6 in.)
- Pico de gallo
- Optional toppings: Lime wedges, queso fresco and additional cilantro

1. Cut the roast in half. Mix the next 9 ingredients; rub over roast. Place in a 5-qt. slow cooker. Add stock and beer. Cook, covered, until meat is tender, 6-8 hours.
2. Remove roast; shred with 2 forks. Reserve 3 cups cooking juices; discard remaining juices. Skim fat from reserved juices. Return beef and reserved juices to slow cooker; heat through.
3. Serve with tortillas and pico de gallo. If desired, serve with lime wedges, queso fresco and additional cilantro.

FREEZE OPTION Place shredded beef in freezer containers. Cool and freeze. To use, partially thaw in refrigerator overnight. Heat through in a covered saucepan, stirring gently; add broth if necessary.

2 FILLED TORTILLAS 361 cal., 10g fat (3g sat. fat), 101mg chol., 652mg sod., 28g carb. (4g sugars, 4g fiber), 38g pro.

NOTES

22g Pro

PRESSURE-COOKER BEEF & FARRO STEW

This pressure-cooked stew is loaded with tender beef and lots of veggies. It's comforting and filling, so it's sure to become a family favorite.
—Kaylen Friederich, Reno, NV

PREP: 40 MIN.
COOK: 30 MIN. + RELEASING
MAKES: 12 SERVINGS (4 QT.)

- 1 boneless beef chuck roast (about 2 lbs.), cut into 1-in. pieces
- 1½ tsp. salt
- ½ tsp. pepper
- 2 Tbsp. olive oil, divided
- 6 large carrots, cut into ½-in. pieces
- 3 celery ribs, chopped
- 1 large onion, chopped
- 6 garlic cloves, minced
- ¼ cup tomato paste
- 1 cup dry red wine
- 6 cups beef stock
- 4 large Yukon Gold potatoes, peeled and cut into 1-in. pieces
- ½ lb. fresh mushrooms, sliced
- ¾ cup farro, rinsed
- 3 bay leaves
- 1 tsp. garlic powder
- 1 tsp. dried thyme

1. Sprinkle beef with salt and pepper. Select saute or browning setting on a 6-qt. electric pressure cooker. Adjust for medium heat; add 1 Tbsp. oil. When oil is hot, brown beef in batches. Set aside.
2. Add remaining 1 Tbsp. oil and carrots, celery and onion to pressure cooker; cook and stir until vegetables are crisp-tender, 5-7 minutes.
3. Add the garlic; cook 1 minute longer. Add tomato paste. Cook and stir until fragrant, about 1 minute. Add wine, stirring to loosen browned bits.
4. Return beef to pressure cooker. Stir in stock, potatoes, mushrooms, farro, bay leaves, garlic powder and thyme. Press cancel.
5. Lock lid; close pressure-release valve. Adjust to pressure-cook on high for 30 minutes. Let the pressure release naturally for 15 minutes; quick-release any remaining pressure. If desired, skim fat from stew. Discard bay leaves.

FREEZE OPTION Freeze cooled stew in freezer containers. To use, partially thaw in refrigerator overnight. Heat through in a saucepan, stirring occasionally; add broth or water if necessary.

1⅓ CUPS 360 cal., 10g fat (3g sat. fat), 49mg chol., 619mg sod., 43g carb. (6g sugars, 5g fiber), 22g pro.

EASY SQUASH PREP

If you don't have a pressure cooker, pop the squash halves into the microwave on high for 15-20 minutes or roast them in the oven upside down until tender.

25g Pro

BEEF & BLACK BEAN SPAGHETTI SQUASH

I've been working on developing healthier recipes that still taste delicious—and keep me satisfied. This squash tossed with beef, beans and kale has so much flavor it's easy to forget it's good for you!
—Charlotte Cravins, Opelousas, LA

PREP: 10 MIN. • **COOK:** 20 MIN.
MAKES: 4 SERVINGS

- 1 medium spaghetti squash (about 4 lbs.)
- ¾ lb. lean ground beef (90% lean)
- ½ cup chopped red onion
- 2 Tbsp. yellow mustard
- 2 to 3 tsp. Louisiana-style hot sauce
- 4 small garlic cloves, minced
- 1 can (15 oz.) no-salt-added black beans, rinsed and drained
- 2 cups chopped fresh kale
- ¼ cup plain Greek yogurt

1. Trim ends of the squash and halve lengthwise; discard seeds. Place squash, cut side down, on a trivet insert in a 6-qt. electric pressure cooker. Add 1 cup water to cooker. Lock lid; close pressure-release valve. Adjust to pressure-cook on high for 7 minutes. Quick-release pressure. Set squash aside.

2. In a large skillet, crumble beef and cook with onion over medium heat until no longer pink, 4-6 minutes; drain. Add mustard, hot sauce and garlic; cook 1 minute more. Stir in black beans and kale; cook just until wilted, 2-3 minutes.

3. Using a fork, separate strands of spaghetti squash; combine with meat mixture. Dollop servings with Greek yogurt.

1½ CUPS 312 cal., 10g fat (4g sat. fat), 57mg chol., 283mg sod., 32g carb. (6g sugars, 8g fiber), 25g pro.

21g Pro

MEXI-STRONI SOUP

If you're a fan of classic minestrone but love bold Mexican flavors, this soup's for you! It's pumped up with spices, veggies and pasta for a filling bowl of fun.
—Darlene Island, Lakewood, WA

PREP: 25 MIN. • **COOK:** 7½ HOURS
MAKES: 10 SERVINGS (3¾ QT.)

- 1½ lbs. beef stew meat (1-in. pieces)
- 1½ cups shredded carrots
- ½ cup chopped onion
- 1 jalapeno pepper, seeded and minced, optional
- 1 tsp. ground cumin
- 1 tsp. chili powder
- ¾ tsp. seasoned salt
- ½ tsp. Italian seasoning
- 2 cans (10 oz. each) diced tomatoes and green chiles, undrained
- 2 cups spicy hot V8 juice
- 1 carton (32 oz.) reduced-sodium beef broth
- 1 medium zucchini, halved and thinly sliced
- 2 cups finely shredded cabbage
- 2 celery ribs, thinly sliced
- 1 can (16 oz.) kidney beans, rinsed and drained
- 1 can (15 oz.) black beans, rinsed and drained
- 1 cup small pasta shells
- ¼ cup chopped fresh cilantro

Place first 11 ingredients, including jalapeno if desired, in a 6- or 7-qt. slow cooker. Cook, covered, on low until meat is tender, 7-9 hours. Stir in zucchini, cabbage, celery, beans and pasta. Cook, covered, on high until vegetables and pasta are tender, 30-45 minutes, stirring occasionally. Stir in cilantro.

1½ CUPS 249 cal., 5g fat (2g sat. fat), 44mg chol., 816mg sod., 29g carb. (5g sugars, 6g fiber), 21g pro.

TURN UP THE HEAT

The V8 and diced tomatoes with green chiles add nice heat. If you like it spicier still, go ahead and add the optional jalapeno.

NOTES

Great family food. I really enjoyed topping it with the sliced jalapeno and pepper jack cheese along with a dollop of sour cream and a sprinkle of corn chips.
—RENEEMURBY, TASTEOFHOME.COM

27g Pro

SLOW-COOKER CHILI MAC

This recipe has regularly appeared on my family menus for more than 40 years, and it's never failed to please at potlucks and bring-a-dish gatherings. Sometimes I turn it into soup by adding a can of beef broth.
—Marie Posavec, Berwyn, IL

PREP: 15 MIN. • **COOK:** 6 HOURS
MAKES: 6 SERVINGS

- 1 lb. lean ground beef (90% lean), cooked and drained
- 2 cans (16 oz. each) hot chili beans, undrained
- 2 large green peppers, chopped
- 1 large onion, chopped
- 4 celery ribs, chopped
- 1 can (8 oz.) no-salt-added tomato sauce
- 2 Tbsp. chili seasoning mix
- 2 garlic cloves, minced
- 1 pkg. (7 oz.) elbow macaroni, cooked and drained
- Salt and pepper to taste
- Optional: Shredded pepper jack cheese and sliced jalapeno pepper

In a 5-qt. slow cooker, combine the first 8 ingredients. Cook, covered, on low for 6 hours or until heated through. Stir in macaroni. Season with salt and pepper. If desired, top servings with cheese and sliced jalapenos.

1 SERVING 348 cal., 8g fat (3g sat. fat), 47mg chol., 713mg sod., 49g carb. (8g sugars, 12g fiber), 27g pro.

19g Pro

SLOW-COOKER BEEF STEW

When there's a chill in the air, I love to make my slow-cooked stew. It's loaded with tender chunks of beef, potatoes and carrots.
—Earnestine Wilson, Waco, TX

PREP: 25 MIN. • **COOK:** 7 HOURS
MAKES: 8 SERVINGS (2 QT.)

- 1½ lbs. potatoes, peeled and cubed
- 6 medium carrots, cut into 1-in. lengths
- 1 medium onion, coarsely chopped
- 3 celery ribs, coarsely chopped
- 3 Tbsp. all-purpose flour
- 1½ lbs. beef stew meat, cut into 1-in. cubes
- 3 Tbsp. canola oil
- 1 can (14½ oz.) diced tomatoes, undrained
- 1 can (14½ oz.) beef broth
- 1 tsp. ground mustard
- ½ tsp. salt
- ½ tsp. pepper
- ½ tsp. dried thyme
- ½ tsp. browning sauce, optional
- Minced fresh thyme, optional

1. Layer the potatoes, carrots, onion and celery in a 5-qt. slow cooker. Place flour in a large shallow dish. Add stew meat; turn to coat evenly. In a large skillet, brown meat in oil in batches. Place over vegetables.

2. In a large bowl, combine the tomatoes, broth, mustard, salt, pepper, thyme and, if desired, browning sauce. Pour over beef. Cover and cook on low 7-8 hours or until the meat and vegetables are tender. If desired, sprinkle with fresh thyme before serving.

1 CUP 272 cal., 12g fat (3g sat. fat), 53mg chol., 541mg sod., 23g carb. (6g sugars, 4g fiber), 19g pro.

33g Pro

SMOKED BRISKET

This is always a crowd favorite—it really melts in your mouth!
—Jodi Abel, La Jolla, CA

PREP: 20 MIN. + CHILLING
GRILL: 8 HOURS + STANDING
MAKES: 20 SERVINGS

- 2 Tbsp. olive oil
- 1 fresh beef brisket (7 to 8 lbs.)

RUB

- 2 Tbsp. garlic powder
- 2 Tbsp. onion powder
- 2 Tbsp. chili powder
- 1 Tbsp. ground mustard
- 1 Tbsp. ground cumin
- 1 Tbsp. paprika
- 1 Tbsp. smoked sea salt

MOP SAUCE

- 2 cups beef broth
- ¼ cup olive oil
- 2 Tbsp. Worcestershire sauce
- 2 Tbsp. hickory-flavored liquid smoke

1. Brush olive oil over brisket. Combine rub ingredients; rub over both sides of beef. Place brisket on a rimmed baking sheet. Cover and refrigerate overnight or up to 2 days. Meanwhile, in a small saucepan, combine the mop sauce ingredients. Simmer 15 minutes, stirring occasionally. Refrigerate until ready to grill.

2. Soak hickory and mesquite chips or pellets; add to smoker according to manufacturer's directions. Heat to 225°. Uncover brisket. Place the brisket in smoker fat side up; smoke for 2 hours. Brush generously with mop sauce; turn meat. Smoke for 2 more hours; brush generously with mop sauce again. Wrap brisket securely in heavy-duty aluminum foil; smoke until a thermometer inserted in beef reads 190°, 4-5 hours longer.

3. Let beef stand 20-30 minutes before slicing; cut diagonally across the grain into thin slices.

NOTE This is a fresh beef brisket, not corned beef.

4 OZ. COOKED BEEF 252 cal., 11g fat (3g sat. fat), 68mg chol., 472mg sod., 2g carb. (0 sugars, 1g fiber), 33g pro.

NOTES

14g Pro

HEARTY BEEF & BARLEY SOUP

Barley soup is a popular menu item in our house throughout the year. Everyone savors the flavor.
—Elizabeth Kendall, Carolina Beach, NC

PREP: 20 MIN. • **COOK:** 1 HOUR 50 MIN.
MAKES: 9 SERVINGS (2¼ QT.)

- 1 Tbsp. canola oil
- 1 lb. beef top round steak, cut into ½-in. cubes
- 3 cans (14½ oz. each) beef broth
- 2 cups water
- ⅓ cup medium pearl barley
- ¾ tsp. salt
- ⅛ tsp. pepper
- 1 cup chopped carrots
- ½ cup chopped celery
- ¼ cup chopped onion
- 3 Tbsp. minced fresh parsley
- 1 cup frozen peas

1. In a large saucepan, heat oil over medium heat. Brown beef on all sides; drain. Stir in broth, water, barley, salt and pepper. Bring to a boil. Reduce heat; cover and simmer for 1 hour.

2. Add carrots, celery, onion and parsley; cover and simmer until the meat and vegetables are tender, 30-40 minutes. Stir in peas; heat through.

1 CUP 133 cal., 4g fat (1g sat. fat), 28mg chol., 859mg sod., 10g carb. (2g sugars, 2g fiber), 14g pro.

31g Pro

SLOW-COOKER FAJITAS

I love fajitas from Mexican restaurants, but when I tried preparing them at home, the meat was always too chewy. Then I tried this recipe in my slow cooker, and my husband and I enjoyed every bite.
—Katie Urso, Seneca, IL

PREP: 25 MIN. • **COOK:** 8 HOURS
MAKES: 8 SERVINGS

- 1 each medium green, sweet red and yellow peppers, cut into ½-in. strips
- 1 sweet onion, cut into ½-in. strips
- 2 lbs. beef top sirloin steaks, cut into thin strips
- ¾ cup water
- 2 Tbsp. red wine vinegar
- 1 Tbsp. lime juice
- 1 tsp. ground cumin
- 1 tsp. chili powder
- ½ tsp. salt
- ½ tsp. garlic powder
- ½ tsp. pepper
- ½ tsp. cayenne pepper
- 8 flour tortillas (8 in.), warmed
- ½ cup salsa
- ½ cup shredded reduced-fat cheddar cheese
- 8 tsp. fresh cilantro leaves

1. Place the peppers and onion in a 5-qt. slow cooker. Top with the beef. Combine water, vinegar, lime juice and seasonings; pour over meat. Cover and cook on low until meat is tender, 8-10 hours.

2. Using a slotted spoon, place about ¾ cup meat mixture down the center of each tortilla. Top with salsa, cheese and cilantro; roll up.

1 FAJITA 361 cal., 10g fat (4g sat. fat), 51mg chol., 555mg sod., 35g carb. (4g sugars, 3g fiber), 31g pro.

25g Pro

TERIYAKI SIRLOIN STEAK

Since a co-worker shared this recipe with me, I seldom make steak any other way. It's an excellent entree for folks like my husband who really savor tasty meat, and it's earned me many compliments on my cooking.
—Nilah Lewis, Calgary, AB

PREP: 10 MIN. + MARINATING
GRILL: 10 MIN. • **MAKES:** 6 SERVINGS

- ½ cup soy sauce
- ¼ cup canola oil
- ¼ cup packed brown sugar
- 2 tsp. ground mustard
- 2 tsp. ground ginger
- 1 tsp. garlic powder
- 1 beef top sirloin steak (1½ lbs.)

1. In a shallow dish, combine the first 6 ingredients; add the steak and turn to coat. Cover and refrigerate for 8 hours or overnight.
2. Drain steak, discarding marinade. Grill steak, covered, over medium heat until meat reaches desired doneness (for medium-rare, a thermometer should read 135°; medium, 140°; medium-well, 145°), 5-8 minutes on each side.
3 OZ. COOKED BEEF 178 cal., 7g fat (2g sat. fat), 46mg chol., 370mg sod., 2g carb. (2g sugars, 0 fiber), 25g pro.

40g Pro 5i

EASY & ELEGANT TENDERLOIN ROAST

I love the simplicity of the rub in this recipe—olive oil, garlic, salt and pepper. Just add the tenderloin and pop it in the oven. In an hour or so you've got an impressive main dish to feed a crowd. This means less time fussing in the kitchen, leaving you with more time to visit with family.
—Mary Kandell, Huron, OH

PREP: 10 MIN.
BAKE: 45 MIN. + STANDING
MAKES: 12 SERVINGS

- 1 beef tenderloin (5 lbs.)
- 2 Tbsp. olive oil
- 4 garlic cloves, minced
- 2 tsp. sea salt
- 1½ tsp. coarsely ground pepper

1. Preheat oven to 425°. Place roast on a rack in a shallow roasting pan. In a small bowl, mix the oil, garlic, salt and pepper; rub over roast.
2. Roast until meat reaches desired doneness (for medium-rare, a thermometer should read 135°; medium, 140°; medium-well, 145°), 45-65 minutes. Remove from oven; tent with foil. Let stand 15 minutes before slicing.
5 OZ. COOKED BEEF 294 cal., 13g fat (5g sat. fat), 82mg chol., 394mg sod., 1g carb. (0 sugars, 0 fiber), 40g pro.

18g Pro

BEST SHEPHERD'S PIE

I received the recipe for this economical dish from a friend who was a whiz at pinching pennies without sacrificing hearty flavor.
—Valerie Merrill, Topeka, KS

PREP: 40 MIN. • **BAKE:** 30 MIN.
MAKES: 10 SERVINGS

- 2½ lbs. potatoes, peeled and cooked
- 1 cup reduced-fat sour cream
- Salt and pepper to taste
- 2 lbs. ground sirloin
- ½ cup chopped onion
- 1 medium sweet red pepper, chopped
- 1 tsp. garlic salt
- 1 can (10½ oz.) condensed cream of mushroom soup, undiluted
- 1 can (15¼ oz.) whole kernel corn, drained
- ½ cup 2% milk
- 2 Tbsp. butter, melted
- Chopped fresh parsley, optional

1. Preheat oven to 350°. In a large bowl, mash potatoes with sour cream. Add salt and pepper. In a large skillet, cook beef with onion and red pepper, crumbling beef, until meat is no longer pink and vegetables are tender; drain. Stir garlic salt into meat mixture. Stir in soup, corn and milk.

2. Spread meat mixture into a 13x9-in. baking dish. Top with mashed potatoes; drizzle with melted butter.

3. Bake, uncovered, until heated through, 30-35 minutes. If desired, sprinkle with parsley.

1 CUP 274 cal., 9g fat (4g sat. fat), 45mg chol., 620mg sod., 32g carb. (6g sugars, 4g fiber), 18g pro.

35g Pro

SLOW-COOKER BEEF TOSTADAS

I dedicate these slow-simmered tostadas to my husband, the only Italian man I know who can't get enough of Mexican flavors. Pile on your best toppings.
—Teresa DeVono, Red Lion, PA

PREP: 20 MIN. • **COOK:** 6 HOURS
MAKES: 6 SERVINGS

- 1 large onion, chopped
- ¼ cup lime juice
- 1 jalapeno pepper, seeded and minced
- 1 serrano pepper, seeded and minced
- 1 Tbsp. chili powder
- 3 garlic cloves, minced
- ½ tsp. ground cumin
- 1 beef top round steak (about 1½ lbs.)
- 1 tsp. salt
- ½ tsp. pepper
- ¼ cup chopped fresh cilantro
- 12 corn tortillas (6 in.)
- Cooking spray

TOPPINGS

- 1½ cups shredded lettuce
- 1 medium tomato, finely chopped
- ¾ cup shredded sharp cheddar cheese
- ¾ cup reduced-fat sour cream, optional

1. Place the first 7 ingredients in a 3- or 4-qt. slow cooker. Cut steak in half and sprinkle with salt and pepper; add to slow cooker. Cook, covered, on low until meat is tender, 6-8 hours.

2. Remove meat; cool slightly. Shred meat with 2 forks. Return beef to slow cooker and stir in cilantro; heat through. Spritz both sides of tortillas with cooking spray. Place in a single layer on baking sheets; broil 1-2 minutes on each side or until crisp. Spoon beef mixture over tortillas; top with lettuce, tomato, cheese and, if desired, sour cream.

NOTE Wear disposable gloves when cutting hot peppers; the oils can burn skin. Avoid touching your face.

2 TOSTADAS 372 cal., 13g fat (6g sat. fat), 88mg chol., 602mg sod., 30g carb. (5g sugars, 5g fiber), 35g pro.

38g Pro

ALL-DAY BRISKET WITH POTATOES

I think the slow cooker was invented with brisket in mind. This sweet and savory version is perfection itself, because it melts in your mouth. It's very important to buy first-cut or flat-cut brisket, which has far less fat than other cuts.

—Lana Gryga, Glen Flora, WI

PREP: 30 MIN. • **COOK:** 8 HOURS
MAKES: 8 SERVINGS

- 2 medium potatoes, peeled and cut into ¼-in. slices
- 2 celery ribs, sliced
- 1 fresh beef brisket (3 lbs.)
- 1 Tbsp. canola oil
- 1 large onion, sliced
- 2 garlic cloves, minced
- 1 can (12 oz.) beer
- ½ tsp. beef bouillon granules
- ¾ cup stewed tomatoes
- ⅓ cup tomato paste
- ¼ cup red wine vinegar
- 3 Tbsp. brown sugar
- 3 Tbsp. Dijon mustard
- 3 Tbsp. soy sauce
- 2 Tbsp. molasses
- ½ tsp. paprika
- ¼ tsp. salt
- ⅛ tsp. pepper
- 1 bay leaf

1. Place potatoes and celery in a 5-qt. slow cooker. Cut brisket in half. In a large skillet, brown beef in oil on all sides; transfer to slow cooker. In the same pan, saute onion until tender. Add garlic; cook 1 minute longer. Add to slow cooker.

2. Add beer and bouillon granules to skillet, stirring to loosen browned bits from pan; pour over meat. In a large bowl, combine remaining ingredients; add to slow cooker.

3. Cover and cook on low until meat and vegetables are tender, 8-10 hours. Discard bay leaf. To serve, thinly slice across the grain.

NOTE This is a fresh beef brisket, not corned beef.

1 SERVING 352 cal., 9g fat (3g sat. fat), 72mg chol., 722mg sod., 25g carb. (13g sugars, 2g fiber), 38g pro.

NOTES

25g Pro

SLOW-COOKED CHILI

This hearty chili can cook for up to 10 hours on low in the slow cooker. It's so good to come home to its wonderful aroma after a long day away.
—Sue Call, Beech Grove, IN

PREP: 20 MIN. • **COOK:** 8 HOURS
MAKES: 10 SERVINGS (2½ QT.)

- 2 lbs. lean ground beef (90% lean)
- 2 cans (16 oz. each) kidney beans, rinsed and drained
- 2 cans (14½ oz. each) diced tomatoes, undrained
- 1 can (8 oz.) tomato sauce
- 2 medium onions, chopped
- 1 medium green pepper, chopped
- 2 garlic cloves, minced
- 2 Tbsp. chili powder
- 1 tsp. salt
- 1 tsp. pepper
- Optional: Shredded cheddar cheese, sliced green onions, chopped red onion, sliced jalapeno peppers and sour cream

1. In a large skillet, cook the beef over medium heat until no longer pink, 10-12 minutes, breaking into crumbles; drain.
2. Transfer to a 5-qt. slow cooker. Add the next 9 ingredients. Cover and cook on low for 8-10 hours. Serve with toppings as desired.

1 CUP 260 cal., 8g fat (3g sat. fat), 57mg chol., 712mg sod., 23g carb. (6g sugars, 7g fiber), 25g pro.

31g Pro

SPECIAL OCCASION BEEF BOURGUIGNON

I've found many rich and satisfying variations for beef Bourguignon, including an intriguing peasant version that used beef cheeks for the meat and a rustic table wine. To make this stew gluten free, use white rice flour instead of all-purpose.
—Leo Cotnoir, Johnson City, NY

PREP: 50 MIN. • **BAKE:** 2 HOURS
MAKES: 8 SERVINGS

- 4 bacon strips, chopped
- 1 beef sirloin tip roast (2 lbs.), cut into 1½-in. cubes and patted dry
- ¼ cup all-purpose flour
- ½ tsp. salt
- ½ tsp. pepper
- 1 Tbsp. canola oil
- 2 medium onions, chopped
- 2 medium carrots, coarsely chopped
- ½ lb. medium fresh mushrooms, quartered
- 4 garlic cloves, minced
- 1 Tbsp. tomato paste
- 2 cups dry red wine
- 1 cup beef stock
- 2 bay leaves
- ½ tsp. dried thyme
- 8 oz. uncooked egg noodles
- Minced fresh parsley

1. Preheat oven to 325°. In a Dutch oven, cook bacon over medium-low heat until crisp, stirring occasionally. Remove with a slotted spoon, reserving drippings; drain on paper towels.
2. In batches, brown beef in drippings over medium-high heat; remove from pan. Toss with flour, salt and pepper.
3. In same pan, heat 1 Tbsp. oil over medium heat; saute onions, carrots and mushrooms until onions are tender, 4-5 minutes. Add garlic and tomato paste; cook and stir 1 minute. Add wine and stock, stirring to loosen browned bits from pan. Add herbs, bacon and beef; bring to a boil.
4. Transfer to oven; bake, covered, until meat is tender, 2-2¼ hours. Remove bay leaves.
5. To serve, cook noodles according to package directions; drain. Serve stew with noodles; sprinkle with parsley.

FREEZE OPTION Freeze cooled stew in freezer containers. To use, partially thaw in refrigerator overnight. Heat through in a saucepan, stirring occasionally; add stock or broth if necessary.

⅔ CUP STEW WITH ⅔ CUP NOODLES
422 cal., 14g fat (4g sat. fat), 105mg chol., 357mg sod., 31g carb. (4g sugars, 2g fiber), 31g pro.

36g Pro

BEEF ROAST DINNER

Because this healthy dish is slow-cooked, you can use less expensive roasts with results as mouthwatering as the more costly cuts. Change up the veggies for variety, nutrition or to suit your tastes!
—Sandra Dudley, Bemidji, MN

PREP: 25 MIN. • **COOK:** 7 HOURS
MAKES: 8 SERVINGS

- 1 lb. red potatoes (3-4 medium), cubed
- 1½ cups fresh baby carrots
- 1 medium green pepper, chopped
- 1 medium parsnip, chopped
- ¼ lb. small fresh mushrooms
- 1 small red onion, chopped
- 1 beef rump roast or bottom round roast (3 lbs.)
- 1 can (14½ oz.) beef broth
- ¾ tsp. salt
- ¾ tsp. dried oregano
- ¼ tsp. pepper
- 3 Tbsp. cornstarch
- ¼ cup cold water

1. Place vegetables in a 5-qt. slow cooker. Cut roast in half; place over vegetables. Mix broth and seasonings; pour over roast. Cook, covered, on low until meat and vegetables are tender, 7-9 hours.

2. Remove roast and vegetables from slow cooker; keep warm. Transfer the cooking juices to a small saucepan; bring to a boil. Mix cornstarch and water until smooth; stir into cooking juices. Return to a boil; cook and stir until thickened, 1-2 minutes. Serve with roast and vegetables.

1 SERVING 304 cal., 8g fat (3g sat. fat), 101mg chol., 533mg sod., 19g carb. (4g sugars, 3g fiber), 36g pro.

STOVETOP BEEF ROAST DINNER In a Dutch oven, brown the roast on all sides in 1-2 Tbsp. canola oil. Add the broth, salt, oregano, pepper and onion; bring to a boil. Reduce the heat, cover and simmer for 2 hours. Add the potatoes, mushrooms, carrots, green pepper and parsnip; cover and simmer 45-60 minutes longer or until the meat is tender. Remove the meat and vegetables to a serving platter and keep warm. For gravy, pour pan drippings and loosened browned bits into a measuring cup; skim and discard fat. Transfer to a small saucepan. Combine cornstarch and cold water until smooth; gradually stir into drippings. Bring to a boil; cook and stir for 2 minutes or until thickened. Slice beef; serve with gravy.

PORK, LAMB & MORE

36g Pro

PINEAPPLE PORK TENDERLOIN

You need just a few ingredients to pull off this special entree of juicy grilled pineapple slices and ginger-flavored pork tenderloin.
—Donna Noel, Gray, ME

PREP: 10 MIN. + MARINATING
GRILL: 30 MIN. • **MAKES:** 4 SERVINGS

- 1 cup unsweetened pineapple juice
- ¼ cup minced fresh gingerroot
- ¼ cup reduced-sodium soy sauce
- 4 garlic cloves, minced
- 1 tsp. ground mustard
- 2 pork tenderloins (¾ lb. each)
- 1 fresh pineapple, cut into 12 slices

1. In a small bowl, combine the first 5 ingredients. Pour ⅔ cup marinade into a large dish. Add the pork; turn to coat. Refrigerate for 8 hours or overnight. Cover and refrigerate remaining marinade.
2. Drain the pork, discarding marinade. Lightly grease the grill rack.
3. Prepare grill for indirect heat, using a drip pan. Place pork over drip pan and grill, covered, over indirect medium heat for 25-30 minutes or until a thermometer reads 160°, basting occasionally with the reserved marinade. Let stand for 5 minutes before slicing.
4. Meanwhile, grill pineapple slices for 2-3 minutes on each side or until heated through; serve with pork.
5 OZ. COOKED PORK WITH 3 PINEAPPLE SLICES 295 cal., 6g fat (2g sat. fat), 95mg chol., 523mg sod., 23g carb. (16g sugars, 2g fiber), 36g pro.

35g Pro

PORK CHOP CACCIATORE

It's hard to believe that so much flavor can come from such an easy recipe. Serve it with noodles and a simple green salad, and dinner is solved!
—Tracy Hiatt Grice, Somerset, WI

PREP: 30 MIN. • **COOK:** 4 HOURS
MAKES: 6 SERVINGS

- 6 bone-in pork loin chops (7 oz. each)
- ¾ tsp. salt, divided
- ¼ tsp. pepper
- 1 Tbsp. olive oil
- 1 cup sliced fresh mushrooms
- 1 small onion, chopped
- 1 celery rib, chopped
- 1 small green pepper, chopped
- 2 garlic cloves, minced
- 1 can (14½ oz.) diced tomatoes
- ½ cup water, divided
- ½ tsp. dried basil
- 2 Tbsp. cornstarch
- 4½ cups cooked egg noodles

1. Sprinkle chops with ½ tsp. salt and ¼ tsp. pepper. In a large skillet, brown chops in oil in batches. Transfer to a 4-or 5-qt. slow cooker coated with cooking spray. In same skillet, cook and stir mushrooms, onion, celery and green pepper in drippings until tender. Add garlic; cook 1 minute longer. Stir in tomatoes, ¼ cup water, basil and remaining ¼ tsp. salt; pour over chops.
2. Cover and cook on low for 4-6 hours or until pork is tender. Remove meat to a serving platter; keep warm. Skim fat from cooking juices if necessary. Transfer juices to a small saucepan; bring to a boil. Combine cornstarch and remaining ¼ cup water until smooth. Gradually stir into pan. Bring to a boil; cook and stir for 2 minutes or until thickened. Serve with meat and noodles.
1 PORK CHOP WITH ¾ CUP NOODLES AND ½ CUP SAUCE 371 cal., 12g fat (4g sat. fat), 110mg chol., 458mg sod., 29g carb. (4g sugars, 3g fiber), 35g pro.

18g Pro

HEARTY PORK BEAN SOUP

It's wonderful to come home to a pork bean soup dinner simmering away in a slow cooker. This soup uses dried beans and is simple to throw together in the morning before work. When you get home, just add a few more ingredients, and in about half an hour dinner will be ready!
—Colleen Delawder, Herndon, VA

PREP: 20 MIN. + SOAKING
COOK: 6¼ HOURS
MAKES: 12 SERVINGS (4 QT.)

- 1 pkg. (16 oz.) dried great northern beans
- 1 large sweet onion, chopped
- 3 medium carrots, chopped
- 3 celery ribs, chopped
- 1 pork tenderloin (1 lb.)
- 1 tsp. garlic powder
- 1 Tbsp. fresh minced chives or 1 tsp. dried chives
- 1 tsp. dried oregano
- ½ tsp. dried thyme
- 1 tsp. pepper
- 1 carton (32 oz.) reduced-sodium chicken broth
- 1 can (14½ oz.) reduced-sodium chicken broth
- 1 bottle (12 oz.) extra pale ale
- 1 can (14½ oz.) diced tomatoes, drained
- 5 oz. fresh spinach
- 1½ to 2 tsp. salt

1. Rinse and sort beans. Place in a large saucepan; add water to cover by 2 in. Let soak, covered, overnight. Drain and rinse beans, discarding liquid.
2. Return beans to saucepan; add water to cover by 2 in. Bring to a boil. Boil for 15 minutes. Drain and rinse beans, discarding liquid.
3. In a 6-qt. slow cooker, layer beans, onion, carrots, celery and pork. Add the seasonings, broth and ale. Cook, covered, on low until beans and pork are tender, 6-8 hours.
4. Remove pork; shred with 2 forks. Stir in tomatoes, spinach and salt. Return pork to slow cooker. Cook, covered, on low for 15-20 minutes or until heated through.

1⅓ CUPS 207 cal., 2g fat (1g sat. fat), 21mg chol., 695mg sod., 30g carb. (5g sugars, 9g fiber), 18g pro.

NOTES

34g Pro

MAPLE-GLAZED PORK TENDERLOIN

My husband and I think this roasted pork tenderloin tastes like a fancy restaurant dish, but it couldn't be simpler to make at home. The maple glaze makes it extra special.

—Colleen Mercier, Salmon Arm, BC

TAKES: 30 MIN. • **MAKES:** 4 SERVINGS

- ¾ tsp. salt
- ¾ tsp. rubbed sage
- ½ tsp. pepper
- 2 pork tenderloins (¾ lb. each)
- 1 tsp. butter
- ¼ cup maple syrup
- 3 Tbsp. cider vinegar
- 1¾ tsp. Dijon mustard

1. Preheat oven to 425°. Mix seasonings; sprinkle over pork. In a large nonstick skillet, heat butter over medium heat; brown tenderloins on all sides. Transfer to a foil-lined 15x10x1-in. pan. Roast for 10 minutes.

2. Meanwhile, for glaze, in same skillet, mix syrup, vinegar and mustard; bring to a boil, stirring to loosen browned bits from pan. Cook and stir until slightly thickened, 1-2 minutes; remove from heat.

3. Brush 1 Tbsp. glaze over pork; continue roasting until a thermometer inserted in pork reads 145°, 7-10 minutes, brushing halfway through with remaining glaze. Let stand 5 minutes before slicing.

5 OZ. COOKED PORK 264 cal., 7g fat (3g sat. fat), 98mg chol., 573mg sod., 14g carb. (12g sugars, 0 fiber), 34g pro.

34g Pro

PORK CHOPS WITH APRICOT GLAZE

This quick recipe is fantastic! The seasonings add just the right amount of flavor, and the apricot preserves offer a touch of sweetness. The glaze is also tasty on grilled chicken.
—Kathy Harding, Richmond, MO

TAKES: 30 MIN. • **MAKES:** 6 SERVINGS

- 1½ tsp. ground ginger
- 1 tsp. salt
- ½ tsp. garlic powder
- ½ tsp. pepper
- 6 boneless pork loin chops (6 oz. each)
- 1 cup apricot preserves
- 2 Tbsp. hoisin sauce
- ½ tsp. crushed red pepper flakes
- 2 green onions, chopped
- 3 Tbsp. chopped unsalted peanuts

1. Mix ginger, salt, garlic powder and pepper; rub onto both sides of chops. In a small saucepan, combine preserves, hoisin sauce and pepper flakes; cook and stir over medium heat until blended. Reserve ½ cup for brushing chops after grilling.

2. On a lightly oiled grill rack, grill pork chops, covered, over medium heat or broil 4 in. from heat 4-5 minutes on each side or until a thermometer reads 145°, basting frequently with remaining sauce during the last 4 minutes of cooking. Let stand 5 minutes before serving. Brush chops with reserved ½ cup sauce; sprinkle with green onions and peanuts.

1 PORK CHOP 399 cal., 12g fat (4g sat. fat), 82mg chol., 549mg sod., 39g carb. (21g sugars, 1g fiber), 34g pro.

13g Pro

BEAN SOUP WITH SAUSAGE

This soup is so simple to put together, and it uses ingredients that are easy to keep on hand. The tomatoey broth is loaded with meat, potatoes and veggies.
—Gail Wilkerson, House Springs, MO

PREP: 10 MIN. • **COOK:** 25 MIN.
MAKES: 10 SERVINGS (2½ QT.)

- 8 oz. bulk lean turkey breakfast sausage
- 1 medium onion, chopped
- 1 medium green pepper, chopped
- 2 cans (16 oz. each) kidney beans, rinsed and drained
- 1 medium potato, peeled and cubed
- 4 cups water
- 1 bay leaf
- ½ tsp. each garlic salt, seasoned salt and pepper
- ½ tsp. dried thyme
- 1 can (28 oz.) diced tomatoes, undrained

1. In a large saucepan, cook sausage, onion and green pepper over medium heat 4-6 minutes or until vegetables are tender and sausage is no longer pink, breaking up sausage into crumbles; drain.

2. Stir in beans, potato, water and seasonings; bring to a boil. Reduce heat; simmer, uncovered, 10-15 minutes or until potato is tender. Stir in tomatoes and heat through. Discard bay leaf.

1 CUP 160 cal., 2g fat (1g sat. fat), 24mg chol., 645mg sod., 23g carb. (5g sugars, 6g fiber), 13g pro.

31g Pro 5i

EASY SLOW-COOKED PORK TENDERLOIN

I find simple dinners are the best comfort foods that my family of seven really desires. Everyday, good ingredients are the key to my success in the kitchen. Three ingredients poured over the pork and—voila!
—Grace Neltner, Lakeside Park, KY

PREP: 5 MIN.
COOK: 1¾ HOURS + STANDING
MAKES: 6 SERVINGS

- ¼ cup olive oil
- 2 Tbsp. soy sauce
- 1 Tbsp. Montreal steak seasoning
- 2 pork tenderloins (1 lb. each)
  Cooked wild rice or mashed potatoes

In a 5-qt. slow cooker, mix oil, soy sauce and steak seasoning. Add pork; turn to coat. Cook, covered, on low until a thermometer inserted in pork reads 145°, 1¾-2¼ hours. Let stand 10 minutes before slicing. Serve with cooking juices if desired and wild rice or mashed potatoes.

5 OZ. COOKED PORK 259 cal., 14g fat (3g sat. fat), 85mg chol., 707mg sod., 0 carb. (0 sugars, 0 fiber), 31g pro.

MOISTURE MATTERS

A thin coating of oil keeps pork from drying out in the slow cooker. Unlike water-based liquids, which create steam, oil coats the surface of the meat, limiting evaporation and locking in moisture.

31g Pro

APPLE-GLAZED HOLIDAY HAM

Each Christmas I'm asked to prepare this entree. I'm happy to oblige because it is easy to assemble, bakes for a few hours unattended and is simply delicious.
—Emory Doty, Jasper, GA

PREP: 10 MIN. • **BAKE:** 2½ HOURS
MAKES: 15 SERVINGS

- 1 spiral-sliced fully cooked bone-in ham (7 to 9 lbs.)
- ½ cup packed brown sugar
- ½ cup unsweetened applesauce
- ½ cup unsweetened apple juice
- ¼ cup maple syrup
- ¼ cup molasses
- 1 Tbsp. Dijon mustard
- Dash ground ginger
- Dash ground cinnamon

1. Place ham on a rack in a shallow roasting pan. Bake, uncovered, at 325° for 2 hours.

2. For glaze, in a small saucepan, combine the remaining ingredients. Cook and stir over medium heat until heated through. Brush ham with some glaze; bake 30-60 minutes longer or until a thermometer reads 140°, brushing occasionally with remaining glaze.

4 OZ. HAM 242 cal., 6g fat (2g sat. fat), 93mg chol., 1138mg sod., 17g carb. (15g sugars, 0 fiber), 31g pro.

TEST KITCHEN TIP

For a juicier, more flavorful ham, leave the skin on during the first 2 hours of cooking. This allows the layer of fat underneath the skin to slowly cook and flavor the meat while retaining the moisture. About 30 to 60 minutes before the ham is done, remove it from the oven and let it cool just enough to handle. Use a sharp knife to trim the skin and fat. Apply the glaze and return to the oven to finish baking. This last stint in the oven lets the glaze's flavor permeate the meat and forms a nice crispy crust on top without cooking too much.

31g Pro

CUBAN-STYLE PORK CHOPS

These are like Cuban sandwiches without the bread, so they're a bit more elegant. Let your family customize the chops with pickles, mustard and other condiments.
—Erica Allen, Tuckerton, NJ

PREP: 15 MIN. + MARINATING
GRILL: 10 MIN. • **MAKES:** 4 SERVINGS

- 1 Tbsp. Dijon mustard
- 1 Tbsp. lime juice
- 1 tsp. adobo seasoning
- 4 boneless pork loin chops (4 oz. each)
- 4 slices deli ham (about 3 oz.)
- 4 slices Swiss cheese
- 2 Tbsp. chopped fresh cilantro
- Optional: Mayonnaise, additional Dijon mustard and thinly sliced dill pickles

1. Mix mustard, lime juice and adobo seasoning. Lightly pound pork chops with a meat mallet to ½-in. thickness; spread both sides with mustard mixture. Refrigerate, covered, 3-4 hours.
2. Grill pork chops, covered, over medium heat 3 minutes. Turn pork and top with ham; grill 2 minutes longer. Top with cheese and cilantro; grill, covered, 30-60 seconds longer or until cheese is melted and a thermometer inserted in chops reads 145°. Let stand 5 minutes before serving. If desired, serve with mayonnaise, mustard and pickles.
1 SERVING 247 cal., 12g fat (5g sat. fat), 84mg chol., 700mg sod., 2g carb. (1g sugars, 0 fiber), 31g pro.

30g Pro

BAJA PORK TACOS

This delicious recipe is my copycat version of the most excellent Mexican food we ever had in Flagstaff, Arizona. The original recipe used beef instead of pork, but this comes mighty close to the same taste.
—Ariella Winn, Mesquite, TX

PREP: 10 MIN. • **COOK:** 8 HOURS
MAKES: 12 SERVINGS

- 1 boneless pork sirloin roast (3 lbs.)
- 5 cans (4 oz. each) chopped green chiles
- 2 Tbsp. reduced-sodium taco seasoning
- 3 tsp. ground cumin
- 24 corn tortillas (6 in.), warmed
- 3 cups shredded lettuce
- 1½ cups shredded part-skim mozzarella cheese

1. Cut roast in half; place in a 3- or 4-qt. slow cooker. Mix chiles, taco seasoning and cumin; spoon over pork. Cook, covered, on low 8-10 hours or until meat is tender.
2. Remove pork; cool slightly. Skim fat from cooking juices. Shred meat with 2 forks. Return to slow cooker; heat through. Serve in tortillas with lettuce and cheese.
FREEZE OPTION Place cooled pork mixture in freezer containers; freeze up to 3 months. To use, partially thaw in refrigerator overnight. Heat through in a covered saucepan, stirring gently; add broth or water if necessary.
2 TACOS 320 cal., 11g fat (4g sat. fat), 77mg chol., 434mg sod., 26g carb. (1g sugars, 4g fiber), 30g pro.

HEALTH TIP

Using reduced-sodium taco seasoning saves about 80mg sodium per serving.

31g Pro

HONEY-GLAZED PORK TENDERLOINS

Honey, smoky chipotle pepper and soy sauce help to flavor this no-fuss pork tenderloin. Serve it with veggies or rice for a satisfying meal.
—Diane Cotton, Franklin, NC

PREP: 15 MIN. • **BAKE:** 20 MIN.
MAKES: 6 SERVINGS

- ½ tsp. garlic powder
- ½ tsp. ground chipotle pepper
- ½ tsp. pepper
- 2 pork tenderloins (1 lb. each)
- 1 Tbsp. canola oil
- ½ cup honey
- 2 Tbsp. reduced-sodium soy sauce
- 1 Tbsp. balsamic vinegar
- 1 tsp. sesame oil

1. Preheat oven to 350°. Combine the first 3 ingredients; rub over pork. In a large ovenproof skillet, brown pork in canola oil on all sides.

2. In a small bowl, combine honey, soy sauce, vinegar and sesame oil; spoon over pork. Bake, uncovered, 20-25 minutes or until a thermometer reads 145°, basting occasionally with pan juices. Let stand 5 minutes before slicing. Serve with pan juices if desired.

4 OZ. COOKED PORK 288 cal., 8g fat (2g sat. fat), 84mg chol., 265mg sod., 24g carb. (24g sugars, 0 fiber), 31g pro.

33g Pro

SKILLET PORK CHOPS WITH APPLES & ONION

Simple recipes that land on the table fast are a lifesaver. I serve skillet pork chops with veggies and, when there's time, cornbread stuffing.
—Tracey Karst, Ponderay, ID

TAKES: 20 MIN. • **MAKES:** 4 SERVINGS

- 4 boneless pork loin chops (6 oz. each)
- 3 medium apples, cut into wedges
- 1 large onion, cut into thin wedges
- ¼ cup water
- ⅓ cup balsamic vinaigrette
- ½ tsp. salt
- ¼ tsp. pepper

1. Place a large nonstick skillet over medium heat; brown pork chops on both sides, about 4 minutes. Remove from pan.

2. In same skillet, combine apples, onion and water. Place pork chops over apple mixture; drizzle chops with vinaigrette. Sprinkle with salt and pepper. Reduce heat; simmer, covered, until a thermometer inserted into chops reads 145°, 3-5 minutes.

1 PORK CHOP WITH ¾ CUP APPLE MIXTURE 360 cal., 15g fat (4g sat. fat), 82mg chol., 545mg sod., 22g carb. (15g sugars, 3g fiber), 33g pro.

STAUB
PROTEIN BOOST
PAGE 320
STAUB

10g Pro

SHORTCUT MINESTRONE

This soup is hearty and makes a comforting lunch or dinner on a brisk day. The spaghetti sauce provides rich flavor without a long simmering time. I further cut the prep time by using my food processor to chop the vegetables.
—Barbara Jellison, Bellevue, WA

PREP: 20 MIN. • **COOK:** 15 MIN.
MAKES: 10 SERVINGS (2½ QT.)

- 4 bacon strips, diced
- 1 large onion, chopped
- 3 medium carrots, chopped
- 3 garlic cloves, minced
- 1 jar (28 oz.) spaghetti sauce
- 1 carton (32 oz.) beef broth
- 1 can (16 oz.) kidney beans, rinsed and drained
- 1 can (15 oz.) garbanzo beans or chickpeas, rinsed and drained
- ⅔ cup uncooked small shell pasta
- 2 tsp. brown sugar
- ½ tsp. dried basil
- ½ tsp. dried oregano
- 1 cup frozen cut green beans
- Grated Parmesan cheese, optional

1. In a Dutch oven or soup kettle, cook bacon over medium heat until crisp. Using a slotted spoon, remove to paper towels. Drain, reserving 2 Tbsp. drippings; set bacon aside. In the drippings, saute onion and carrots until tender, 3-4 minutes. Add garlic; cook 2 minutes longer.

2. Stir in the spaghetti sauce, broth and beans. Bring to a boil. Add the pasta, brown sugar, basil and oregano. Cook, uncovered, until pasta is tender, 8-10 minutes, stirring occasionally. Add green beans; cook until heated through, about 5 minutes longer. Garnish with bacon and, if desired, Parmesan cheese.

1 CUP 188 cal., 3g fat (1g sat. fat), 2mg chol., 560mg sod., 31g carb., 7g fiber), 10g pro.

MAKE IT YOUR OWN

Make this soup your own by adding any vegetables you like. Zucchini, yellow squash, butternut squash, acorn squash, sweet potatoes, russet potatoes and kale are all great options. Make the soup even heartier by adding cooked and crumbled ground beef or Italian sausage.

33g Pro

FRUITY PORK ROAST

I like using the slow cooker because it gives me time for other preparations and frees up the oven. Plus, it usually doesn't matter if you serve the food later than planned. This pork roast, which I created by adapting other recipes, gets a special flavor from the fruit.
—Mary Jeppesen-Davis, St. Cloud, MN

PREP: 25 MIN.
COOK: 5 HOURS + STANDING
MAKES: 8 SERVINGS

- ½ medium lemon, sliced
- ½ cup dried cranberries
- ⅓ cup golden raisins
- ⅓ cup unsweetened apple juice
- 3 Tbsp. sherry or additional unsweetened apple juice
- 1 tsp. minced garlic
- ½ tsp. ground mustard
- 1 boneless pork loin roast (3 lbs.)
- ½ tsp. salt
- ¼ tsp. pepper
- ⅛ to ¼ tsp. ground ginger
- 1 medium apple, peeled and sliced
- ½ cup packed fresh parsley sprigs

1. In a small bowl, combine the first 7 ingredients. Cut roast in half; sprinkle with salt, pepper and ginger.
2. Transfer to a 5-qt. slow cooker. Pour fruit mixture over roast. Place apple slices and parsley sprigs around roast. Cover and cook on low until meat is tender, 5-6 hours.
3. Transfer meat to a serving platter. Let stand for 10-15 minutes before slicing.

5 OZ. COOKED PORK WITH ¼ CUP FRUIT MIXTURE 272 cal., 8g fat (3g sat. fat), 85mg chol., 200mg sod., 15g carb. (12g sugars, 1g fiber), 33g pro.

NOTES

33g Pro

ONE-SKILLET PORK CHOP SUPPER

My husband, Clark, and I reserve this recipe for Sundays after the grandkids have gone home and we're too tired to prepare a big meal. It's comforting and quick.
—Kathy Thompson, Port Orange, FL

PREP: 10 MIN. • **COOK:** 30 MIN.
MAKES: 4 SERVINGS

- 1 Tbsp. butter
- 4 pork loin chops (½ in. thick and 7 oz. each)
- 3 medium red potatoes, cut into small wedges
- 3 medium carrots, cut into ½-in. slices, or 2 cups fresh baby carrots
- 1 medium onion, cut into wedges
- 1 can (10¾ oz.) condensed cream of mushroom soup, undiluted
- ½ cup water
- Optional: Cracked black pepper and chopped fresh parsley

1. In a large cast-iron or other heavy skillet, heat butter over medium heat. Brown pork chops on both sides; remove from pan, reserving drippings.
2. In same pan, saute vegetables in drippings until lightly browned. Whisk together soup and water; stir into vegetables. Bring to a boil. Reduce heat; simmer, covered, just until vegetables are tender, 15-20 minutes.
3. Add chops; cook, covered, until a thermometer inserted in pork reads 145°, 8-10 minutes. Remove from heat; let stand 5 minutes. If desired, sprinkle with pepper and parsley.
1 SERVING 390 cal., 15g fat (6g sat. fat), 97mg chol., 700mg sod., 28g carb. (6g sugars, 4g fiber), 33g pro.

22g Pro 5i

BEST EVER LAMB CHOPS

My mom just loved a good lamb chop, and this easy recipe was her favorite way to make them. I've also grilled these chops with amazing results.
—Kim Mundy, Visalia, CA

PREP: 10 MIN. + CHILLING
BROIL: 10 MIN. • **MAKES:** 4 SERVINGS

- 1 tsp. each dried basil, marjoram and thyme
- ½ tsp. salt
- 8 lamb loin chops (3 oz. each)
- Mint jelly, optional

1. Combine herbs and salt; rub over lamb chops. Cover and refrigerate for 1 hour.
2. Broil 4-6 in. from the heat until meat reaches desired doneness, 5-8 minutes on each side (for medium-rare, a thermometer should read 135°; medium, 140°; medium-well, 145°). Serve with mint jelly if desired.
2 LAMB CHOPS 157 cal., 7g fat (2g sat. fat), 68mg chol., 355mg sod., 0 carb. (0 sugars, 0 fiber), 22g pro.
HONEY-GLAZED LAMB CHOPS Omit herbs and salt; skip step 1. In a small saucepan, combine ⅓ cup honey, ⅓ cup prepared mustard, 1 tsp. minced garlic, ½ tsp. onion salt and ½ tsp. pepper. Stir for 2-3 minutes or until heated through. Brush sauce over both sides of lamb chops. Proceed as directed in step 2.

POWER PLAY

Lamb loin chops are a lean source of protein and provide immune-supporting nutrients like zinc, selenium and iron.

43g Pro

PORK SOUVLAKI

This popular Greek dish features pork tenderloin marinated in an aromatic sauce and grilled to perfection. Serve it with pita bread and a side of tzatziki sauce for the whole experience.
—Taste of Home *Test Kitchen*

PREP: 15 MIN. + MARINATING
GRILL: 15 MIN. • **MAKES:** 4 SKEWERS

PORK SOUVLAKI
- 1/3 cup olive oil
- 1/4 cup red wine vinegar
- 1/4 cup lemon juice
- 4 garlic cloves, minced
- 2 Tbsp. fresh thyme sprigs
- 2 tsp. salt
- 2 tsp. dried oregano
- 1 tsp. paprika
- 1/2 tsp. pepper
- 1 1/2 lbs. pork tenderloin, cut into 2-in. cubes
- 4 wooden skewers

TZATZIKI SAUCE
- 1 cup plain Greek yogurt
- 1/4 medium English cucumber, finely chopped
- 1 Tbsp. lemon juice
- 1/2 Tbsp. olive oil
- 1/4 tsp. salt
- 1 Tbsp. minced fresh mint, optional

PITAS
- 4 whole pita breads
- 2 medium tomatoes, sliced
- 1 medium red onion, thinly sliced

1. In a large bowl, whisk together olive oil, vinegar, lemon juice, garlic, thyme, salt, oregano, paprika and pepper. Add cubed pork tenderloin; toss to coat. Cover; refrigerate at least 1 hour.
2. Preheat grill to 400°. On 4 metal or soaked wooden skewers, thread cubed pork tenderloin; brush with excess marinade. Grill 4-5 minutes per side or until pork is cooked through, brushing with additional marinade as desired; discard remaining marinade.
3. For tzatziki sauce, in a small bowl, whisk together yogurt, cucumber, lemon juice, olive oil, salt and, if desired, mint.
4. Serve with pita bread, tomatoes, red onion and tzatziki sauce. Refrigerate remaining tzatziki sauce for up to 1 week.

1 SKEWER PORK WITH 1 PITA BREAD AND 2 TBSP. TZATZIKI SAUCE 637 cal., 32g fat (8g sat. fat), 110mg chol., 1758mg sod., 45g carb. (7g sugars, 3g fiber), 43g pro.

NOTES

> I loved this recipe. Bean soup is one of my favorite things to eat. I made a big skillet of cornbread to eat with it. So delicious!
>
> —QUEENLALISA, TASTEOFHOME.COM

20g Pro

OLD-FASHIONED HAM & BEAN SOUP

This old-fashioned version of ham and bean soup starts with dried navy beans, but you could start with great northern beans instead. The first soak of the beans softens them, but they won't get tender until after they are simmered in the second step.
—Taste of Home *Test Kitchen*

PREP: 15 MIN. + SOAKING
COOK: 1½ HOURS
MAKES: 10 SERVINGS (2½ QT.)

- 1 lb. dried navy beans
- 1 Tbsp. canola oil
- 2 medium onions, chopped
- 2 celery ribs, chopped
- 8 cups water
- 1 medium carrot, chopped
- 2 bay leaves
- 1 tsp. dried thyme
- ½ tsp. pepper
- 2 smoked ham hocks
- 2 cups cubed fully cooked ham
- ½ tsp. salt

1. Place beans in a Dutch oven; add water to cover by 2 in. Bring to a boil; boil for 2 minutes. Remove from the heat; cover and let stand for 1-4 hours or until beans are softened. Drain and rinse beans, discarding liquid.
2. In the same pan, heat oil over medium heat; add onions and celery. Cook and stir until crisp-tender, 3-5 minutes. Stir in softened beans, 8 cups water, carrot, bay leaves, thyme and pepper. Add ham hocks. Bring to a boil. Reduce heat; cover and simmer for 1¼-1½ hours or until beans are tender.
3. Discard bay leaves. Remove ham hocks; set aside until cool enough to handle. Remove ham from bones and cut into cubes; discard bones. Stir cubed ham and salt into soup; heat through.
1 CUP 230 cal., 4g fat (1g sat. fat), 25mg chol., 521mg sod., 31g carb. (3g sugars, 8g fiber), 20g pro.

BEAN-POWERED THICKNESS

As the beans cook, they will naturally thicken the soup. If using canned beans, consider pureeing ⅓ of the beans before adding them to the soup for a thicker texture.

30g Pro 5i

CHILI PORK TENDERLOIN

Just because a dish is good for you doesn't mean it has to be tough and without flavor. My family can't get enough of this tender pork meal.
—Renee Barfield, Thomaston, GA

PREP: 10 MIN. • **BAKE:** 25 MIN.
MAKES: 3 SERVINGS

- 1 Tbsp. lime juice
- 1 tsp. chili powder
- 1 tsp. reduced-sodium soy sauce
- ½ tsp. sugar
- ½ tsp. salt
- ¼ tsp. pepper
- 1 pork tenderloin (1 lb.)
- 1 Tbsp. canola oil

1. In a small bowl, combine the first 6 ingredients; brush over pork.
2. In a large ovenproof skillet, brown pork in oil on all sides.
3. Bake at 375° for 25-30 minutes or until a thermometer reads 145°. Let stand for 5 minutes before slicing.
4 OZ. COOKED PORK 224 cal., 10g fat (2g sat. fat), 84mg chol., 529mg sod., 2g carb. (1g sugars, 0 fiber), 30g pro.

31g Pro

MEDITERRANEAN PORK & ORZO

On a really busy day, this meal in a bowl is one of my top picks. It's quick to put together, leaving me a lot more time to relax at the table.
—Mary Relyea, Canastota, NY

TAKES: 30 MIN. • **MAKES:** 6 SERVINGS

- 1½ lbs. pork tenderloin
- 1 tsp. coarsely ground pepper
- 2 Tbsp. olive oil
- 3 qt. water
- 1¼ cups uncooked orzo pasta
- ¼ tsp. salt
- 1 pkg. (6 oz.) fresh baby spinach
- 1 cup grape tomatoes, halved
- ¾ cup crumbled feta cheese

1. Rub pork with pepper; cut into 1-in. cubes. In a large nonstick skillet, heat oil over medium heat. Add pork; cook and stir until no longer pink, 8-10 minutes.
2. Meanwhile, in a Dutch oven, bring water to a boil. Stir in orzo and salt; cook, uncovered, 8 minutes. Stir in spinach; cook until orzo is tender and spinach is wilted, 45-60 seconds longer. Drain.
3. Add tomatoes to pork; heat through. Stir in orzo mixture and cheese.
1⅓ CUPS 372 cal., 11g fat (4g sat. fat), 71mg chol., 306mg sod., 34g carb. (2g sugars, 3g fiber), 31g pro.

35g Pro

PORK CHOPS & MUSHROOMS

My mother-in-law gave me this recipe years ago, and I have used it ever since. Tarragon is such a special flavor—my family loves it.
—Hilary Rigo, Wickenburg, AZ

TAKES: 25 MIN. • **MAKES:** 4 SERVINGS

- 4 boneless pork loin chops (6 oz. each)
- ¾ tsp. salt, divided
- ⅛ tsp. white pepper
- 3 tsp. butter, divided
- ¾ lb. sliced fresh mushrooms
- ½ cup dry white wine or reduced-sodium chicken broth
- ½ tsp. dried tarragon

1. Sprinkle pork with ½ tsp. salt and the white pepper. In a large nonstick skillet, heat 2 tsp. butter over medium heat. Add pork chops; cook for 5-6 minutes on each side or until a thermometer reads 145°. Remove from pan.

2. In the same skillet, heat remaining 1 tsp. butter over medium-high heat. Add mushrooms; cook and stir for 6-8 minutes or until tender. Add wine, tarragon and remaining ¼ tsp. salt, stirring to loosen browned bits from pan. Bring to a boil; cook until liquid is reduced by half. Return chops to pan; heat through.

1 PORK CHOP WITH ⅓ CUP MUSHROOMS
299 cal., 13g fat (5g sat. fat), 89mg chol., 515mg sod., 4g carb. (1g sugars, 1g fiber), 35g pro.

23g Pro

FRENCH MARKET SOUP

An old friend gave me this recipe. I think it tastes best the next day, so I recommend preparing it the day before you plan to serve it. Leftovers also freeze well.
—Terri Lowe, Lumberton, TX

PREP: 20 MIN. + SOAKING
COOK: 4½ HOURS
MAKES: 12 SERVINGS (4½ QT.)

- 3 cups assorted dried beans for soup
- 2 smoked ham hocks
- 12 cups water
- 1½ tsp. salt
- ½ tsp. pepper
- 1 can (28 oz.) crushed tomatoes, undrained
- 2 medium onions, chopped
- ¼ to ⅓ cup lemon juice
- 2 garlic cloves, minced
- ½ tsp. chili powder
- 1 lb. smoked kielbasa, chopped
- 1½ cups cubed cooked chicken
- ½ cup dry red wine or chicken broth
- ½ cup minced fresh parsley

1. Sort beans and rinse in cold water. Place beans in a Dutch oven and add water to cover by 2 in. Bring to a boil; boil for 2 minutes. Remove from the heat. Cover and let stand for 1-4 hours or until beans are softened.

2. Drain and rinse beans, discarding liquid; return beans to pan. Add the ham hocks, water, salt and pepper; bring to a boil. Reduce heat. Cover and simmer for 3 hours or until beans are tender.

3. Remove ham hocks; set aside until cool enough to handle. Add tomatoes, onions, lemon juice, garlic and chili powder to the beans. Simmer 1 hour longer.

4. Remove ham from bones and cut into cubes; discard bones. Return ham to soup. Stir in kielbasa, chicken, wine and parsley. Simmer for 30-40 minutes or until heated through and as thick as desired.

1½ CUPS 291 cal., 14g fat (5g sat. fat), 52mg chol., 840mg sod., 32g carb. (3g sugars, 18g fiber), 23g pro.

NOTES

28g Pro

PROSCIUTTO-PEPPER PORK CHOPS

Here's a dish that's easy, fast and, most importantly, delicious. Serve these cheesy chops with a green salad for a light and satisfying meal.
—Donna Prisco, Randolph, NJ

TAKES: 20 MIN. • **MAKES:** 4 SERVINGS

- 4 boneless pork loin chops (4 oz. each)
- ⅛ tsp. garlic powder
- ⅛ tsp. pepper
- 2 tsp. canola oil
- 4 thin slices prosciutto or deli ham
- ½ cup julienned roasted sweet red peppers
- 2 slices reduced-fat provolone cheese, cut in half

1. Sprinkle pork chops with garlic powder and pepper. In a large nonstick skillet, cook chops in oil over medium heat until a thermometer inserted in pork reads 145°, 4-5 minutes on each side.

2. Top each pork chop with prosciutto, red peppers and cheese. Cover and cook for 1-2 minutes or until cheese is melted. Let stand 5 minutes before serving.

1 PORK CHOP 237 cal., 12g fat (4g sat. fat), 72mg chol., 483mg sod., 1g carb. (1g sugars, 0 fiber), 28g pro.

23g Pro

CLASSIC COBB SALAD

Making this salad is a lot like putting in a garden. I plant everything in nice, neat sections, just as I do with seedlings.
—Patricia Kile, Elizabethtown, PA

TAKES: 20 MIN. • **MAKES:** 4 SERVINGS

- 6 cups torn iceberg lettuce
- 2 medium tomatoes, chopped
- 1 medium ripe avocado, peeled and chopped
- ¾ cup diced fully cooked ham
- 2 hard-boiled large eggs, chopped
- ¾ cup diced cooked turkey
- 1¼ cups sliced fresh mushrooms
- ½ cup crumbled blue cheese
- Salad dressing of choice
- Optional: Sliced ripe olives and lemon wedges

Place lettuce on a platter or in a large serving bowl. Arrange next 7 ingredients in rows or sections as desired. Serve with salad dressing of choice. If desired, add olives and serve with lemon wedges.

1 SERVING 260 cal., 15g fat (5g sat. fat), 148mg chol., 586mg sod., 10g carb. (5g sugars, 4g fiber), 23g pro.

PROTEIN BOOST
PAGE 320

44g Pro

BAKED PORK CHOPS

The flavorful rub on these pork chops is sweet, salty and savory. It goes nicely on any cut of pork you have.
—Taste of Home *Test Kitchen*

PREP: 10 MIN. • **BAKE:** 25 MIN.
MAKES: 4 SERVINGS

- 2 Tbsp. brown sugar
- 2 tsp. paprika
- 1 tsp. salt
- 1 tsp. onion powder
- 1 tsp. garlic powder
- 1 tsp. dried thyme
- ½ tsp. pepper
- 4 bone-in pork loin chops (8 oz. each)
- 1 Tbsp. olive oil

1. Preheat oven to 350°. Combine the first 7 ingredients. Drizzle chops with oil; rub spice mixture over both sides of pork chops. Place in a greased 13x9-in. baking dish.
2. Bake, uncovered until a thermometer reads 145°, 25-30 minutes. Let stand 5 minutes before serving.

1 PORK CHOP 361 cal., 16g fat (5g sat. fat), 109mg chol., 538mg sod., 7g carb. (6g sugars, 1g fiber), 44g pro.

This recipe is simple and truly delicious. Keeps my stove top free for preparing the rest of the meal.

—TRICIA1240, TASTEOFHOME.COM

37g Pro

SPICY LAMB CURRY

I've tweaked this curry over the years using a blend of aromatic spices. Fenugreek seeds can be found in specialty spice stores and are common in many curries and chutneys, but you can leave them out of this recipe if you prefer.
—Janis Kracht, Slaterville Spring, NY

PREP: 25 MIN. + MARINATING
COOK: 1 HOUR • **MAKES:** 6 SERVINGS

- 3 Tbsp. ground cumin
- 2 Tbsp. ground ginger
- 1 Tbsp. ground coriander
- 1 Tbsp. ground fenugreek
- 4 garlic cloves, minced
- 1 tsp. ground cloves
- ½ tsp. ground cinnamon
- 2 lbs. lamb stew meat, cut into ¾-in. pieces
- 1 Tbsp. olive oil
- 2 large onions, chopped
- ½ cup water
- 2 Tbsp. paprika
- 2 Tbsp. tomato paste
- 1 tsp. salt
- 1 tsp. ground mustard
- 1 tsp. chili powder
- 1 cup plain yogurt
- 3 cups hot cooked brown rice
- Optional toppings: Cubed fresh pineapple, flaked coconut and toasted sliced almonds

1. In a large bowl, combine the first 7 ingredients. Add the lamb; turn to coat. Cover; refrigerate for 8 hours or overnight.
2. In a Dutch oven, brown meat in oil in batches; remove and keep warm. In the same pan, cook onions in drippings until tender. Add the water, paprika, tomato paste, salt, mustard and chili powder.
3. Return lamb to pan. Bring to a boil. Reduce heat; cover and simmer for 1-1½ hours or until meat is tender. Remove from the heat; stir in yogurt. Serve with rice. Top with pineapple, coconut and almonds if desired.

NOTE The color of lamb can be an indication of the age of the animal, which translates into tenderness and flavor of the meat. Lamb is usually pinkish-red, baby lamb is pale pink and mutton is light to dark red.

¾ CUP CURRY WITH ½ CUP RICE 419 cal., 14g fat (4g sat. fat), 104mg chol., 534mg sod., 36g carb. (5g sugars, 6g fiber), 37g pro.

17g Pro

PRESSURE-COOKER ANDOUILLE LENTIL CHILI

This recipe has been in my family for a number of years, and it's still a hit today. The smoky flavor of the andouille sausage adds a lot to the humble lentils. And you can make it in either a pressure cooker or a slow cooker.
—Melody Gow, Mead, WA

PREP: 20 MIN.
COOK: 15 MIN. + RELEASING
MAKES: 12 SERVINGS

- 1 pkg. fully cooked andouille sausage links (14½ oz.), cut into ⅛-in. slices
- 1 medium onion, chopped
- ¼ medium green pepper, seeded and finely chopped
- 3 Tbsp. plus 4 cups water, divided
- 2 cups dried lentils, rinsed
- 2 cans (15 oz. each) tomato sauce
- 2 cans (14½ oz. each) stewed tomatoes
- ¼ cup packed dark brown sugar
- ¼ cup Worcestershire sauce
- ¼ cup red wine vinegar
- 2 Tbsp. chili powder
- 3 garlic cloves, finely minced
- Optional toppings: Sour cream, jalapeno slices and cilantro

1. Select saute or browning setting on a 6-qt. electric pressure cooker; adjust for medium heat. Cook and stir sausage, onion and green pepper with 3 Tbsp. water until vegetables are caramelized, 6-8 minutes. Stir in remaining 4 cups water and the next 8 ingredients.

2. Lock lid; close pressure-release valve. Adjust to pressure-cook on high for 15 minutes. Let pressure release naturally for 10 minutes; quick-release any remaining pressure. If desired, top with sour cream, jalapeno slices and cilantro.

FREEZE OPTION Freeze cooled chili in freezer containers. To use, partially thaw in refrigerator overnight. Heat through in a saucepan, stirring occasionally; add water if necessary.

1 CUP 267 cal., 8g fat (2g sat. fat), 44mg chol., 849mg sod., 38g carb. (11g sugars, 6g fiber), 17g pro.

SLOW COOKER METHOD

In a large skillet, cook and stir sausage, onion and green pepper with 3 Tbsp. water until vegetables are caramelized, 6-8 minutes. Transfer sausage and vegetables to a 5-qt. slow cooker; stir in remaining water and next 8 ingredients. Cook, covered, on high until lentils are tender, 8-10 hours. Top as desired.

PROTEIN
BOOST
PAGE 320

28g Pro

KASHMIRI LAMB CURRY STEW

I was taught that spicy foods are for lovers. So after I got married, this was the first meal I made for my husband.
—Amber El, Pittsburgh, PA

PREP: 25 MIN. + MARINATING
COOK: 8 HOURS
MAKES: 11 SERVINGS (2¾ QT.)

- 1 cup plain yogurt
- 2 Tbsp. ghee or butter, melted
- ¼ cup lemon juice
- 4 tsp. curry powder
- 1 Tbsp. cumin seeds
- 1 tsp. each coriander seeds, ground ginger, ground cloves, ground cardamom, sugar and salt
- ½ tsp. each ground cinnamon and pepper
- 3 lbs. lamb stew meat, cut into 1-in. cubes
- 1 large onion, sliced
- 1 medium sweet potato, quartered
- 1 medium Yukon Gold potato, quartered
- 1 large tomato, chopped
- 1 cup frozen peas and carrots
- 3 garlic cloves, minced
- 2 dried hot chiles
- ½ cup chicken broth
- 1½ Tbsp. garam masala
- Optional: Hot cooked basmati rice, sliced green onion, mango chutney and raisins

1. In a large bowl, combine yogurt, ghee and lemon juice. Add curry powder, cumin seeds, coriander, ginger, cloves, cardamom, sugar, salt, cinnamon and pepper. Add next 8 ingredients; mix gently to coat. Cover and refrigerate for up to 24 hours.
2. Transfer lamb mixture and marinade to 6-qt. slow cooker; stir in broth and garam masala. Cook, covered, on low until meat is tender, 8-9 hours. If desired, serve with rice, green onion, mango chutney and raisins.

FREEZE OPTION Freeze cooled stew in freezer containers. To use, partially thaw in refrigerator overnight. Heat through in a saucepan, stirring occasionally; add broth if necessary.

1 CUP 261 cal., 10g fat (4g sat. fat), 89mg chol., 384mg sod., 15g carb. (5g sugars, 3g fiber), 28g pro.

NOTES

14g Pro

OLD-FASHIONED SPLIT PEA SOUP WITH HAM BONE

The old-fashioned favorite is a snap to make, and it's economical too. Carrots, celery and onion accent the subtle flavor of the split peas, while a ham bone adds a meaty touch to this hearty soup. It's sure to chase away autumn's chill.
—Laurie Todd, Columbus, MS

PREP: 15 MIN. + STANDING
COOK: 2¼ HOURS
MAKES: 10 SERVINGS (ABOUT 2½ QT.)

- 1 pkg. (16 oz.) dried green split peas
- 1 meaty ham bone
- 1 large onion, chopped
- 1 tsp. salt
- ½ tsp. pepper
- ½ tsp. dried thyme
- 1 bay leaf
- 1 cup chopped carrot
- 1 cup chopped celery

1. Sort peas and rinse with cold water. Place peas in a Dutch oven; add water to cover by 2 in. Bring to a boil; boil for 2 minutes. Remove from heat; cover and let stand for 1-4 hours or until peas are softened. Drain and rinse peas, discarding liquid.

2. Return peas to Dutch oven. Add 2½ qt. water, ham bone, onion, salt, pepper, thyme and bay leaf. Bring to a boil. Reduce heat; cover and simmer for 1½ hours, stirring occasionally.

3. Remove the ham bone; when cool enough to handle, remove meat from bone. Discard bone; dice meat and return to soup. Add carrot and celery. Simmer, uncovered, for 45-60 minutes or until soup reaches desired thickness and vegetables are tender. Discard bay leaf.

1 CUP 202 cal., 3g fat (1g sat. fat), 11mg chol., 267mg sod., 31g carb. (6g sugars, 12g fiber), 14g pro.

33g Pro

LEMON-GARLIC PORK CHOPS

My son James created these zesty chops spiced with paprika and cayenne. He keeps the spice rub in a jar to use with chops or chicken.
—Molly Seidel, Edgewood, NM

TAKES: 20 MIN. • **MAKES:** 4 SERVINGS

- 2 Tbsp. lemon juice
- 2 garlic cloves, minced
- 1 tsp. salt
- 1 tsp. paprika
- ½ tsp. pepper
- ¼ tsp. cayenne pepper
- 4 boneless pork loin chops (6 oz. each)

1. Preheat broiler. In a small bowl, mix the first 6 ingredients; brush over pork chops. Place in a 15x10x1-in. baking pan.
2. Broil 4-5 in. from heat until a thermometer reads 145°, 4-5 minutes on each side. Let stand 5 minutes before serving.

1 PORK CHOP 233 cal., 10g fat (4g sat. fat), 82mg chol., 638mg sod., 2g carb. (0 sugars, 0 fiber), 33g pro.

35g Pro

SLOW-COOKED PORK CHOPS & SCALLOPED POTATOES

Here's a meal that feels homey and Sunday-special. When my sister gave me this recipe, it was for a casserole baked in the oven, but I've adapted it to the slow cooker as well as the stovetop. Everyone who tastes it seems to love it.
—Elizabeth Johnston, Glendale, AZ

PREP: 30 MIN. • **COOK:** 8 HOURS
MAKES: 6 SERVINGS

- 4 medium potatoes, peeled and thinly sliced
- 6 bone-in pork loin chops (7 oz. each)
- 1 Tbsp. canola oil
- 2 large onions, sliced and separated into rings
- 2 tsp. butter
- 3 Tbsp. all-purpose flour
- ¼ tsp. salt
- ¼ tsp. pepper
- 1 can (14½ oz.) reduced-sodium chicken broth
- 1 cup fat-free milk

1. Place potatoes in a 5- or 6-qt. slow cooker coated with cooking spray. In a large nonstick skillet, brown pork chops in oil in batches.
2. Place chops over potatoes. Saute onions in drippings until tender; place over chops. Melt butter in skillet. Combine the flour, salt, pepper and broth until smooth. Stir into pan. Add milk. Bring to a boil; cook and stir for 2 minutes or until thickened.
3. Pour sauce over onions. Cover and cook on low for 8-10 hours or until pork is tender. Skim fat and thicken cooking juices if desired.

1 SERVING 372 cal., 12g fat (4g sat. fat), 90mg chol., 389mg sod., 29g carb. (6g sugars, 2g fiber), 35g pro.

35g Pro

CITRUS-HERB PORK ROAST

The genius combination of seasonings and citrus in this tender roast reminds us why we cherish tasty recipes.
—Laura Brodine, Colorado Springs, CO

PREP: 25 MIN. • **COOK:** 4 HOURS
MAKES: 8 SERVINGS

- 1 boneless pork sirloin roast (3 to 4 lbs.)
- 1 tsp. dried oregano
- ½ tsp. ground ginger
- ½ tsp. pepper
- 2 medium onions, cut into thin wedges
- 1 cup plus 3 Tbsp. orange juice, divided
- 1 Tbsp. sugar
- 1 Tbsp. white grapefruit juice
- 1 Tbsp. steak sauce
- 1 Tbsp. reduced-sodium soy sauce
- 1 tsp. grated orange zest
- ½ tsp. salt
- 3 Tbsp. cornstarch
- Hot cooked egg noodles
- Minced fresh oregano, optional

1. Cut roast in half. In a small bowl, combine the oregano, ginger and pepper; rub over pork. In a large skillet coated with cooking spray, brown roast on all sides. Transfer to a 4-qt. slow cooker; add onions.

2. In a small bowl, combine 1 cup orange juice, sugar, grapefruit juice, steak sauce and soy sauce; pour over top. Cover and cook on low for 4-5 hours or until meat is tender. Remove meat and onions to a serving platter; keep warm.

3. Skim fat from cooking juices; transfer to a small saucepan. Add orange zest and salt. Bring to a boil. Combine cornstarch and the remaining 3 Tbsp. orange juice until smooth. Gradually stir into the pan. Bring to a boil; cook and stir for 2 minutes or until thickened. Serve with pork and noodles; if desired, sprinkle with fresh oregano.

5 OZ. COOKED PORK WITH 2 TBSP. GRAVY
289 cal., 10g fat (4g sat. fat), 102mg chol., 326mg sod., 13g carb. (8g sugars, 1g fiber), 35g pro.

NOTES

23g Pro

ASPARAGUS-STUFFED PORK TENDERLOIN

Fresh asparagus looks amazing tucked inside a rolled pork tenderloin. A homemade seasoning mix dresses up this eye-catching entree you'll be proud to serve any time. *—Tonya Farmer, IA City, IA*

PREP: 20 MIN. • **GRILL:** 20 MIN.
MAKES: 4 SERVINGS

- ¼ tsp. each onion powder, garlic powder, chili powder, salt, seasoned salt and poultry seasoning
- ⅛ tsp. cayenne pepper
- 1 pork tenderloin (1 lb.)
- 8 to 10 fresh asparagus spears, trimmed

1. In a small bowl, combine all of the seasonings; set aside. Cut a lengthwise slit down the center of pork tenderloin to within ½ in. of bottom. Open so meat lies flat; cover with plastic wrap. Flatten to ¼-in. thickness. Remove plastic; sprinkle ½ tsp. seasoning mix over meat.

2. In a large skillet, bring 1 cup water to a boil. Add asparagus; cover and cook for 2 minutes. Drain asparagus and immediately place in ice water; drain and pat dry. Place asparagus lengthwise over tenderloin.

3. Fold meat over asparagus, starting with a long side, and secure with kitchen string. Sprinkle with remaining seasoning. Grill, covered, over indirect medium heat for 20-25 minutes or until a thermometer reads 160°, turning occasionally. Let stand for 5 minutes before slicing.

1 SERVING 140 cal., 4g fat (1g sat. fat), 64mg chol., 296mg sod., 2g carb. (0 sugars, 1g fiber), 23g pro.

36g Pro

BLACKENED PORK CAESAR SALAD

When I cook, the goal is to have enough leftovers for lunch the next day. This Caesar salad with pork has fantastic flavor even when the meat is chilled. *—Penny Hedges, Dewdney, BC*

TAKES: 30 MIN. • **MAKES:** 2 SERVINGS

- 2 Tbsp. mayonnaise
- 1 Tbsp. olive oil
- 1 Tbsp. lemon juice
- 1 garlic clove, minced
- ⅛ tsp. seasoned salt
- ⅛ tsp. pepper

SALAD

- ¾ lb. pork tenderloin, cut into 1-in. cubes
- 1 Tbsp. blackened seasoning
- 1 Tbsp. canola oil
- 6 cups torn romaine
- Optional: Salad croutons and shredded Parmesan cheese

1. For dressing, in a small bowl, mix the first 6 ingredients until blended.

2. Toss pork with blackened seasoning. In a large skillet, heat oil over medium-high heat. Add pork; cook and stir until tender, 5-7 minutes.

3. To serve, place romaine in a large bowl; add dressing and toss to coat. Top with pork and, if desired, croutons and cheese.

2½ CUPS 458 cal., 31g fat (5g sat. fat), 100mg chol., 464mg sod., 8g carb. (2g sugars, 3g fiber), 36g pro.

38g Pro

SALSA SKILLET PORK CHOPS

There's nothing better than turning out a super quick skillet supper that totally delivers on a meal that'll please the whole family on a busy weeknight. It's a keeper.
—Deanna Ellett, Boynton Beach, FL

TAKES: 30 MIN. • **MAKES:** 6 SERVINGS

- 6 boneless pork loin chops (6 oz. each)
- ½ tsp. salt
- ¼ tsp. pepper
- 2 cups fresh whole kernel corn
- 1 can (15 oz.) pinto beans, rinsed and drained
- 1¼ cups chunky salsa
- 2 Tbsp. water
- 1 tsp. ground cumin

1. Sprinkle pork chops with salt and pepper. Heat a large skillet coated with cooking spray over medium heat. Brown chops on both sides in batches.

2. Return all chops to pan. Add remaining ingredients; bring to a boil. Reduce heat; simmer, covered, 6-8 minutes or until thermometer inserted in pork reads 145°. Let stand 5 minutes before serving.

1 PORK CHOP WITH ½ CUP CORN MIXTURE 366 cal., 11g fat (4g sat. fat), 82mg chol., 548mg sod., 29g carb. (5g sugars, 4g fiber), 38g pro.

22g Pro

SOUTHWEST PORK TENDERLOIN

When living in Europe, I missed classic southwestern flavors. Using what I had, I made spicy pork tenderloin, and it's been a staple ever since.
—John Cox, New Braunfels, TX

PREP: 10 MIN. • **BAKE:** 25 MIN. + STANDING
MAKES: 8 SERVINGS

- 2 pork tenderloins (1 lb. each)
- 2 Tbsp. canola oil
- 1 envelope taco seasoning
- 3 medium limes, cut into wedges

1. Preheat oven to 425°. Rub tenderloins with oil; sprinkle with taco seasoning. Place on a rack in a shallow roasting pan.

2. Roast 25-30 minutes or until a thermometer reads 145°. Remove tenderloins from oven; tent with foil. Let stand 10 minutes before slicing. Squeeze lime wedges over pork.

3 OZ. COOKED PORK 184 cal., 7g fat (2g sat. fat), 63mg chol., 446mg sod., 6g carb. (0 sugars, 1g fiber), 22g pro.

33g Pro

JALAPENO JELLY-GLAZED PORK CHOPS

Jalapeno jelly makes a fabulous glaze. The chops have a beautiful golden color, and my husband says they're good enough to keep everyone quiet at the dinner table.
—Shannon Bruce, Mooresville, IN

TAKES: 25 MIN. • **MAKES:** 4 SERVINGS

- 1 lb. fresh green beans, trimmed
- 2 tsp. olive oil
- ¾ tsp. salt, divided
- ⅛ tsp. plus ¼ tsp. pepper, divided
- 4 boneless pork loin chops (¾ in. thick and 6 oz. each)
- 4 Tbsp. jalapeno pepper jelly, divided

1. Preheat oven to 425°. Place green beans in a 15x10x1-in. baking pan coated with cooking spray; toss with oil, ¼ tsp. salt and ⅛ tsp. pepper. Roast 15-20 minutes or until tender and lightly browned, stirring occasionally.

2. Meanwhile, sprinkle pork chops with remaining ½ tsp. salt and ¼ tsp. pepper. Place a large skillet coated with cooking spray over medium heat. Add chops; cook, uncovered, 4 minutes. Turn chops over; spread tops with half of the jalapeno jelly.

3. Cook, uncovered, 2-3 minutes longer or until a thermometer reads 145°. Turn chops over; spread tops with remaining jelly. Let stand 5 minutes. Serve with green beans.

1 SERVING 328 cal., 10g fat (4g sat. fat), 82mg chol., 354mg sod., 27g carb. (19g sugars, 0 fiber), 33g pro.

25g Pro

PORK TENDERLOIN WITH SWEET POTATO RAGOUT

With the taste of sweet potatoes and pork, this combination is a perfect dish to serve on a fall evening.
—Greg Fontenot, The Woodlands, TX

PREP: 1 HOUR • **GRILL:** 20 MIN.
MAKES: 6 SERVINGS (3 CUPS RAGOUT)

- 2 Tbsp. olive oil
- 1 large onion, chopped
- 2 garlic cloves, minced
- 1 large navel orange
- ¼ cup packed brown sugar
- ¼ cup balsamic vinegar
- ⅛ tsp. plus ½ tsp. salt, divided
- 1 can (15¾ oz.) cut sweet potatoes in syrup, undrained
- 1 can (14½ oz.) diced tomatoes, undrained
- 2 medium tart apples, peeled and chopped
- 2 pork tenderloins (¾ lb. each)
- ½ tsp. pepper

1. In a large skillet, heat oil over medium heat. Add onion; cook and stir 4-5 minutes or until softened. Reduce heat to medium-low; cook 20-25 minutes or until golden brown, stirring occasionally. Add garlic; cook 1 minute longer.

2. Finely grate zest from orange. Cut orange crosswise in half; squeeze juice from orange. Stir brown sugar, vinegar, ⅛ tsp. salt, orange zest and orange juice into onion mixture. Bring to a boil; cook 6-8 minutes or until liquid is almost evaporated.

3. Stir in sweet potatoes, tomatoes and apples. Return to a boil. Reduce heat; simmer, uncovered, 20-25 minutes or until apples are tender and liquid is almost evaporated, stirring occasionally.

4. Sprinkle pork with pepper and remaining ½ tsp. salt. Grill, covered, over medium heat 18-22 minutes or until a thermometer reads 145°, turning occasionally. Let stand 5 minutes before slicing. Serve with ragout.

3 OZ. COOKED PORK WITH ½ CUP RAGOUT
344 cal., 9g fat (2g sat. fat), 64mg chol., 436mg sod., 42g carb. (34g sugars, 5g fiber), 25g pro.

NOTES

23g Pro

CURRIED HAM & SPLIT PEA SOUP

This soup is great for stocking in the freezer and the curry gives it a warmer flavor, which goes so nicely with the salty ham.
—Trisha Kruse, Eagle, ID

PREP: 10 MIN. • **COOK:** 7 HOURS
MAKES: 8 SERVINGS (2 QT.)

- 2 Tbsp. butter
- 1 medium onion, chopped
- 4 garlic cloves, minced
- 1 Tbsp. curry powder
- 1 pkg. (16 oz.) dried green split peas
- 2 cups cubed fully cooked ham
- 1 cup sliced fresh carrots
- 4 cups reduced-sodium beef broth
- 2 cups water
- ½ tsp. pepper

1. In a skillet, heat butter over medium heat. Add onion; cook and stir 3-4 minutes or until tender. Add garlic and curry powder; cook 1 minute longer.
2. Transfer to a 4- or 5-qt. slow cooker. Add remaining ingredients. Cook, covered, on low 7-9 hours or until peas are tender. Stir before serving.
FREEZE OPTION Freeze cooled soup in freezer containers. To use, partially thaw in refrigerator overnight. Heat through in a saucepan, stirring occasionally and adding a little water if necessary.
1 CUP 288 cal., 5g fat (2g sat. fat), 31mg chol., 683mg sod., 39g carb. (7g sugars, 16g fiber), 23g pro.

20g Pro

DENVER OMELET SALAD

I love this recipe. It's not your typical breakfast, but it has all the right elements. It's easy, healthy and fast. Turn your favorite omelet ingredients into a morning salad!
—Pauline Custer, Duluth, MN

TAKES: 25 MIN. • **MAKES:** 4 SERVINGS

- 8 cups fresh baby spinach
- 1 cup chopped tomatoes
- 2 Tbsp. olive oil, divided
- 1½ cups chopped fully cooked ham
- 1 small onion, chopped
- 1 small green pepper, chopped
- 4 large eggs
- Salt and pepper to taste

1. Arrange spinach and tomatoes on a platter; set aside. In a large skillet, heat 1 Tbsp. olive oil over medium-high heat. Add ham, onion and green pepper; saute until ham is heated through and vegetables are tender, 5-7 minutes. Spoon over spinach and tomatoes.
2. In same skillet, heat remaining 1 Tbsp. olive oil over medium heat. Break eggs, 1 at a time, into a small cup, then gently slide into skillet. Immediately reduce heat to low; season eggs with salt and pepper. To prepare sunny-side up eggs, cover pan and cook until whites are completely set and yolks thicken but are not hard. Top salad with fried eggs.
1 SERVING 229 cal., 14g fat (3g sat. fat), 217mg chol., 756mg sod., 7g carb. (3g sugars, 2g fiber), 20g pro.

PROTEIN
BOOST
PAGE 320

FISH & SEAFOOD

34g Pro

TILAPIA TACOS

I absolutely love fish tacos and wanted to create a slimmed-down recipe so I could enjoy them anytime I wanted. I never have any complaints when I serve these for dinner.
—Jade Peterson, Portland, OR

TAKES: 30 MIN. • **MAKES:** 4 SERVINGS

- 1 large egg
- 1 Tbsp. fat-free milk
- ½ tsp. green hot pepper sauce
- ½ cup cornmeal
- 2 Tbsp. all-purpose flour
- ¼ tsp. ground cumin
- ¼ tsp. pepper
- 4 tilapia fillets (4 oz. each), cut lengthwise in half
- 4 tsp. olive oil
- 1 can (15 oz.) Southwest or seasoned recipe black beans
- 8 corn tortillas (6 in.), warmed
- 3 plum tomatoes, chopped
- 2 cups shredded cabbage
- ½ cup salsa verde
- ¼ cup minced fresh cilantro
- Lime wedges

1. Preheat oven to 375°. In a shallow bowl, whisk egg, milk and pepper sauce. In another shallow bowl, mix cornmeal, flour, cumin and pepper. Dip tilapia in egg mixture, then in cornmeal mixture, patting to help coating adhere. Place on a baking sheet coated with cooking spray. Drizzle tops with oil. Bake 15-20 minutes or until fish flakes easily with a fork.
2. Meanwhile, place beans in a small saucepan; heat through over medium-low heat, stirring occasionally. Serve tilapia in tortillas; top with beans, tomatoes, cabbage, salsa verde and cilantro. Serve with lime wedges.
2 TACOS 438 cal., 9g fat (2g sat. fat), 87mg chol., 567mg sod., 57g carb. (3g sugars, 12g fiber), 34g pro.

40g Pro 5i

GARLIC HERBED GRILLED TUNA STEAKS

After enjoying yellowfin tuna at a restaurant in southwest Florida, I came up with this recipe so I could enjoy the flavor of my favorite fish at home.
—Jan Huntington, Painesville, OH

PREP: 10 MIN. + MARINATING
GRILL: 10 MIN. • **MAKES:** 4 SERVINGS

- 2 Tbsp. lemon juice
- 1 Tbsp. olive oil
- 2 garlic cloves, minced
- 2 tsp. minced fresh thyme or ½ tsp. dried thyme
- 4 tuna steaks (6 oz. each)
- ¼ tsp. salt
- ¼ tsp. pepper

1. In a container with a lid, combine the lemon juice, oil, garlic and thyme. Add the tuna and turn to coat. Cover and refrigerate for up to 30 minutes, turning tuna occasionally.
2. Remove tuna from bag; sprinkle with salt and pepper. Drain tuna, discarding marinade. On a lightly greased grill rack, grill tuna, covered, over medium-hot heat or broil 4 in. from the heat for 3-4 minutes on each side for medium-rare or until slightly pink in the center.
1 SERVING 218 cal., 5g fat (1g sat. fat), 77mg chol., 211mg sod., 1g carb. (0 sugars, 0 fiber), 40g pro.

ASIAN SPIN

Craving Asian flavors? Add ½ tsp. minced fresh ginger to the sauce and use sesame oil instead of olive oil.

31g Pro

SWEET & TANGY SALMON WITH GREEN BEANS

I'm always up for new ways to cook salmon. In this dish, a sweet sauce gives the fish and green beans some down-home barbecue tang. Even our kids love it.
—Aliesha Caldwell, Robersonville, NC

PREP: 20 MIN. • **BAKE:** 15 MIN.
MAKES: 4 SERVINGS

- 4 salmon fillets (6 oz. each)
- 1 Tbsp. butter
- 2 Tbsp. brown sugar
- 2 Tbsp. reduced-sodium soy sauce
- 2 Tbsp. Dijon mustard
- 1 Tbsp. olive oil
- ½ tsp. pepper
- ⅛ tsp. salt
- 1 lb. fresh green beans, trimmed

1. Preheat oven to 425°. Place fillets in a 15x10x1-in. baking pan coated with cooking spray. In a small skillet, melt butter; stir in brown sugar, soy sauce, mustard, oil, pepper and salt. Brush half of the mixture over the salmon.
2. Place green beans in a large bowl; drizzle with remaining brown sugar mixture and toss to coat. Arrange green beans around fillets. Roast until fish just begins to flake easily with a fork and green beans are crisp-tender, 14-16 minutes.

1 FILLET WITH ¾ CUP GREEN BEANS 394 cal., 22g fat (5g sat. fat), 93mg chol., 661mg sod., 17g carb. (10g sugars, 4g fiber), 31g pro.

21g Pro

SCALLOPS WITH SNOW PEAS

The vibrant, crisp pea pods are a nice contrast with the soft scallops. This dish looks and tastes bright and fresh.
—Barb Carlucci, Orange Park, FL

TAKES: 30 MIN. • **MAKES:** 4 SERVINGS

- 2 Tbsp. cornstarch
- 2 Tbsp. reduced-sodium soy sauce
- ⅔ cup water
- 4 tsp. canola oil, divided
- 1 lb. bay scallops
- ½ lb. fresh snow peas, halved diagonally
- 2 medium leeks (white portion only), cut into 3x½-in. strips
- 1½ tsp. minced fresh gingerroot
- 3 cups hot cooked brown rice

1. Mix cornstarch, soy sauce and water. In a large nonstick skillet, heat 2 tsp. oil over medium-high heat; stir-fry scallops until firm and opaque, 1-2 minutes. Remove from pan.
2. In same pan, heat remaining 2 tsp. oil over medium-high heat; stir-fry snow peas, leeks and ginger until peas are just crisp-tender, 4-6 minutes. Stir cornstarch mixture; add to pan. Cook and stir until sauce is thickened, about 1 minute. Add scallops; heat through. Serve with rice.

1 CUP STIR-FRY WITH ¾ CUP RICE 378 cal., 7g fat (1g sat. fat), 27mg chol., 750mg sod., 57g carb. (4g sugars, 5g fiber), 21g pro.

34g Pro

BLACKENED TILAPIA WITH ZUCCHINI NOODLES

I love quick meals like this one-skillet wonder. Homemade pico de gallo is easy to make the night before.
—Tammy Brownlow, Dallas, TX

TAKES: 30 MIN. • **MAKES:** 4 SERVINGS

- 2 large zucchini (about 1½ lbs.)
- 1½ tsp. ground cumin
- ¾ tsp. salt, divided
- ½ tsp. smoked paprika
- ½ tsp. pepper
- ¼ tsp. garlic powder
- 4 tilapia fillets (6 oz. each)
- 2 tsp. olive oil
- 2 garlic cloves, minced
- 1 cup pico de gallo

1. Trim ends of zucchini. Using a spiralizer, cut zucchini into thin strands.
2. Mix cumin, ½ tsp. salt, smoked paprika, pepper and garlic powder; sprinkle mixture generously onto both sides of tilapia. In a large nonstick skillet, heat oil over medium-high heat. In batches, cook tilapia until fish just begins to flake easily with a fork, 2-3 minutes per side. Remove from pan; keep warm.
3. In same pan, cook zucchini with garlic over medium-high heat until zucchini is slightly softened, 1-2 minutes, tossing constantly with tongs (do not overcook). Sprinkle with remaining ¼ tsp. salt. Serve with tilapia and pico de gallo.
NOTE If a spiralizer is not available, zucchini may also be cut into ribbons using a vegetable peeler. Saute as directed, increasing time as necessary.
1 SERVING 203 cal., 4g fat (1g sat. fat), 83mg chol., 522mg sod., 8g carb. (5g sugars, 2g fiber), 34g pro.

NOTES

What a delicious dinner! When I make tilapia, it's usually bland. This blend of spices along with the zucchini noodles makes for a creative tilapia.
—JENNIFER084, TASTEOFHOME.COM

23g Pro

AIR-FRYER BREADED SHRIMP

These quick air-fryer shrimp are so good you won't even miss the fat! Eat them alone with cocktail sauce or put them on a salad or sandwich.
—Rashanda Cobbins, Aurora, CO

PREP: 25 MIN. • **COOK:** 10 MIN./BATCH
MAKES: 4 SERVINGS

- ½ cup all-purpose flour
- ½ tsp. seafood seasoning
- ½ tsp. dill weed
- ½ tsp. pepper
- 1 large egg
- ½ cup 2% milk
- 1 tsp. hot pepper sauce
- 1 cup panko bread crumbs
- 1 lb. uncooked shrimp (26-30 per lb.), peeled and deveined
- Cooking spray
- Optional: Seafood cocktail sauce and lemon wedges

1. Preheat air fryer to 375°. In a shallow bowl, mix flour, seafood seasoning, dill weed and pepper. In a separate shallow bowl, whisk egg, milk and hot pepper sauce. Place bread crumbs in a third shallow bowl. Dip shrimp into flour mixture to coat both sides; shake off excess. Dip into egg mixture, then into bread crumbs, patting to help adhere.

2. In batches, arrange shrimp in a single layer on a greased tray in air-fryer basket; spritz with cooking spray. Cook until lightly browned and shrimp turn pink, 3-4 minutes on each side. If desired, serve with cocktail sauce and lemon wedges.

1 SERVING (ABOUT 7 SHRIMP) 198 cal., 4g fat (1g sat. fat), 171mg chol., 287mg sod., 15g carb. (2g sugars, 1g fiber), 23g pro.

19g Pro

SKILLET FISH DINNER

This healthy recipe takes very little time. We enjoy it with a spinach salad and whole wheat rolls.
—Janet Cooper Claggett, Olney, MD

TAKES: 20 MIN. • **MAKES:** 2 SERVINGS

- 1 celery rib, chopped
- ½ cup chopped green pepper
- ½ cup chopped onion
- 1 tsp. olive oil
- 2 to 3 plum tomatoes, chopped
- ¼ tsp. salt
- Dash pepper
- ½ lb. cod, haddock or orange roughy fillets
- ¼ to ½ tsp. seafood seasoning
- Hot cooked rice
- Hot pepper sauce, optional

In a skillet, saute the celery, green pepper and onion in oil until almost tender. Add tomatoes; cook and stir for 1-2 minutes. Sprinkle with salt and pepper. Top with fish fillets and sprinkle with seafood seasoning. Reduce heat; cover and simmer for 6 minutes. Break fish into chunks. Cook about 3 minutes longer or until fish flakes easily with a fork. Serve over rice. Serve with hot pepper sauce if desired.

1 SERVING 142 cal., 3g fat (1g sat. fat), 43mg chol., 461mg sod., 9g carb. (4g sugars, 3g fiber), 19g pro.

35g Pro

MAHI MAHI & VEGGIE SKILLET

Cooking mahi mahi with a mix of vegetables may seem complex, but I developed a skillet recipe to bring out the wow factor without the hassle and fuss.
—Solomon Wang, Arlington, TX

TAKES: 30 MIN. • **MAKES:** 4 SERVINGS

- 3 Tbsp. olive oil, divided
- 4 mahi mahi or salmon fillets (6 oz. each)
- 3 medium sweet red peppers, cut into thick strips
- ½ lb. sliced baby portobello mushrooms
- 1 large sweet onion, cut into thick rings and separated
- ⅓ cup lemon juice
- ¾ tsp. salt, divided
- ½ tsp. pepper
- ¼ cup minced fresh chives
- ⅓ cup pine nuts, optional

1. In a large skillet, heat 2 Tbsp. oil over medium-high heat. Add fillets; cook until fish just begins to flake easily with a fork, 4-5 minutes per side. Remove from pan.
2. Add remaining 1 Tbsp. oil, peppers, mushrooms, onion, lemon juice and ¼ tsp. salt. Cook, covered, over medium heat until vegetables are tender, stirring occasionally, 6-8 minutes.
3. Place fish over vegetables; sprinkle with pepper and remaining ½ tsp. salt. Cook, covered, until heated through, about 2 minutes longer. Sprinkle with chives and, if desired, pine nuts before serving.

1 SERVING 307 cal., 12g fat (2g sat. fat), 124mg chol., 606mg sod., 15g carb. (9g sugars, 3g fiber), 35g pro.

> *It was delicious. I took a risk cooking it for a dinner party for the first time, and I was very pleased with the results. I will make it again.*
>
> —POLINA, TASTEOFHOME.COM

24g Pro

LAUREN'S BOUILLABAISSE

This golden-colored soup brimming with an assortment of seafood is paired with sourdough toast with a savory, colorful spread.
—Lauren Covas, New Brunswick, NJ

PREP: 30 MIN. • **COOK:** 20 MIN.
MAKES: 12 SERVINGS (5 QT.)

- ⅔ cup chopped roasted sweet red pepper, drained
- ¼ cup reduced-fat mayonnaise

TOASTS

- 6 slices sourdough bread
- 1 garlic clove, halved

BOUILLABAISSE

- 1 medium onion, chopped
- 1 Tbsp. olive oil
- 2 garlic cloves, minced
- 2 plum tomatoes, chopped
- ½ tsp. saffron threads or 2 tsp. ground turmeric
- 3½ cups cubed red potatoes
- 2½ cups thinly sliced fennel bulb
- 1 carton (32 oz.) reduced-sodium chicken broth
- 3 cups clam juice
- 2 tsp. dried tarragon
- 24 fresh littleneck clams
- 24 fresh mussels, scrubbed and beards removed
- 1 lb. red snapper fillet, cut into 2-in. pieces
- ¾ lb. uncooked large shrimp, peeled and deveined
- ¼ cup minced fresh parsley

1. Place red pepper and mayonnaise in a food processor; cover and process until smooth. Refrigerate until serving.
2. For toasts, rub 1 side of each bread slice with garlic; discard garlic. Cut bread slices in half. Place on an ungreased baking sheet. Bake at 400° for 4-5 minutes on each side or until lightly browned.
3. In a stockpot, saute onion in oil until tender. Add garlic; cook 1 minute longer. Reduce heat; stir in tomatoes and saffron. Add the potatoes, fennel, broth, clam juice and tarragon. Bring to a boil. Reduce heat; simmer, uncovered, for 10-12 minutes or until potatoes are almost tender.
4. Add the clams, mussels, snapper and shrimp. Cook, stirring occasionally, for 10-15 minutes or until clams and mussels open and fish flakes easily with a fork. Discard any unopened clams or mussels. Spoon into bowls; sprinkle with parsley. Spread pepper mayo over toasts; serve with bouillabaisse.

1⅔ CUPS WITH 1 PIECE TOAST AND 2 TSP. SPREAD 239 cal., 5g fat (1g sat. fat), 70mg chol., 684mg sod., 23g carb. (3g sugars, 2g fiber), 24g pro.

NOTES

18g Pro

LIGHT-BUT-HEARTY TUNA CASSEROLE

My boyfriend grew up loving his mom's tuna casserole and says he can't even tell that this one is so light! We have it at least once a month. I usually serve it with a salad, but it has enough veggies to stand on its own.
—Heidi Carofano, Brooklyn, NY

PREP: 20 MIN. • **BAKE:** 25 MIN.
MAKES: 4 SERVINGS

- 3 cups uncooked yolk-free noodles
- 1 can (10¾ oz.) reduced-fat, reduced-sodium condensed cream of mushroom soup, undiluted
- ½ cup fat-free milk
- 2 Tbsp. reduced-fat mayonnaise
- ½ tsp. ground mustard
- 1 jar (6 oz.) sliced mushrooms, drained
- 1 can (5 oz.) albacore white tuna in water
- ¼ cup chopped roasted sweet red pepper

TOPPING

- ¼ cup dry bread crumbs
- 1 Tbsp. butter, melted
- ½ tsp. paprika
- ¼ tsp. Italian seasoning
- ¼ tsp. pepper

1. Preheat oven to 400°. Cook noodles according to package directions.
2. In a large bowl, combine soup, milk, mayonnaise and mustard. Stir in the mushrooms, tuna and red pepper. Drain noodles; add to soup mixture and stir until blended. Transfer to a greased 8-in. square baking dish.
3. Combine topping ingredients; sprinkle over casserole. Bake until bubbly, 25-30 minutes.

1½ CUPS 322 cal., 9g fat (3g sat. fat), 32mg chol., 843mg sod., 39g carb. (7g sugars, 4g fiber), 18g pro.

MAKE IT YOUR OWN

Chopped onion is a great, flavorful addition to a light tuna casserole, but don't stop there. Feel free to mix in other vegetables such as peas, carrots or corn for extra color and texture. Even a light sprinkle of cheese won't hurt.

PROTEIN
BOOST
PAGE 320

34g Pro

TUNA ARTICHOKE MELTS

After sampling a similar open-faced sandwich at a restaurant, I created my own version of lemon-seasoned tuna salad with artichoke hearts. Serve these melts on the patio for lunch with a friend.
—Evelyn Basinger, Linville, VA

TAKES: 15 MIN. • **MAKES:** 2 SERVINGS

- 1 can (6 oz.) light water-packed tuna, drained and flaked
- ⅓ cup coarsely chopped water-packed artichoke hearts, rinsed and drained
- 2 Tbsp. mayonnaise
- ½ cup shredded Mexican cheese blend, divided
- ¼ tsp. lemon-pepper seasoning
- ⅛ tsp. dried oregano
- 2 English muffins, split and toasted

1. Preheat broiler. In a small bowl, combine the tuna, artichokes, mayonnaise, ¼ cup cheese, lemon pepper and oregano. Spread over English muffin halves.

2. Place on a baking sheet. Broil 4-6 in. from the heat until heated through, 3-5 minutes. Sprinkle with remaining ¼ cup cheese; broil until cheese is melted, 1-2 minutes longer.

2 TOPPED MUFFIN HALVES 335 cal., 8g fat (4g sat. fat), 47mg chol., 989mg sod., 31g carb. (3g sugars, 2g fiber), 34g pro.

25g Pro

COCONUT-MANGO TILAPIA

Friends always request the recipe for this dish, with its intriguing tropical taste. A sweet mango-lime puree nicely complements the couscous and fish.
—Jess Apfe, Berkeley, CA

PREP: 20 MIN. + MARINATING
GRILL: 10 MIN. • **MAKES:** 4 SERVINGS

- ½ cup light coconut milk
- 2 Tbsp. lime juice
- 2 large mangoes, peeled and diced
- 3 Tbsp. brown sugar
- 4½ tsp. minced fresh gingerroot
- 4 tilapia fillets (4 oz. each)

COUSCOUS

- ¾ cup light coconut milk
- 1½ tsp. minced fresh gingerroot
- ⅔ cup uncooked couscous
- 2 Tbsp. minced fresh cilantro

1. Place the first 5 ingredients in a blender; cover and process until smooth. Pour 1 cup mixture into a large resealable plastic bag. Add fish; seal bag and turn to coat. Refrigerate at least 2 hours. Cover and refrigerate remaining mixture for sauce.

2. Drain fish, discarding marinade in bag. Moisten a paper towel with cooking oil; using long-handled tongs, rub on grill rack to coat lightly. Grill fish, covered, over high heat or broil 3-4 in. from heat 3-5 minutes or until fish just begins to flake easily with a fork.

3. Meanwhile, in a small saucepan, bring coconut milk and ginger to a boil. Stir in couscous. Remove from heat; let stand, covered, 5-10 minutes or until liquid is absorbed. Add cilantro; fluff with a fork. Serve fish with couscous and reserved sauce.

1 FILLET WITH ½ CUP COUSCOUS AND ABOUT 1 TBSP. SAUCE 350 cal., 10g fat (7g sat. fat), 55mg chol., 72mg sod., 40g carb. (17g sugars, 2g fiber), 25g pro.

32g Pro

BAKED LEMON HADDOCK

After testing out a ton of haddock recipes, I've decided this baked version is the best. The crunchy, lemony topping is just delicious.
—Jean Ann Perkins, Newburyport, MA

TAKES: 30 MIN. • **MAKES:** 6 SERVINGS

- 2 lbs. haddock fillets
- 1 cup seasoned dry bread crumbs
- ¼ cup butter, melted
- 2 Tbsp. dried parsley flakes
- 2 tsp. grated lemon zest
- ½ tsp. garlic powder

Preheat oven to 350°. Cut fish into 6 serving-sized pieces. Place in a greased 11x7-in. baking dish. Combine remaining ingredients; sprinkle over fish. Bake until fish just begins to flake easily with a fork, 20-25 minutes.

4 OZ. COOKED FISH 269 cal., 9g fat (5g sat. fat), 108mg chol., 446mg sod., 13g carb. (1g sugars, 1g fiber), 32g pro.

28g Pro

BAKED SALMON CAKES

Made in muffin tins and served with sauce on the side, these little salmon patties make a fantastic light meal. You can also bake a double batch and freeze some for a quick supper later on.
—Nikki Haddad, Germantown, MD

TAKES: 30 MIN. • **MAKES:** 4 SERVINGS

- 1 can (14¾ oz.) salmon, drained, bones and skin removed
- 1½ cups soft whole wheat bread crumbs
- ½ cup finely chopped sweet red pepper
- ½ cup egg substitute
- 3 green onions, thinly sliced
- ¼ cup finely chopped celery
- ¼ cup minced fresh cilantro
- 3 Tbsp. fat-free mayonnaise
- 1 Tbsp. lemon juice
- 1 garlic clove, minced
- ⅛ to ¼ tsp. hot pepper sauce

SAUCE

- 2 Tbsp. fat-free mayonnaise
- ¼ tsp. capers, drained
- ¼ tsp. dill weed
- Dash lemon juice

1. In a large bowl, combine the first 11 ingredients. Place ⅓ cup salmon mixture into each of 8 muffin cups coated with cooking spray. Bake at 425° for 10-15 minutes or until a thermometer reads 160°.
2. Meanwhile, combine the sauce ingredients. Serve with salmon.

2 SALMON CAKES 266 cal., 9g fat (2g sat. fat), 48mg chol., 914mg sod., 17g carb. (5g sugars, 3g fiber), 28g pro.

NO-FAIL PATTIES

The key to salmon patties that hold together is the right balance of wet and dry ingredients. If the mixture feels too wet, add a little more bread crumbs. If it's dry and crumbly, stir in a bit more mayonnaise.

20g Pro

SPICY TUNA CRUNCH WRAPS

These quick-to-fix wraps are ideal for lunch or dinner. They're versatile too—you can replace the tuna with chicken, turkey or ham. Adapt them to whatever you have on hand for a fun alternative to sandwiches.
—Amy Smeltzer, Frostburg, MD

TAKES: 15 MIN. • **MAKES:** 4 SERVINGS

- 4 pouches (2.6 oz. each) sweet and spicy chunk light tuna
- 1½ cups coleslaw mix
- ⅓ cup chopped salted peanuts
- 1 Tbsp. rice vinegar
- ¼ tsp. crushed red pepper flakes
- ⅛ tsp. pepper
- 12 Bibb or Boston lettuce leaves (about 1 medium head)
- Reduced-sodium soy sauce

In a small bowl, combine first 6 ingredients; toss lightly to combine. Serve in lettuce leaves with soy sauce.

3 LETTUCE WRAPS 179 cal., 7g fat (1g sat. fat), 35mg chol., 495mg sod., 10g carb. (6g sugars, 2g fiber), 20g pro.

34g Pro

SAVORY TOMATO-BRAISED TILAPIA

I shared this recipe with my bunco group, and now one of my friends makes it all the time. I think that's the perfect testament to how good this dish is.
—Nancy Shively, Shorewood, IL

TAKES: 30 MIN. • **MAKES:** 4 SERVINGS

- 4 tilapia fillets (6 oz. each)
- ¼ tsp. seasoned salt
- 1 Tbsp. lemon juice
- 2 Tbsp. olive oil
- 1 small red onion, chopped
- 1 can (10 oz.) diced tomatoes and green chiles, undrained
- ¾ cup chopped roasted sweet red peppers
- ½ cup chicken broth
- ¼ cup tomato paste
- 1 tsp. garlic powder
- 1 tsp. dried oregano
- Hot cooked pasta, optional

1. Sprinkle fillets with seasoned salt; drizzle with lemon juice. In a large skillet, heat oil over medium-high heat. Add onion; cook and stir until tender. Add tomatoes, peppers, broth, tomato paste, garlic powder and oregano; cook and stir 2-3 minutes longer.

2. Place fillets over tomato mixture; cook, covered, 6-8 minutes or until fish flakes easily with a fork. If desired, serve with pasta.

1 FILLET WITH ½ CUP SAUCE 254 cal., 8g fat (2g sat. fat), 83mg chol., 740mg sod., 10g carb. (4g sugars, 2g fiber), 34g pro.

23g Pro

EASY GRILLED SALMON SALAD

Try this grilled salmon salad with your favorite herb vinaigrette or creamy Caesar salad dressing. You can add berries during the summer months when they are in season, or citrus when berries aren't available.
—Susan Bronson, Rhinelander, WI

TAKES: 30 MIN. • **MAKES:** 4 SERVINGS

- 4 salmon fillets (4 oz. each)
- 2 garlic cloves, minced
- ½ cup teriyaki sauce
- 1 pkg. (10 oz.) hearts of romaine salad mix
- 1 medium cucumber, sliced
- 1 pint cherry or grape tomatoes, halved
- ½ medium red onion, thinly sliced
- Salad dressing of your choice
- Optional: Crumbled feta cheese, fresh dill and lemon slices

1. Rub salmon with garlic; place in a shallow bowl. Add teriyaki sauce; turn salmon to coat. Let stand 10 minutes.
2. Place salmon on an oiled grill rack. Grill salmon, covered, over medium-high heat or broil 3-4 in. from heat until fish just begins to flake easily with a fork, 4-5 minutes on each side.
3. Toss salad mix, cucumber, tomatoes and onion with salad dressing; place on 4 salad plates. Top with salmon and desired toppings.

1 SERVING 221 cal., 11g fat (2g sat. fat), 57mg chol., 242mg sod., 10g carb. (4g sugars, 4g fiber), 23g pro.

29g Pro

SEAFOOD CIOPPINO

If you're looking for a great seafood recipe for your slow cooker, this classic fish stew is just the ticket. It's brimming with clams, crab, fish and shrimp, and it is fancy enough to be an elegant meal.
—Lisa Moriarty, Wilton, NH

PREP: 20 MIN. • **COOK:** 4 HOURS 20 MIN.
MAKES: 8 SERVINGS (2½ QT.)

- 1 can (28 oz.) diced tomatoes, undrained
- 2 medium onions, chopped
- 3 celery ribs, chopped
- 1 bottle (8 oz.) clam juice
- 1 can (6 oz.) tomato paste
- ½ cup white wine or ½ cup vegetable broth
- 5 garlic cloves, minced
- 1 Tbsp. red wine vinegar
- 1 Tbsp. olive oil
- 1 to 2 tsp. Italian seasoning
- 1 bay leaf
- ½ tsp. sugar
- 1 lb. haddock fillets, cut into 1-in. pieces
- 1 lb. uncooked shrimp (41-50 per lb.), peeled and deveined
- 1 can (6 oz.) chopped clams, undrained
- 1 can (6 oz.) lump crabmeat, drained
- 2 Tbsp. minced fresh parsley

1. In a 4- or 5-qt. slow cooker, combine the first 12 ingredients. Cook, covered, on low 4-5 hours.
2. Stir in seafood. Cook, covered, until fish just begins to flake easily with a fork and shrimp turn pink, 20-30 minutes longer.
3. Remove bay leaf. Stir in parsley.

1¼ CUPS 205 cal., 3g fat (1g sat. fat), 125mg chol., 483mg sod., 15g carb. (8g sugars, 3g fiber), 29g pro.

FLAVOR SWAPS

For a little more heat, add red pepper flakes or hot sauce. Instead of haddock, use cod, tilapia or another firm white fish. Boost the seafood with lobster, scallops, mussels or even octopus. When tomatoes are at their best, toss in diced ripe plum tomatoes. And for more flavor depth, add diced carrots, sliced fennel or a splash of dry vermouth or red wine.

> *Our first grilled meal of the season! And we'll be hard-pressed to find a better one, no matter how often we grill this year.*
>
> —BROWNS19FAN, TASTEOFHOME.COM

19g Pro

TROPICAL SEAFOOD SALAD

A fruity dressing makes this seafood salad shine. Served on a bed of greens, the scrumptious combination of grilled seafood, veggies and macadamia nuts is the perfect way to celebrate a special summer occasion.
—Jackie Pressinger, Stuart, WI

PREP: 35 MIN. • **COOK:** 5 MIN.
MAKES: 2 SERVINGS

- 2 Tbsp. diced peeled mango
- 1 Tbsp. diced fresh pineapple
- 1½ tsp. mango chutney
- 1½ tsp. olive oil
- 1 tsp. rice vinegar
- ¾ tsp. lime juice
- Dash salt
- Dash crushed red pepper flakes
- 3 cups torn Bibb or Boston lettuce
- 1 cup chopped peeled cucumber
- ½ medium ripe avocado, peeled and sliced
- 2 Tbsp. coarsely chopped macadamia nuts, toasted
- 1 Tbsp. finely chopped red onion
- 1 Tbsp. minced fresh cilantro
- 2 Tbsp. canola oil
- 1½ tsp. Caribbean jerk seasoning
- 6 uncooked large shrimp, peeled and deveined
- 6 sea scallops, halved

1. Place the first 8 ingredients in a blender. Cover and process until blended. Divide the lettuce, cucumber, avocado, nuts, onion and cilantro between 2 serving plates.

2. In a small bowl, combine oil and jerk seasoning. Thread shrimp and scallops onto 2 metal or soaked wooden skewers; brush with oil mixture.

3. Grill skewers, covered, over medium heat until shrimp turn pink and scallops are firm and opaque, 2-3 minutes on each side. Place on salads; drizzle with dressing.

1 SALAD 413 cal., 32g fat (4g sat. fat), 96mg chol., 523mg sod., 16g carb. (6g sugars, 5g fiber), 19g pro.

NOTES

34g Pro

CRISPY DILL TILAPIA

Every week I try to serve a new healthy fish. With its delicious panko bread crumb herb crust with fresh dill, this dish with mild tilapia is a winner.
—Tamara Huron, New Market, AL

TAKES: 20 MIN. • **MAKES:** 4 SERVINGS

- 1 cup panko bread crumbs
- 2 Tbsp. olive oil
- 2 Tbsp. snipped fresh dill
- ¼ tsp. salt
- ⅛ tsp. pepper
- 4 tilapia fillets (6 oz. each)
- 1 Tbsp. lemon juice
- Lemon wedges

1. Preheat oven to 400°. Toss together first 5 ingredients.
2. Place tilapia in a 15x10x1-in. baking pan coated with cooking spray; brush with lemon juice. Top with crumb mixture, patting to help adhere.
3. Bake, uncovered, on an upper oven rack until fish just begins to flake easily with a fork, 12-15 minutes. Serve with lemon wedges.

1 FILLET 256 cal., 9g fat (2g sat. fat), 83mg chol., 251mg sod., 10g carb. (1g sugars, 1g fiber), 34g pro.

28g Pro

MINI SCALLOP CASSEROLES

Tiny and tender bay scallops take center stage in these miniature dishes. They're reminiscent of potpies—very creamy, and packed with flavorful veggies in every bite.
—Vivian Manary, Nepean, ON

PREP: 30 MIN. • **BAKE:** 20 MIN.
MAKES: 4 SERVINGS

- 3 celery ribs, chopped
- 1 cup sliced fresh mushrooms
- 1 medium green pepper, chopped
- 1 small onion, chopped
- 2 Tbsp. butter
- ⅓ cup all-purpose flour
- ¼ tsp. salt
- ¼ tsp. pepper
- 2 cups fat-free milk
- 1 lb. bay scallops

TOPPING

- 1 cup soft bread crumbs
- 1 Tbsp. butter, melted
- ¼ cup shredded cheddar cheese

1. In a large skillet, saute celery, mushrooms, green pepper and onion in butter until tender. Stir in flour, salt and pepper until blended; gradually add milk. Bring to a boil; cook and stir 2 minutes or until thickened.
2. Reduce heat; add scallops. Cook, stirring occasionally, 3-4 minutes or until scallops are firm and opaque.
3. Preheat oven to 350°. Divide mixture among four 10-oz. ramekins or custard cups. In a small bowl, combine bread crumbs and butter; sprinkle over scallop mixture.
4. Bake, uncovered, 15-20 minutes or until bubbly. Sprinkle with cheese; bake 5 minutes longer or until cheese is melted.

1 SERVING 332 cal., 12g fat (7g sat. fat), 70mg chol., 588mg sod., 27g carb. (9g sugars, 2g fiber), 28g pro.

> Loved this! I made the recipe with shrimp. My husband and I loved this to death. And it was so much fun using the ramekins. I've never had so much fun with a recipe that was so great tasting.
>
> —BONNIEKENK, TASTEOFHOME.COM

23g Pro

AIR-FRYER FISH & FRIES

Looking for easy air-fryer recipes? Try this simple fish and chips. The fish fillets have a fuss-free coating that's healthier but just as crunchy and golden as the deep-fried kind. The crispy fries are simply seasoned and perfect on the side.
—Janice Mitchell, Aurora, CO

PREP: 15 MIN. • **COOK:** 25 MIN.
MAKES: 4 SERVINGS

- 1 lb. potatoes (about 2 medium)
- 2 Tbsp. olive oil
- ¼ tsp. pepper
- ¼ tsp. salt

FISH

- ⅓ cup all-purpose flour
- ¼ tsp. pepper
- 1 large egg
- 2 Tbsp. water
- ⅔ cup crushed cornflakes
- 1 Tbsp. grated Parmesan cheese
- ⅛ tsp. cayenne pepper
- 1 lb. haddock or cod fillets
- ¼ tsp. salt
- Tartar sauce, optional

1. Preheat air fryer to 400°. Peel and cut potatoes lengthwise into ½-in.-thick slices; cut slices into ½-in.-thick sticks.
2. In a large bowl, toss potatoes with oil, pepper and salt. Working in batches, place potatoes in a single layer on tray in air-fryer basket; cook until just tender, 5-10 minutes Toss potatoes to redistribute; cook until lightly browned and crisp, 5-10 minutes longer.
3. Meanwhile, in a shallow bowl, mix flour and pepper. In another shallow bowl, whisk egg with water. In a third bowl, toss cornflakes with cheese and cayenne. Sprinkle fish with salt. Dip into flour mixture to coat both sides; shake off excess. Dip in egg mixture, then in cornflake mixture, patting to help coating adhere.
4. Remove fries from basket; keep warm. Place fish in a single layer on tray in air-fryer basket. Cook until fish is lightly browned and just beginning to flake easily with a fork, 8-10 minutes, turning halfway through cooking. Do not overcook. Return fries to basket to heat through. Serve immediately. If desired, serve with tartar sauce.

NOTE Cook times vary dramatically among brands of air fryers. Refer to your air-fryer manual for general cook times and adjust if necessary.

1 SERVING 312 cal., 9g fat (2g sat. fat), 85mg chol., 503mg sod., 35g carb. (3g sugars, 1g fiber), 23g pro.

HEALTH TIP

Look for farmed U.S. or Canadian tilapia that's been raised in closed tanks for the least impact on the environment.

32g Pro

GRILLED TILAPIA PICCATA

We aren't big fish eaters, but a friend made this for us, and we couldn't believe how wonderful it was! Now we eat it regularly. I love making it for guests because it's simple, looks lovely and tastes like a fancy dish from a restaurant.
—Beth Cooper, Columbus, OH

TAKES: 25 MIN. • **MAKES:** 4 SERVINGS

- ½ tsp. grated lemon zest
- 3 Tbsp. lemon juice
- 2 Tbsp. olive oil
- 2 garlic cloves, minced
- 2 tsp. capers, drained
- 3 Tbsp. minced fresh basil, divided
- 4 tilapia fillets (6 oz. each)
- ½ tsp. salt
- ¼ tsp. pepper

1. In a small bowl, whisk lemon zest, lemon juice, oil and garlic until blended; stir in capers and 2 Tbsp. basil. Reserve 2 Tbsp. mixture for drizzling cooked fish. Brush remaining mixture onto both sides of tilapia; sprinkle with salt and pepper.
2. Grill tilapia on a lightly oiled rack, covered, over medium heat or broil 4 in. from heat until fish just begins to flake easily with a fork, 3-4 minutes per side. Drizzle with reserved lemon mixture; sprinkle with remaining 1 Tbsp. basil.

1 FILLET 206 cal., 8g fat (2g sat. fat), 83mg chol., 398mg sod., 2g carb. (0 sugars, 0 fiber), 32g pro.

40g Pro

TUNA WITH CITRUS PONZU SAUCE

I like this Asian-inspired tuna because it's easy to prepare, delicious and healthy, too. It's a popular dish with my friends.
—Diane Halferty, Corpus Christi, TX

TAKES: 20 MIN. • **MAKES:** 4 SERVINGS

- ½ tsp. Chinese five-spice powder
- ¼ tsp. salt
- ¼ tsp. cayenne pepper
- 4 tuna steaks (6 oz. each)
- 1 Tbsp. canola oil
- ¼ cup orange juice
- 2 green onions, thinly sliced
- 1 Tbsp. lemon juice
- 1 Tbsp. reduced-sodium soy sauce
- 2 tsp. rice vinegar
- 1 tsp. brown sugar
- ¼ tsp. minced fresh gingerroot

1. Combine the five-spice powder, salt and cayenne; sprinkle over tuna steaks. In a large skillet over medium heat, cook tuna in oil for 2-3 minutes on each side for medium-rare, or until slightly pink in the center; remove and keep warm.
2. Combine the orange juice, onions, lemon juice, soy sauce, vinegar, brown sugar and ginger; pour into skillet. Cook for 1-2 minutes or until slightly thickened. Serve with tuna.

1 TUNA STEAK WITH 1 TBSP. SAUCE 234 cal., 5g fat (1g sat. fat), 77mg chol., 364mg sod., 5g carb. (3g sugars, 0 fiber), 40g pro.

33g Pro

CHRISTMAS EVE CONFETTI PASTA

Our Christmas Eve tradition is to make linguine with red and green peppers and shrimp. We serve it with a fresh garden salad and garlic bread.
—Ellen Fiore, Montvale, NJ

TAKES: 25 MIN. • **MAKES:** 8 SERVINGS

- 1 pkg. (16 oz.) linguine
- 1 cup chopped sweet red pepper
- 1 cup chopped green pepper
- ⅓ cup chopped onion
- 3 garlic cloves, peeled and thinly sliced
- ¼ tsp. salt
- ¼ tsp. dried oregano
- ⅛ tsp. crushed red pepper flakes
- ⅛ tsp. pepper
- ¼ cup olive oil
- 2 lbs. peeled and deveined cooked shrimp (61-70 per lb.)
- ½ cup shredded Parmesan cheese

1. Cook linguine according to package directions. Meanwhile, in a Dutch oven, saute the peppers, onion, garlic and seasonings in oil until vegetables are tender.
2. Add the shrimp; cook and stir for 2-3 minutes longer or until heated through. Drain linguine; toss with shrimp mixture. Sprinkle with cheese.
1⅓ CUPS 418 cal., 11g fat (2g sat. fat), 176mg chol., 331mg sod., 46g carb. (3g sugars, 3g fiber), 33g pro.

45g Pro

CRAB-STUFFED FLOUNDER WITH HERBED AIOLI

If you like seafood, you'll love this scrumptious flounder. The light and creamy aioli sauce tops it off with fresh tones of chives and garlic.
—Beverly O'Ferrall, Linkwood, MD

PREP: 20 MIN. • **BAKE:** 20 MIN.
MAKES: 6 SERVINGS

- ¼ cup egg substitute
- 2 Tbsp. fat-free milk
- 1 Tbsp. minced chives
- 1 Tbsp. reduced-fat mayonnaise
- 1 Tbsp. Dijon mustard
- Dash hot pepper sauce
- 1 lb. lump crabmeat
- 6 flounder fillets (6 oz. each)
- Paprika

AIOLI

- ⅓ cup reduced-fat mayonnaise
- 2 tsp. minced chives
- 2 tsp. minced fresh parsley
- 2 tsp. lemon juice
- 1 garlic clove, minced

1. In a small bowl, combine the first 6 ingredients; gently fold in crabmeat. Cut the fillets in half widthwise; place 6 halves in a 15x10x1-in. baking pan coated with cooking spray. Spoon crab mixture over fillets; top with remaining fish. Sprinkle with paprika.
2. Bake at 400° for 20-24 minutes or until fish flakes easily with a fork. Meanwhile, combine the aioli ingredients. Serve with fish.
1 STUFFED FILLET WITH 2½ TSP. AIOLI 276 cal., 8g fat (1g sat. fat), 153mg chol., 585mg sod., 3g carb. (1g sugars, 0 fiber), 45g pro.

31g Pro

GRILLED TUNA SALAD

I love serving this tuna spinach salad! Tuna steaks are quick to cook and delicious, and always seem elegant even though they're pretty inexpensive. You can find them at most meat and seafood counters.
—De'Lawrence Reed, Durham, NC

TAKES: 30 MIN. • **MAKES:** 2 SERVINGS

- ½ lb. tuna steaks
- 1 tsp. olive oil
- ⅛ tsp. salt
- ⅛ tsp. pepper
- 3 cups fresh baby spinach
- ½ cup grape tomatoes
- ⅓ cup frozen shelled edamame, thawed
- ¼ cup frozen corn, thawed

CITRUS VINAIGRETTE

- 1 Tbsp. olive oil
- 1½ tsp. minced fresh basil
- 1½ tsp. white wine vinegar
- 1½ tsp. honey
- 1½ tsp. lime juice
- 1½ tsp. lemon juice
- 1½ tsp. orange juice
- ⅛ tsp. salt
- ⅛ tsp. pepper

1. Brush tuna with oil; sprinkle with salt and pepper. Grill, covered, over high heat on a greased grill rack or broil 3-4 in. from the heat for 3-4 minutes on each side for medium-rare or until slightly pink in the center. Let stand for 5 minutes.

2. Meanwhile, in a large bowl, combine the spinach, tomatoes, edamame and corn. In a small bowl, whisk together all the vinaigrette ingredients. Drizzle dressing over salad; toss to coat.

3. Divide salad between 2 plates; slice tuna and arrange over salads. Serve immediately.

2 CUPS SALAD WITH 3 OZ. COOKED TUNA 290 cal., 12g fat (2g sat. fat), 51mg chol., 380mg sod., 16g carb. (7g sugars, 3g fiber), 31g pro.

Yummy! My first time grilling a tuna steak, and it was fantastic!
—MARSHA428, TASTEOFHOME.COM

MAKE IT A MEAL

If you happen to have any leftover shrimp, serve it over hot cooked pasta, polenta or quinoa. A little sprinkle of Parmesan cheese won't hurt, either.

25g Pro

SPINACH, SHRIMP & RICOTTA TACOS

I was looking for a new recipe for tacos, and this version was a perfect solution. With shrimp, green chiles, spinach and ricotta, it's made with ingredients I love that aren't normally associated with traditional tacos.
—Priscilla Gilbert, Indian Harbour Beach, FL

TAKES: 30 MIN. • **MAKES:** 6 SERVINGS

- 1 carton (15 oz.) part-skim ricotta cheese
- 2 Tbsp. minced fresh cilantro
- 4 garlic cloves, minced, divided
- ¼ tsp. salt
- ⅛ tsp. pepper
- 1 Tbsp. canola oil
- 1 medium onion, chopped
- 1 lb. uncooked shrimp (31-40 per lb.), peeled and deveined
- 2 cans (4 oz. each) chopped green chiles
- ¼ tsp. crushed red pepper flakes
- 10 oz. fresh baby spinach (about 12 cups)
- 12 corn tortillas (6 in.), warmed
- Salsa and lime wedges

1. In a large bowl, combine ricotta, cilantro, half the minced garlic, salt and pepper; set aside.
2. In a large skillet, heat oil over medium-high heat. Add onion; cook and stir until softened, 4-5 minutes. Add shrimp, green chiles and pepper flakes; cook 1 minute longer. Add spinach and remaining garlic; cook and stir until shrimp turn pink and spinach is wilted, 2-3 minutes.
3. Serve shrimp mixture in tortillas with ricotta mixture, salsa and lime wedges.

2 TACOS 317 cal., 11g fat (4g sat. fat), 114mg chol., 468mg sod., 32g carb. (2g sugars, 5g fiber), 25g pro.

NOTES

20g Pro

SHRIMP LETTUCE WRAPS WITH PEANUT SAUCE

Tender shrimp meets crisp Bibb lettuce for this light and tasteful lettuce wrap. Shrimp, carrots and cucumbers are layered on a leaf of lettuce and then topped with a flavorful sauce made of peanut butter, soy sauce and brown sugar. It's a simple and easy lunch you have to try!
—Taste of Home *Test Kitchen*

TAKES: 20 MIN. • **MAKES:** 6 SERVINGS

- ⅓ cup water
- 1 Tbsp. reduced-sodium soy sauce
- 1 Tbsp. creamy peanut butter
- 1 Tbsp. packed brown sugar
- 1 Tbsp. canola oil
- 1½ lbs. uncooked shrimp (31-40 per lb.), peeled and deveined
- 1 Tbsp. minced fresh gingerroot
- 2 garlic cloves, minced
- 4 green onions, chopped
- 12 Bibb or butter lettuce leaves
- 1 cup julienned carrot
- 1 small cucumber, cut into strips

1. Whisk together first 4 ingredients until smooth. In a large skillet, heat oil over medium-high heat. Add shrimp; cook and stir until shrimp turn pink, 2-3 minutes. Add ginger and garlic; cook and stir 1 minute. Stir in sauce mixture and green onions; heat through.

2. Serve in lettuce leaves; top with carrot and cucumber. If desired, garnish with additional chopped green onions.

2 WRAPS 163 cal., 5g fat (1g sat. fat), 138mg chol., 260mg sod., 8g carb. (4g sugars, 1g fiber), 20g pro.

Thank you for creating this recipe. I left out the garlic and soy and served them for lunch, and they were delicious.

—ORBS, TASTEOFHOME.COM

24g Pro

THAI SALMON BROWN RICE BOWLS

Turn to this salmon recipe for a quick and nourishing meal. The store-bought sesame ginger dressing saves time and adds extra flavor to this healthy dish.
—Naylet LaRochelle, Miami, FL

TAKES: 15 MIN. • **MAKES:** 4 SERVINGS

- 4 salmon fillets (4 oz. each)
- ½ cup sesame ginger salad dressing, divided
- 3 cups hot cooked brown rice
- ½ cup chopped fresh cilantro
- ¼ tsp. salt
- 1 cup julienned carrot
- Thinly sliced red cabbage, optional

1. Preheat oven to 400°. Place salmon in a foil-lined 15x10x1-in. pan; brush with ¼ cup dressing. Bake until fish just begins to flake easily with a fork, 8-10 minutes. Meanwhile, toss rice with cilantro and salt.

2. To serve, divide rice mixture among 4 bowls. Top with salmon, carrot and, if desired, cabbage. Drizzle with remaining dressing.

1 SERVING 486 cal., 21g fat (4g sat. fat), 57mg chol., 532mg sod., 49g carb. (8g sugars, 3g fiber), 24g pro.

HERB SWAP

People seem to either love or hate cilantro. If it's not your favorite, you can omit the chopped cilantro and add some chopped fresh parsley instead.

PROTEIN BOOST
PAGE 320

Love the flavors in this dish! Plus, it is so simple and light. I swapped in rice for the orzo to make this gluten free.
—LPHJKITCHEN, TASTEOFHOME.COM

25g Pro

GRILLED JERK SHRIMP ORZO SALAD

It doesn't matter what the temperature outside is—you'll feel as if you're in the Caribbean when you take your first bite of this salad.
—Eileen Budnyk, Palm Beach Gardens, FL

PREP: 25 MIN. • **GRILL:** 10 MIN.
MAKES: 2 SERVINGS

- ⅓ cup uncooked whole wheat orzo pasta
- ½ lb. uncooked shrimp (31-40 per lb.), peeled and deveined
- 1 Tbsp. Caribbean jerk seasoning
- 1 medium ear sweet corn, husked
- 1 tsp. olive oil
- 6 fresh asparagus spears, trimmed
- 1 small sweet red pepper, chopped

DRESSING

- 3 Tbsp. lime juice
- 1 Tbsp. water
- 1 Tbsp. olive oil
- ⅛ tsp. salt
- ⅛ tsp. pepper

1. Cook orzo according to package directions. Rinse with cold water; drain well. Meanwhile, toss shrimp with jerk seasoning; thread onto metal or soaked wooden skewers. Brush corn with oil.
2. On a covered grill over medium heat, cook corn until tender and lightly browned, 10-12 minutes, turning occasionally. Cook asparagus until crisp-tender, 5-7 minutes, turning occasionally. Grill shrimp until they turn pink, 1-2 minutes per side.
3. Cut corn from cob; cut asparagus into 1-in. pieces. Remove shrimp from skewers. In a large bowl, combine orzo, grilled vegetables, shrimp and red pepper. Whisk together dressing ingredients; toss with salad.
2 CUPS 340 cal., 12g fat (2g sat. fat), 138mg chol., 716mg sod., 35g carb. (6g sugars, 7g fiber), 25g pro.

NOTES

19g Pro

CAROLINA SHRIMP SOUP

Fresh shrimp from the Carolina coast is one of our favorite foods. We add kale, garlic, red peppers and black-eyed peas to complete this wholesome, filling soup.
—Mary M. Leverette, Columbia, SC

TAKES: 25 MIN. • **MAKES:** 6 SERVINGS

- 4 tsp. olive oil, divided
- 1 lb. uncooked shrimp (31-40 per lb.), peeled and deveined
- 5 garlic cloves, minced
- 1 bunch kale, trimmed and coarsely chopped (about 16 cups)
- 1 medium sweet red pepper, cut into ¾-in. pieces
- 3 cups reduced-sodium chicken broth
- 1 can (15½ oz.) black-eyed peas, rinsed and drained
- ¼ tsp. salt
- ¼ tsp. pepper
- Minced fresh chives, optional

1. In a 6-qt. stockpot, heat 2 tsp. oil over medium-high heat. Add shrimp; cook and stir 2 minutes. Add garlic; cook just until shrimp turn pink, 1-2 minutes longer. Remove from pot.

2. In same pot, heat remaining 2 tsp. oil over medium-high heat. Stir in kale and red pepper; cook, covered, until kale is tender, stirring occasionally, 8-10 minutes. Add broth; bring to a boil. Stir in peas, salt, pepper and shrimp; heat through. If desired, sprinkle servings with chives.

1 CUP 188 cal., 5g fat (1g sat. fat), 92mg chol., 585mg sod., 18g carb. (2g sugars, 3g fiber), 19g pro.

35g Pro 5i

MEDITERRANEAN TILAPIA

I recently became a fan of tilapia. Its mild taste makes it easy to top with my favorite ingredients. Plus, it's low in calories and fat. What's not to love?
—Robin Brenneman, Hilliard, OH

TAKES: 20 MIN. • **MAKES:** 6 SERVINGS

- 6 tilapia fillets (6 oz. each)
- 1 cup canned Italian diced tomatoes
- ½ cup water-packed artichoke hearts, chopped
- ½ cup sliced ripe olives
- ½ cup crumbled feta cheese

Preheat oven to 400°. Place fillets in a 15x10x1-in. baking pan coated with cooking spray. Top with tomatoes, artichoke hearts, olives and cheese. Bake, uncovered, until fish flakes easily with a fork, 15-20 minutes.

1 FILLET 197 cal., 4g fat (2g sat. fat), 88mg chol., 446mg sod., 5g carb. (2g sugars, 1g fiber), 34g pro.

ITALIAN TILAPIA Follow method as directed but top fillets with 1 cup diced tomatoes with roasted garlic, ½ cup each julienned roasted sweet red pepper, sliced fresh mushrooms and diced fresh mozzarella cheese, and ½ tsp. dried basil.

1 FILLET 189 cal., 4g fat (2g sat. fat), 90mg chol., 351mg sod., 4g carb., trace fiber, 34g pro.

SOUTHWEST TILAPIA Follow method as directed but top fillets with 1 cup diced tomatoes with mild green chiles, ½ cup cubed avocado, ½ cup frozen corn (thawed), ½ cup cubed cheddar cheese and ½ tsp. dried cilantro.

1 FILLET 224 cal., 7g fat (3g sat. fat), 93mg chol., 281mg sod., 7g carb., 2g fiber, 35g pro.

32g Pro

SALMON WITH TOMATO-GOAT CHEESE COUSCOUS

With rich goat cheese and fresh tomatoes, this recipe works for a weeknight supper or an elegant company dinner—and can be easily adjusted to serve more people.
—Toni Roberts, La Canada, CA

TAKES: 30 MIN. • **MAKES:** 4 SERVINGS

- 4 salmon fillets (5 oz. each)
- ¼ tsp. salt
- ¼ tsp. garlic salt
- ¼ tsp. pepper
- 1 Tbsp. olive oil
- 1 cup chicken stock
- ¾ cup uncooked whole wheat couscous
- 2 plum tomatoes, chopped
- 4 green onions, chopped
- ¼ cup crumbled goat cheese

1. Sprinkle salmon with salt, garlic salt and pepper. Heat oil in a large skillet over medium-high heat; add salmon skin side up and cook 3 minutes. Turn fish and cook an additional 4 minutes or until fish flakes easily with a fork. Remove from heat and keep warm.

2. In a large saucepan, bring stock to a boil. Stir in couscous. Remove from heat; let stand, covered, until stock is absorbed, about 5 minutes. Stir in tomatoes, green onions and goat cheese. Serve with salmon.

1 FILLET WITH 1 CUP COUSCOUS MIXTURE
414 cal., 19g fat (4g sat. fat), 80mg chol., 506mg sod., 31g carb. (2g sugars, 6g fiber), 32g pro.

CUT TO SIZE

If you can't find small pieces of salmon, buy a large fillet and cut it into 5-oz. portions.

PROTEIN BOOST
PAGE 320

14g Pro

THAI SHRIMP SOUP

This tasty crowd-pleasing soup comes together in minutes, and I like the fact that the ingredients are available in my little local grocery store.
—Jessie Grearson, Falmouth, ME

PREP: 20 MIN. • **COOK:** 20 MIN.
MAKES: 8 SERVINGS (2 QT.)

- 1 medium onion, chopped
- 1 Tbsp. olive oil
- 3 cups reduced-sodium chicken broth
- 1 cup water
- 1 Tbsp. brown sugar
- 1 Tbsp. minced fresh gingerroot
- 1 Tbsp. fish sauce or soy sauce
- 1 Tbsp. red curry paste
- 1 lemongrass stalk
- 1 lb. uncooked large shrimp, peeled and deveined
- 1½ cups frozen shelled edamame
- 1 can (13.66 oz.) light coconut milk
- 1 can (8¾ oz.) whole baby corn, drained and cut in half
- ½ cup bamboo shoots
- ¼ cup fresh basil leaves, julienned
- ¼ cup minced fresh cilantro
- 2 Tbsp. lime juice
- 1½ tsp. grated lime zest
- 1 tsp. curry powder

1. In a Dutch oven, saute onion in oil until tender. Add the broth, water, brown sugar, ginger, fish sauce, curry paste and lemongrass. Bring to a boil. Reduce heat; carefully stir in shrimp and edamame. Cook, uncovered, for 5-6 minutes or until shrimp turn pink.

2. Add the coconut milk, corn, bamboo shoots, basil, cilantro, lime juice, lime zest and curry powder; heat through. Discard lemongrass.

1 CUP 163 cal., 7g fat (3g sat. fat), 69mg chol., 505mg sod., 9g carb. (5g sugars, 2g fiber), 14g pro.

26g Pro

SHRIMP SALAD WITH HOT HONEY AVOCADO DRESSING

This light main dish salad with shrimp uses avocado in place of oil in the dressing and hot honey for a kick. Mix and match your favorite toppings to make this salad your own. Sometimes I like to add sliced black olives and green onions. Plain water can be used in place of the mango sparkling water.
—Jeanne Holt, Mendota Heights, MN

TAKES: 25 MIN. • **MAKES:** 8 SERVINGS

- ½ cup mango sparkling water
- ¼ cup cider vinegar
- ¼ cup hot chile-infused honey
- 3 Tbsp. lime juice
- 1 medium ripe avocado, peeled and cubed
- ¼ cup fresh cilantro leaves
- 1 garlic clove
- 8 cups chopped romaine
- 1 medium mango, peeled and cubed
- 1 medium sweet red pepper, chopped
- 2 lbs. peeled and deveined cooked shrimp (31-40 per lb.)
- ¼ cup salted pepitas

1. In a blender or food processor, combine the first 7 ingredients. Cover and process until smooth.
2. Place lettuce in a large serving bowl. Top with mango, red pepper and shrimp. Drizzle with 1 cup dressing; toss to coat. Sprinkle with pepitas and serve with remaining dressing.
2 CUPS 243 cal., 7g fat (1g sat. fat), 172mg chol., 185mg sod., 21g carb. (16g sugars, 3g fiber), 26g pro.

32g Pro 5i

WALNUT & OAT-CRUSTED SALMON

A crunchy oat and nut crust pairs with tender salmon in this quick and easy dish.
—Cristen Dutcher, Marietta, GA

TAKES: 30 MIN. • **MAKES:** 2 SERVINGS

- 2 salmon fillets (6 oz. each), skin removed
- ¼ tsp. salt
- ¼ tsp. pepper
- 3 Tbsp. quick-cooking oats, crushed
- 3 Tbsp. finely chopped walnuts
- 2 Tbsp. olive oil

Preheat oven to 400°. Place salmon on a baking sheet; sprinkle with salt and pepper. Combine remaining ingredients; press onto salmon. Bake until fish just begins to flake easily with a fork, 12-15 minutes.
1 FILLET 484 cal., 37g fat (6g sat. fat), 85mg chol., 381mg sod., 7g carb. (0 sugars, 2g fiber), 32g pro.

WILD SALMON TIP

When you're shopping, buy wild-caught salmon if it's available. It has a significantly higher vitamin D content than farm-raised salmon. Salmon is also loaded with omega-3 fatty acids, which can help reduce the risk of heart disease.

32g Pro

GRILLED TILAPIA WITH MANGO

Here's a new twist on tilapia that I created for my wife. She enjoys the combination of mango with Parmesan. Somehow it tastes even better outside on the deck with a cold glass of iced tea.
—Gregg May, Columbus, OH

TAKES: 20 MIN. • **MAKES:** 4 SERVINGS

- 4 tilapia fillets (6 oz. each)
- 1 Tbsp. olive oil
- ½ tsp. salt
- ½ tsp. dill weed
- ¼ tsp. pepper
- 1 Tbsp. grated Parmesan cheese
- 1 medium lemon, sliced
- 1 medium mango, peeled and thinly sliced

1. Brush fillets with oil; sprinkle with salt, dill and pepper.
2. Grill tilapia, covered, on a lightly oiled rack over medium heat for 5 minutes. Turn tilapia; top with cheese, lemon and mango. Grill 4-6 minutes longer or until fish flakes easily with a fork.
1 FILLET 213 cal., 5g fat (1g sat. fat), 84mg chol., 377mg sod., 10g carb. (8g sugars, 1g fiber), 32g pro.

HEALTH TIP

Add mango to your regular fruit rotation to boost your intake of important nutrients like vitamin C, vitamin A and potassium.

30g Pro

SEA SCALLOP FETTUCCINE

When we decided to lose weight, my husband and I tried this recipe and loved it so much we had it every Tuesday. It's so easy, he would fix it on nights I was running late.
—Donna Thompson, Laramie, WY

TAKES: 30 MIN. • **MAKES:** 2 SERVINGS

- 4 oz. uncooked fettuccine
- 1 Tbsp. olive oil
- ½ medium sweet red pepper, julienned
- 1 garlic clove, minced
- ½ tsp. grated lemon zest
- ¼ tsp. crushed red pepper flakes
- ½ cup reduced-sodium chicken broth
- ¼ cup white wine or additional broth
- 1 Tbsp. lemon juice
- 6 sea scallops (about ¾ lb.)
- 2 tsp. grated Parmesan cheese

1. Cook fettuccine according to package directions; drain.
2. Meanwhile, in a large skillet, heat oil over medium-high heat. Add red pepper, garlic, lemon zest and pepper flakes; cook and stir 2 minutes. Stir in broth, wine and lemon juice. Bring to a boil. Reduce heat; simmer, uncovered, 5-6 minutes or until liquid is reduced by half.
3. Cut each scallop horizontally in half; add to skillet. Cook, covered, 4-5 minutes or until scallops are firm and opaque, stirring occasionally. Serve with fettuccine. Sprinkle with cheese.
1 SERVING 421 cal., 10g fat (2g sat. fat), 42mg chol., 861mg sod., 49g carb. (4g sugars, 3g fiber), 30g pro.

> *A tasty combination of flavors! Instead of grilling, I baked in the oven at 375 for 10 minutes with the cheese, lemon and mango the entire time. I will make this again.*
>
> —TERRYH1387, TASTEOFHOME.COM

MEATLESS & MIGHTY

15g Pro

VEGETARIAN PEA SOUP

I combined several recipes to make my own version of this soup. It was a real favorite when I was a vegetarian for health reasons. Even my meat-loving husband asked for seconds!
—Corrie Gamache, Palmyra, VA

PREP: 15 MIN. • **COOK:** 7 HOURS
MAKES: 8 SERVINGS (2 QT.)

- 1 pkg. (16 oz.) dried green split peas, rinsed
- 1 medium leek (white portion only), chopped
- 3 celery ribs, chopped
- 1 medium potato, peeled and chopped
- 2 medium carrots, chopped
- 1 garlic clove, minced
- ¼ cup minced fresh parsley
- 2 cartons (32 oz. each) reduced-sodium vegetable broth
- 1½ tsp. ground mustard
- ½ tsp. pepper
- ½ tsp. dried oregano
- 1 bay leaf

In a 5-qt. slow cooker, combine all ingredients. Cover and cook on low for 7-8 hours or until peas are tender. Discard bay leaf. Stir before serving.
1 CUP 248 cal., 1g fat (0 sat. fat), 0 chol., 702mg sod., 46g carb. (7g sugars, 16g fiber), 15g pro.

14g Pro

MUSHROOM BURGERS

Even the most stubborn meat-and-potatoes people have a change of heart when they bite into one of these flavorful, cheddary mushroom burgers.
—Denise Hollebeke, Penhold, AB

TAKES: 25 MIN. • **MAKES:** 4 SERVINGS

- 2 cups finely chopped fresh mushrooms
- 2 large eggs, lightly beaten
- ½ cup dry bread crumbs
- ½ cup shredded cheddar cheese
- ½ cup finely chopped onion
- ¼ cup all-purpose flour
- ½ tsp. salt
- ¼ tsp. dried thyme
- ¼ tsp. pepper
- 1 Tbsp. canola oil
- 4 whole wheat hamburger buns, split
- 4 lettuce leaves
- Optional: Sliced tomatoes, sliced Swiss cheese and mayonnaise

1. In a large bowl, lightly but thoroughly combine the first 9 ingredients. Shape into four ¾-in.-thick patties.
2. In a large cast-iron or other heavy skillet, heat oil over medium heat. Add burgers; cook until crisp and lightly browned, 3-4 minutes on each side. Serve burgers on buns with lettuce and, if desired, tomatoes, cheese and mayonnaise.
1 BURGER 330 cal., 13g fat (5g sat. fat), 121mg chol., 736mg sod., 42g carb. (4g sugars, 5g fiber), 14g pro.

13g Pro

HEARTY ASIAN LETTUCE SALAD

It may sound nutty, but this meatless version of your favorite restaurant salad packs in 13 grams of protein and is bursting with juicy flavor.
—Taste of Home *Test Kitchen*

TAKES: 20 MIN. • **MAKES:** 2 SERVINGS

- 1 cup ready-to-serve brown rice
- 1 cup frozen shelled edamame
- 3 cups spring mix salad greens
- ¼ cup reduced-fat sesame ginger salad dressing
- 1 medium navel orange, peeled and sectioned
- 4 radishes, sliced
- 2 Tbsp. sliced almonds, toasted

1. Prepare rice and edamame according to package directions.
2. In a large bowl, combine the salad greens, rice and edamame. Drizzle with salad dressing and toss to coat. Divide salad mixture between 2 plates; top with orange segments, radishes and almonds.
1 SALAD 329 cal., 10g fat (1g sat. fat), 0 chol., 430mg sod., 44g carb. (12g sugars, 7g fiber), 13g pro.

21g Pro

TOMATO-GARLIC LENTIL BOWLS

An Ethiopian recipe inspired this feel-good dinner that's tangy, creamy and packed with hearty comfort.
—*Rachael Cushing, Portland, OR*

TAKES: 30 MIN. • **MAKES:** 6 SERVINGS

- 1 Tbsp. olive oil
- 2 medium onions, chopped
- 4 garlic cloves, minced
- 2 cups dried brown lentils, rinsed
- 1 tsp. salt
- ½ tsp. ground ginger
- ½ tsp. paprika
- ¼ tsp. pepper
- 3 cups water
- ¼ cup lemon juice
- 3 Tbsp. tomato paste
- ¾ cup fat-free plain Greek yogurt
  Optional: Chopped tomatoes and minced fresh cilantro

1. In a large saucepan, heat oil over medium-high heat; saute the onions 2 minutes. Add garlic; cook 1 minute. Stir in lentils, seasonings and water; bring to a boil. Reduce heat; simmer, covered, until lentils are tender, 25-30 minutes.
2. Stir in lemon juice and tomato paste; heat through. Serve with yogurt and, if desired, tomatoes and cilantro.
¾ CUP 294 cal., 3g fat (0 sat. fat), 0 chol., 419mg sod., 49g carb. (5g sugars, 8g fiber), 21g pro.

HEALTH TIP

This is a perfect cold-weather main dish salad when gardens are still under a layer of frost. For a heartier version, add sauteed shrimp or leftover rotisserie chicken.

PROTEIN BOOST

PAGE 320

18g Pro

SWEET PEPPER BURRITOS

This meatless mainstay is bursting with cheese, rice, onion and peppers. The burritos are a fun change of pace from tacos or sandwiches.
—Marian Platt, Sequim, WA

TAKES: 30 MIN. • **MAKES:** 6 SERVINGS

- 1 medium onion, chopped
- 1 Tbsp. canola oil
- 2 medium sweet red peppers, diced
- 1 medium sweet yellow pepper, diced
- 1 medium green pepper, diced
- 2 tsp. ground cumin
- 2 cups cooked brown rice
- 1½ cups shredded reduced-fat cheddar cheese
- 3 oz. fat-free cream cheese, cubed
- ½ tsp. salt
- ½ tsp. pepper
- 6 flour tortillas (10 in.), warmed
- Salsa, optional

1. In a large nonstick skillet, saute onion in oil for 2 minutes. Add peppers; saute for 5 minutes or until crisp-tender. Sprinkle with cumin; saute 1 minute longer. Stir in the rice, cheeses, salt and pepper.
2. Spoon about ⅔ cup of filling off-center on each tortilla; fold sides and ends over filling and roll up. Place seam side down in a 13x9-in. baking dish coated with cooking spray.
3. Cover and bake at 425° until heated through, 10-15 minutes. Let stand for 5 minutes. Serve with salsa if desired.

1 BURRITO 429 cal., 13g fat (5g sat. fat), 21mg chol., 671mg sod., 54g carb. (0 sugars, 9g fiber), 18g pro.

18g Pro

CONTEST-WINNING EGGPLANT PARMESAN

Because my recipe calls for baking the eggplant instead of frying it, it's much healthier than other Parmesans! The prep time is a little longer than for some recipes, but the Italian flavors and rustic elegance are well worth it.
—Laci Hooten, McKinney, TX

PREP: 40 MIN. • **BAKE:** 25 MIN.
MAKES: 8 SERVINGS

- **3 large eggs, beaten**
- **2½ cups panko bread crumbs**
- **3 medium eggplants, cut into ¼-in. slices**
- **2 jars (4½ oz. each) sliced mushrooms, drained**
- **½ tsp dried basil**
- **⅛ tsp. dried oregano**
- **2 cups shredded part-skim mozzarella cheese**
- **½ cup grated Parmesan cheese**
- **1 jar (28 oz.) spaghetti sauce**

1. Preheat oven to 350°. Place the eggs and bread crumbs in separate shallow bowls. Dip eggplant slices in eggs, then coat in crumbs. Place on baking sheets coated with cooking spray. Bake until tender and golden brown, 15-20 minutes, turning once.

2. In a small bowl, combine mushrooms, basil and oregano. In another small bowl, combine the mozzarella and Parmesan cheeses.

3. Spread ½ cup sauce into a 13x9-in. baking dish coated with cooking spray. Layer with a third of the mushroom mixture, a third of the eggplant, ¾ cup sauce and a third of the cheese mixture. Repeat layers twice.

4. Bake, uncovered, until heated through and cheese is melted, 25-30 minutes.

1 SERVING 305 cal., 12g fat (5g sat. fat), 102mg chol., 912mg sod., 32g carb. (12g sugars, 9g fiber), 18g pro.

16g Pro

CUMIN-SPICED LENTIL BURGERS

I adapted my Turkish daughter-in-law's traditional recipe for lentil logs—typically wrapped in a lettuce leaf and served with a lemon wedge—into vegan burgers. If you prefer a spicier version, add hot chili powder or crushed red chili peppers.
—Sheila Joan Suhan, Scottdale, PA

PREP: 30 MIN. + STANDING
COOK: 10 MIN./BATCH
MAKES: 8 SERVINGS

- 2¼ cups water, divided
- 1 cup dried red lentils, rinsed
- 1 cup bulgur (fine grind)
- 1½ tsp. salt, divided
- 6 Tbsp. canola oil, divided
- 1 large onion, chopped
- 1 Tbsp. ground cumin
- 1 Tbsp. chili powder
- 1 large egg, lightly beaten
- 6 green onions, sliced
- 3 Tbsp. chopped fresh parsley
- 8 flatbread wraps
- 8 Tbsp. Sriracha mayonnaise
- Optional toppings: Lettuce leaves, sliced tomato and sliced onions

1. In a large saucepan, bring 2 cups water and lentils to a boil. Reduce the heat; simmer, uncovered, until lentils are tender, 15-20 minutes, stirring occasionally. Remove from heat; stir in the bulgur and 1 tsp. salt. Cover and let stand until bulgur is tender and liquid is absorbed, 15-20 minutes.
2. Meanwhile, in a large nonstick skillet, heat 2 Tbsp. oil over medium-high heat. Add the onion; cook and stir until tender, 5-7 minutes. Add cumin and chili powder; cook 1 minute longer. Remove from heat. Add onion mixture to lentil mixture. Stir in the egg, green onions, parsley and remaining ½ tsp. salt, mixing lightly but thoroughly. If needed, add remaining ¼ cup water, 1 Tbsp. at a time, to help mixture stay together when squeezed; shape into eight ½-in.-thick patties.
3. In the same skillet, heat remaining 4 Tbsp. oil over medium heat. Add burgers in batches; cook until golden brown, 3-5 minutes on each side. Serve in wraps with Sriracha mayonnaise, and toppings as desired.
1 BURGER 434 cal., 23g fat (2g sat. fat), 1mg chol., 780mg sod., 54g carb. (2g sugars, 16g fiber), 16g pro.

GO TRADITIONAL

Your favorite garnish or sauce may be added, but traditional Turkish dishes are served with tomatoes, lettuce, onions and green pepper strips.

18g Pro

STUFFED VEGETARIAN SHELLS

When my aunt first told me about these shells, they sounded like a lot of work—but the recipe whips up in no time.
—Amelia Hopkin, Salt Lake City, UT

PREP: 20 MIN. • **BAKE:** 30 MIN.
MAKES: 8 SERVINGS

- 24 uncooked jumbo pasta shells
- 1 carton (15 oz.) part-skim ricotta cheese
- 3 cups frozen chopped broccoli, thawed and drained
- 1 cup shredded part-skim mozzarella cheese
- 2 large egg whites
- 1 Tbsp. minced fresh basil or 1 tsp. dried basil
- ½ tsp. garlic salt
- ¼ tsp. pepper
- 1 jar (26 oz.) meatless spaghetti sauce
- 2 Tbsp. shredded Parmesan cheese

1. Cook pasta according to package directions. In a large bowl, combine ricotta, broccoli, mozzarella, egg whites and seasonings. Drain pasta and rinse in cold water.
2. Spread half spaghetti sauce into a 13x9-in. baking dish coated with cooking spray. Stuff pasta shells with ricotta mixture; arrange over spaghetti sauce. Pour remaining sauce over pasta shells.
3. Cover and bake at 375° for 25 minutes. Uncover; sprinkle with the Parmesan cheese. Bake until heated through, about 5 minutes longer.

3 STUFFED SHELLS 279 cal., 8g fat (5g sat. fat), 26mg chol., 725mg sod., 36g carb. (8g sugars, 4g fiber), 18g pro.

NOTES

12g Pro

TUSCAN PORTOBELLO STEW

Here's a healthy one-skillet meal that's quick and easy to prepare yet elegant enough for company. I often take this stew to my school's potlucks, where it is devoured by teachers and students alike. *—Jane Siemon, Viroqua, WI*

PREP: 20 MIN. • **COOK:** 20 MIN.
MAKES: 4 SERVINGS

- 2 large portobello mushrooms, coarsely chopped
- 1 medium onion, chopped
- 3 garlic cloves, minced
- 2 Tbsp. olive oil
- ½ cup white wine or vegetable broth
- 1 can (28 oz.) diced tomatoes, undrained
- 2 cups chopped fresh kale
- 1 bay leaf
- 1 tsp. dried thyme
- ½ tsp. dried basil
- ½ tsp. dried rosemary, crushed
- ¼ tsp. salt
- ¼ tsp. pepper
- 2 cans (15 oz. each) cannellini beans, rinsed and drained

1. In a large skillet, saute mushrooms, onion and garlic in oil until tender. Add wine. Bring to a boil; cook until liquid is reduced by half. Stir in tomatoes, kale and seasonings. Bring to a boil. Reduce heat; cover and simmer for 8-10 minutes.
2. Add beans; heat through. Discard bay leaf.

1¼ CUPS 309 cal., 8g fat (1g sat. fat), 0 chol., 672mg sod., 46g carb. (9g sugars, 13g fiber), 12g pro.

MUSHROOM MAGIC

Because of their large size, portobello mushrooms are well suited for grilling or broiling. Their meaty texture makes them popular as vegetarian burgers and in other vegetarian recipes. Baby portobello mushrooms are also known as cremini mushrooms. They can be used instead of white mushrooms for a flavor boost.

26g Pro

ITALIAN HERB-LENTIL PATTIES WITH MOZZARELLA

My family has requested this meatless recipe over and over again. It is simple to prepare, and even meat lovers like it.
—Geraldine Lucas, Oldsmar, FL

PREP: 50 MIN. • **COOK:** 10 MIN./BATCH
MAKES: 10 SERVINGS

- 3 cups dried lentils, rinsed
- 3 large eggs, lightly beaten
- 1 Tbsp. dried minced onion
- 1 Tbsp. dried parsley flakes
- 1 tsp. dried basil
- 1 tsp. salt
- ½ tsp. dried thyme
- ¼ tsp. pepper
- 2 cups uncooked instant oatmeal
- 2 Tbsp. canola oil
- 10 slices part-skim mozzarella cheese or provolone cheese
- Marinara sauce, warmed, optional

1. Cook lentils according to package directions; drain and cool slightly.
2. In a large bowl, combine eggs and seasonings; gently but thoroughly stir in cooked lentils and oatmeal. Shape into ten ¾-in.-thick patties.
3. In a large nonstick skillet, heat 1 Tbsp. oil over medium heat. Cook patties in batches, 4-6 minutes on each side or until golden brown and a thermometer reads 160°, adding additional oil as needed. Top with cheese; cook until cheese is melted, 1-2 minutes longer. If desired, serve with marinara sauce.
1 PATTY 416 cal., 12g fat (4g sat. fat), 74mg chol., 517mg sod., 54g carb. (2g sugars, 9g fiber), 26g pro.

19g Pro

CHEESE RAVIOLI WITH PUMPKIN ALFREDO SAUCE

When I first made this recipe, people were skeptical of the pumpkin-and-pasta combination. After just one taste, they were sold!
—Cheri Neustifter, Sturtevant, WI

TAKES: 30 MIN. • **MAKES:** 6 SERVINGS

- 1 pkg. (25 oz.) frozen cheese ravioli
- 3 Tbsp. all-purpose flour
- 2 cups fat-free milk
- 1 can (14½ oz.) reduced-sodium chicken broth
- 3 garlic cloves, minced
- 2 Tbsp. butter
- ½ cup shredded Parmesan cheese
- ½ cup canned pumpkin
- ¼ cup minced fresh parsley
- 1½ tsp. minced fresh sage
- Dash ground nutmeg
- ¼ cup pine nuts, toasted
- ¼ cup chopped walnuts, toasted

1. Cook ravioli according to package directions. Meanwhile, in a large bowl, whisk the flour, milk and broth.
2. In a large skillet, saute garlic in butter until tender. Stir in the milk mixture, cheese, pumpkin, parsley, sage and nutmeg. Cook, uncovered, over medium heat for 10-15 minutes or until thickened, stirring occasionally.
3. Drain ravioli and stir into sauce. Sprinkle with nuts.
1 CUP 420 cal., 16g fat (6g sat. fat), 29mg chol., 662mg sod., 50g carb. (6g sugars, 4g fiber), 19g pro.

SOBA SWAP

Soba noodles are made from buckwheat flour and offer a slightly more toothsome texture than spaghetti.

18g Pro

EDAMAME & SOBA NOODLE BOWL

I love the hearty texture of soba noodles in this wholesome bowl.
—Matthew Hass, Ellison Bay, WI

TAKES: 30 MIN. • **MAKES:** 6 SERVINGS

- 1 pkg. (12 oz.) uncooked Japanese soba noodles or whole wheat spaghetti
- 2 Tbsp. sesame oil
- 2 cups fresh small broccoli florets
- 1 medium onion, halved and thinly sliced
- 3 cups frozen shelled edamame, thawed
- 2 large carrots, cut into ribbons with a vegetable peeler
- 4 garlic cloves, minced
- 1 cup reduced-fat Asian toasted sesame salad dressing
- ¼ tsp. pepper
- Sesame seeds, toasted, optional

1. In a 6-qt. stockpot, cook noodles according to package directions; drain and return to pan.
2. Meanwhile, in a large skillet, heat oil over medium heat. Add broccoli and onion; cook and stir until crisp-tender, 4-6 minutes. Add edamame and carrots; cook and stir until tender, 6-8 minutes. Add garlic; cook 1 minute longer. Add vegetable mixture, dressing and pepper to noodles; toss to combine. Sprinkle with sesame seeds if desired.
1 SERVING 414 cal., 12g fat (1g sat. fat), 0 chol., 867mg sod., 64g carb. (12g sugars, 4g fiber), 18g pro.

13g Pro

CARROT & LENTIL CHILI

This is one of my favorite plant-based versions of chili. I love to make this in fall and spring for the satisfying combination of fresh bright orange carrots and hearty earthy lentils. I serve it with yogurt, sour cream or plant-based cheese.
—Rebekah Ranes, Sedona, AZ

PREP: 30 MIN. • **COOK:** 4½ HOURS
MAKES: 8 SERVINGS (2½ QT.)

- 2 Tbsp. olive oil
- 1 medium onion, chopped
- ¾ cup dried green lentils, rinsed
- ¾ cup dried red lentils, rinsed
- 6 garlic cloves, minced
- 6 cups chopped carrots (about 10 medium carrots)
- 1 carton (32 oz.) reduced-sodium vegetable broth
- 1 Tbsp. ground cumin
- 1 tsp. salt
- 2 tsp. paprika
- 1 tsp. chili powder
- 1 can (15 oz.) crushed tomatoes, undrained
- 2 medium ripe avocados, peeled and cubed
- Optional: Sour cream, sliced red onion and additional paprika

1. In a large skillet, heat oil over medium-high heat. Add onion; cook and stir until tender, 4-5 minutes. Add the lentils and garlic; cook 1 minute longer. Transfer to a 5- or 6-qt. slow cooker. Stir in carrots, broth and seasonings. Cook, covered, on low 4-6 hours or until vegetables and lentils are tender.
2. Stir in the crushed tomatoes; cook, covered, 30 minutes longer. Serve with avocados and, if desired, sour cream, red onion and additional paprika.
FREEZE OPTION Freeze cooled chili in freezer containers. To use, partially thaw in refrigerator overnight. Heat through in a saucepan, stirring occasionally; add broth or water if necessary.
1¼ CUPS 310 cal., 10g fat (1g sat. fat), 0 chol., 574mg sod., 47g carb. (11g sugars, 12g fiber), 13g pro.

19g Pro

MAKEOVER MEATLESS LASAGNA

If you have never tried tofu before, go for it with this recipe. The tofu blends in with all the other ingredients, adding protein without the fat and calories of ground beef.
—Mary Lou Moeller, Wooster, OH

PREP: 30 MIN.
BAKE: 45 MIN. + STANDING
MAKES: 12 SERVINGS

- 10 uncooked whole wheat lasagna noodles
- 1½ cups sliced fresh mushrooms
- ¼ cup chopped onion
- 2 garlic cloves, minced
- 1 can (14½ oz.) Italian diced tomatoes, undrained
- 1 can (12 oz.) tomato paste
- 1 pkg. (14 oz.) firm tofu, drained and cubed
- 2 large eggs, lightly beaten
- 3 cups 2% cottage cheese
- ½ cup grated Parmesan cheese
- ½ cup packed fresh parsley leaves
- ½ tsp. pepper
- 2 cups shredded part-skim mozzarella cheese, divided

1. Preheat oven to 375°. Cook noodles according to package directions for al dente. Meanwhile, in a large saucepan, cook the mushrooms and onion over medium heat until tender. Add garlic; cook 1 minute. Add tomatoes and tomato paste; cook and stir until heated through.
2. Pulse tofu in a food processor until smooth. Add next 5 ingredients; pulse until combined. Drain noodles.
3. Place 5 noodles into a 13x9-in. baking dish coated with cooking spray, overlapping as needed. Layer with half the tofu mixture, half the sauce and half the mozzarella. Top with remaining noodles, tofu mixture and sauce.
4. Bake, covered, 35 minutes. Sprinkle with the remaining mozzarella. Bake, uncovered, 10-15 minutes or until cheese is melted. Let stand 10 minutes before serving.

1 PIECE 258 cal., 9g fat (4g sat. fat), 48mg chol., 498mg sod., 26g carb. (9g sugars, 3g fiber), 19g pro.

TOFU TRICK

If you don't tell your guests, they'll never know there is tofu in this. Pureed with cottage cheese, it has a very similar taste and texture to ricotta. There are many types of tofu on the market, so you'll want to make sure to pick up one marked firm and not soft.

18g Pro

AVOCADO EGG SALAD TOAST

After purchasing far too many unripe avocados for an event, I had a surplus of ripe ones in my kitchen for a week after! I was making some egg salad sandwiches for lunch on one of these day, and I had the great idea to use avocado instead of traditional mayonnaise to bind it together. Not only was this version unbelievably delicious, but also the healthy fats, vitamins and fiber in the avocado make this a more nutritious option than the traditional mayo-laden version.
—Shannon Dobos, Calgary, AB

TAKES: 20 MIN. • **MAKES:** 4 SERVINGS

- 1 medium ripe avocado, peeled and cubed
- 6 hard-boiled large eggs, chopped
- 1 green onion, finely chopped
- 1 tsp. lemon juice
- ¼ tsp. salt
- ⅛ tsp. pepper
- 4 large slices sourdough bread, halved and toasted

In a large bowl, mash avocado to desired consistency. Gently stir in eggs, green onion, lemon juice, salt and pepper. Spread over toast. Serve immediately.

2 PIECES 367 cal., 15g fat (4g sat. fat), 280mg chol., 671mg sod., 41g carb. (4g sugars, 4g fiber), 18g pro.

18g Pro

BROCCOLI CHEESEBURGERS WITH SPICY SWEET POTATOES

These faux burgers are so packed with flavor that nobody notices they're also packed with protein, fiber and vitamins.
—Pamela Vachon, Astoria, NY

PREP: 10 MIN. • **COOK:** 30 MIN.
MAKES: 4 SERVINGS

- 2 medium sweet potatoes, cut into 12 wedges each
- Cooking spray
- 1 tsp. salt-free spicy seasoning blend or reduced-sodium Creole seasoning
- 4 tsp. extra virgin olive oil, divided
- 1 shallot, minced
- 1 cup fresh broccoli florets, cut into ¾-in. pieces
- 1 large egg, beaten
- 1 cup canned cannellini beans, rinsed and drained
- 1 cup ready-to-serve quinoa
- ¾ cup shredded reduced-fat cheddar cheese
- 4 whole wheat hamburger buns, split
- Optional toppings: Lettuce leaves, tomato slices, ketchup, mustard and reduced-fat mayonnaise

1. Preheat oven to 450°. Spritz sweet potato wedges with cooking spray until lightly coated. Sprinkle with seasoning blend; toss to coat. Arrange wedges in a single layer on a 15x10x1-in. baking sheet. Bake, turning wedges halfway through cooking, until tender and lightly spotted, 30-35 minutes.

2. Meanwhile, in a large nonstick skillet, heat 2 tsp. olive oil over medium heat. Add shallot; cook until translucent, about 2 minutes. Add broccoli; cook just until it turns bright green, about 3 minutes longer.

3. Transfer broccoli mixture to a food processor. Add egg and beans; pulse until ingredients are blended but not pureed. Pour broccoli mixture into a large bowl. Add quinoa and cheddar cheese; mix lightly but thoroughly. Shape into four ½-in.-thick patties.

4. In a large nonstick skillet, heat remaining oil over medium-high heat. Add burger patties to skillet; cook until golden and heated through, about 3 minutes on each side.

5. Serve burgers immediately on whole wheat buns with sweet potato wedges. If desired, add optional toppings.

1 BURGER WITH 6 SWEET POTATO WEDGES 457 cal., 14g fat (4g sat. fat), 62mg chol., 550mg sod., 65g carb. (14g sugars, 11g fiber), 18g pro.

> *Easy to make. We did the bread crumb topping. It hardly took any extra time at all and it added a nice crunch. I used unseasoned homemade bread crumbs.*
>
> —NH-RESCUE, TASTEOFHOME.COM

18g Pro

MAKEOVER CREAMY MAC & CHEESE

Macaroni and cheese just may be king of the comfort foods. This sensational version is bubbling with creamy goodness, but is lighter on calories.
—April Taylor, Holcomb, KS

PREP: 30 MIN. • **BAKE:** 25 MIN.
MAKES: 10 SERVINGS

- 1 pkg. (16 oz.) elbow macaroni
- ⅓ cup all-purpose flour
- ½ tsp. garlic powder
- ½ tsp. pepper
- ¼ tsp. salt
- 2 cups fat-free half-and-half
- 2 Tbsp. butter
- 2 cups fat-free milk
- 3 cups shredded reduced-fat sharp cheddar cheese

OPTIONAL TOPPING

- 2 Tbsp. butter
- 1 medium onion, chopped
- 3 cups soft bread crumbs
- ½ cup shredded reduced-fat cheddar cheese

OPTIONAL GARNISH

Sliced cherry tomatoes and minced chives

1. Preheat oven to 350°. Cook macaroni according to package directions; drain.
2. Meanwhile, in small bowl, whisk the flour, seasonings and half-and-half until smooth. In a large saucepan, melt butter over medium heat. Stir in half-and-half mixture. Add milk. Bring to a gentle boil, stirring constantly; remove from heat. Add cheese; stir until melted. Stir in macaroni. Transfer to a 13x9-in. baking dish coated with cooking spray.
3. For optional topping, in a large skillet, heat butter over medium-high heat. Add onion; cook and stir until tender. Add bread crumbs; cook and stir 2 minutes longer. Sprinkle over macaroni mixture; top with cheese.
4. Bake, uncovered, until heated through, 25-30 minutes. Garnish as desired.
1 CUP 343 cal., 11g fat (6g sat. fat), 31mg chol., 354mg sod., 45g carb. (8g sugars, 2g fiber), 18g pro.

CREAMY YOUR WAY

This mac and cheese is extremely creamy. If you prefer yours a little less creamy, reduce the half-and-half or milk down to 1 cup.

18g Pro

HERBED PORTOBELLO PASTA

This makes a colorful, hearty side dish or a lovely meatless main. The ingredient list seems long, but the whole dish totals up to about $10!
—Laurie Trombley, Stonyford, CA

PREP: 20 MIN. • **COOK:** 15 MIN.
MAKES: 4 SERVINGS

- ½ lb. uncooked multigrain angel hair pasta
- 4 large portobello mushrooms (¾ lb.), stems removed
- 1 Tbsp. olive oil
- 2 garlic cloves, minced
- 4 plum tomatoes, chopped
- ¼ cup pitted Greek olives
- ¼ cup minced fresh basil
- 1 tsp. minced fresh rosemary or ¼ tsp. dried rosemary, crushed
- 1 tsp. minced fresh thyme or ¼ tsp. dried thyme
- ¼ tsp. salt
- ⅛ tsp. pepper
- ⅔ cup crumbled feta cheese
- ¼ cup shredded Parmesan cheese

1. Cook pasta according to package directions for al dente. Meanwhile, cut mushrooms in half and thinly slice. In a large skillet, heat oil over medium heat. Add mushrooms; saute 8-10 minutes or until tender. Add garlic; cook 1 minute longer. Stir in tomatoes and olives. Reduce heat to low; cook, uncovered, until slightly thickened, about 5 minutes. Stir in herbs, salt and pepper.
2. Drain pasta, reserving ¼ cup pasta water. Toss pasta with mushroom mixture, adjusting consistency with reserved pasta water. Sprinkle with cheeses.
1½ CUPS 375 cal., 12g fat (4g sat. fat), 14mg chol., 585mg sod., 48g carb. (5g sugars, 7g fiber), 18g pro.

13g Pro

BLACK BEAN-PUMPKIN SOUP

This recipe is packed with protein from the beans, and vitamins from the pumpkin. The dollop of light sour cream adds a satisfying touch.
—Jennifer Fisher, Austin, TX

PREP: 30 MIN. • **COOK:** 30 MIN.
MAKES: 8 SERVINGS (2 QT.)

- 2 cans (15 oz. each) black beans, rinsed and drained
- 1 can (14½ oz.) diced tomatoes, drained
- 2 medium onions, finely chopped
- 1 tsp. olive oil
- 3 garlic cloves, minced
- 1 tsp. ground cumin
- 3 cups vegetable broth
- 1 can (15 oz.) pumpkin
- 2 Tbsp. cider vinegar
- ½ tsp. pepper
- 2 Tbsp. bourbon, optional
- ½ cup reduced-fat sour cream
- ½ cup thinly sliced green onions
- ½ cup roasted salted pumpkin seeds

1. Place beans and tomatoes in a food processor; cover and process until blended. Set aside.
2. In a Dutch oven, saute onions in oil until tender. Add the garlic and cumin; saute 1 minute longer. Stir in the broth, pumpkin, vinegar, pepper and bean mixture. Bring to a boil. Reduce heat; cover and simmer for 20 minutes.
3. Stir in bourbon if desired. Garnish each serving with sour cream, green onions and pumpkin seeds.
1 CUP 238 cal., 8g fat (2g sat. fat), 5mg chol., 716mg sod., 30g carb. (9g sugars, 9g fiber), 13g pro.

22g Pro

CURRY POMEGRANATE PROTEIN BOWL

This simple and beautiful recipe blends together a lot of unique flavors to create a taste sensation that is out of this world. You can substitute other roasted, salted nuts for the soy nuts, and use warmed berry jam in place of the molasses.
—Mary Baker, Wauwatosa, WI

PREP: 25 MIN. • **COOK:** 25 MIN.
MAKES: 4 SERVINGS

- 3 cups cubed peeled butternut squash (½-in. cubes)
- 2 Tbsp. olive oil, divided
- ½ tsp. salt, divided
- ¼ tsp. pepper
- ½ small onion, chopped
- 1 Tbsp. curry powder
- 1 Tbsp. ground cumin
- 1 garlic clove, minced
- 1 tsp. ground coriander
- 3 cups water
- 1 cup dried red lentils, rinsed
- ½ cup salted soy nuts
- ½ cup dried cranberries
- ⅓ cup thinly sliced green onions
- ⅓ cup pomegranate molasses
- ½ cup crumbled feta cheese
- ½ cup pomegranate seeds
- ¼ cup chopped fresh cilantro

1. Preheat oven to 375°. Place squash on a greased 15x10x1-in. baking pan. Drizzle with 1 Tbsp. oil; sprinkle with ¼ tsp. salt and pepper. Roast for 25-30 minutes or until tender, turning once.
2. Meanwhile, in a skillet, heat remaining 1 Tbsp. oil over medium-high heat.
3. Add onion; cook and stir until crisp-tender, 4-6 minutes. Add curry powder, cumin, garlic, coriander and remaining ¼ tsp. salt; cook 1 minute longer. Add water and lentils; bring to a boil. Reduce heat; simmer, covered, 15 minutes or until the lentils are tender and water is absorbed. Gently stir in the next 3 ingredients and roasted squash.
4. Divide among serving bowls. Drizzle with molasses and top with feta, pomegranate seeds and cilantro.

1¼ CUP 550 cal., 14g fat (3g sat. fat), 8mg chol., 490mg sod., 90g carb. (34g sugars, 14g fiber), 22g pro.

18g Pro

CREAMY AVOCADO MANICOTTI

I am always looking for creative ways to make vegetarian dinners a little different. I grow my own basil, and avocados are a versatile favorite, so this recipe is a fantastic way to make manicotti that's a little unusual.
—Jennifer Coduto, Kent, OH

PREP: 25 MIN. • **BAKE:** 45 MIN.
MAKES: 7 SERVINGS

- 1 pkg. (8 oz.) manicotti shells
- 1 small onion, finely chopped
- 1 Tbsp. olive oil
- 2 garlic cloves, minced
- 1 can (28 oz.) crushed tomatoes
- ½ cup minced fresh basil or 3 Tbsp. dried basil
- ⅓ cup dry red wine or vegetable broth
- 1 Tbsp. brown sugar
- ½ tsp. salt
- ½ tsp. pepper

FILLING

- 1 carton (15 oz.) reduced-fat ricotta cheese
- 1 medium ripe avocado, peeled and mashed
- ½ cup grated Parmesan cheese
- ¼ tsp. salt
- ¼ tsp. pepper
- 1 cup shredded part-skim mozzarella cheese
- 1 medium ripe avocado, sliced, optional

1. Cook manicotti according to package directions. Meanwhile, in a large skillet, saute onion in oil until tender. Add the garlic; cook 1 minute longer. Stir in the tomatoes, basil, wine, brown sugar, salt and pepper. Bring to a boil. Reduce heat; simmer, uncovered, for 10-15 minutes, stirring occasionally.

2. Drain manicotti. In a small bowl, combine the ricotta cheese, avocado, Parmesan cheese, salt and pepper. Stuff cheese mixture into manicotti shells. Spread 1 cup sauce into a greased 13x9-in. baking dish. Arrange manicotti over sauce. Pour remaining sauce over top.

3. Cover and bake at 350° for 35 minutes or until bubbly. Uncover; sprinkle with mozzarella cheese. Bake 10-15 minutes longer or until cheese is melted. If desired, garnish with avocado slices.

2 PIECES 359 cal., 13g fat (5g sat. fat), 29mg chol., 625mg sod., 41g carb. (7g sugars, 5g fiber), 18g pro.

This was relatively easy to make. The flavor of the sauce was very tasty. The avocado gave the filling a nice but very mild flavor; I'd probably do 1½ avocados next time.

—SCUBACAS, TASTEOFHOME.COM

19g Pro

TASTY LENTIL TACOS

My husband has to watch his cholesterol. Finding dishes that are healthy for him and yummy for our five children is a challenge sometimes, but this fun taco recipe is a huge hit with everyone.
—Michelle Thomas, Bangor, ME

PREP: 15 MIN. • **COOK:** 40 MIN.
MAKES: 6 SERVINGS

- 1 tsp. canola oil
- 1 medium onion, finely chopped
- 1 garlic clove, minced
- 1 cup dried lentils, rinsed
- 1 Tbsp. chili powder
- 2 tsp. ground cumin
- 1 tsp. dried oregano
- 2½ cups vegetable or reduced-sodium chicken broth
- 1 cup salsa
- 12 taco shells
- 1½ cups shredded lettuce
- 1 cup chopped fresh tomatoes
- 1½ cups shredded reduced-fat cheddar cheese
- 6 Tbsp. fat-free sour cream

1. In a large nonstick skillet, heat oil over medium heat; saute onion and garlic until tender. Add lentils and seasonings; cook and stir 1 minute. Stir in broth; bring to a boil. Reduce heat; simmer, covered, until lentils are tender, 25-30 minutes.
2. Cook, uncovered, until mixture is thickened, 6-8 minutes, stirring occasionally. Mash lentils slightly; stir in salsa and heat through. Serve in taco shells. Top with remaining ingredients.
2 TACOS 365 cal., 12g fat (5g sat. fat), 21mg chol., 777mg sod., 44g carb. (5g sugars, 6g fiber), 19g pro.

18g Pro

QUINOA & BLACK BEAN STUFFED PEPPERS

If you're thinking about a meatless meal, give these no-fuss peppers a try. They come together with just a few ingredients and put a tasty spin on a low-fat dinner.
—Cindy Reams, Philipsburg, PA

TAKES: 30 MIN. • **MAKES:** 4 SERVINGS

- 1½ cups water
- 1 cup quinoa, rinsed
- 4 large green peppers
- 1 jar (16 oz.) chunky salsa, divided
- 1 can (15 oz.) black beans, rinsed and drained
- ½ cup reduced-fat ricotta cheese
- ½ cup shredded Monterey Jack cheese, divided

1. Preheat oven to 400°. In a small saucepan, bring water to a boil. Add quinoa. Reduce heat; simmer, covered, until water is absorbed, 10-12 minutes.
2. Meanwhile, cut and discard tops from peppers; remove the seeds. Place in a greased 8-in. square baking dish, cut side down. Microwave, uncovered, on high until crisp-tender, 3-4 minutes. Turn peppers cut side up.
3. Reserve ⅓ cup salsa; add remaining salsa to quinoa. Stir in beans, ricotta cheese and ¼ cup Monterey Jack cheese. Spoon mixture into peppers; sprinkle with remaining ¼ cup cheese. Bake, uncovered, until filling is heated through, 10-15 minutes. Top with reserved salsa.
1 STUFFED PEPPER 393 cal., 8g fat (4g sat. fat), 20mg chol., 774mg sod., 59g carb. (10g sugars, 10g fiber), 18g pro.

19g Pro

SPINACH PIZZA QUESADILLAS

This simple five-ingredient dinner is special to me because my daughter and I created it together. You can make variations with other veggies you might have at home. It's a smart way to get kids to eat healthier.
—Tanna Mancini, Gulfport, FL

TAKES: 20 MIN. • **MAKES:** 6 SERVINGS

- 6 whole wheat tortillas (8 in.)
- 3 cups shredded part-skim mozzarella cheese
- 3 cups chopped fresh spinach
- 1 can (8 oz.) pizza sauce

1. Preheat oven to 400°. On half of each tortilla, layer ½ cup cheese, ½ cup spinach and about 2 Tbsp. sauce. Fold each tortilla in half over filling. Place on baking sheets coated with cooking spray.
2. Bake 10-12 minutes or until cheese is melted. If desired, serve with additional pizza sauce.
1 QUESADILLA 301 cal., 13g fat (7g sat. fat), 36mg chol., 650mg sod., 29g carb. (3g sugars, 4g fiber), 19g pro.

12g Pro

JUMPIN' ESPRESSO BEAN CHILI

I love experimenting with chili and creating different takes on the classic hearty dish. This meatless version is low in fat but high in flavor. Everyone tries to guess the secret ingredient, but no one ever thinks it's coffee!
—Jess Apfe, Berkeley, CA

PREP: 15 MIN. • **COOK:** 35 MIN.
MAKES: 7 SERVINGS

- 3 medium onions, chopped
- 2 Tbsp. olive oil
- 2 Tbsp. brown sugar
- 2 Tbsp. chili powder
- 2 Tbsp. ground cumin
- 1 Tbsp. instant espresso powder or instant coffee granules
- 1 Tbsp. baking cocoa
- ¾ tsp. salt
- 2 cans (14½ oz. each) no-salt-added diced tomatoes
- 1 can (15 oz.) black beans, rinsed and drained
- 1 can (15 oz.) kidney beans, rinsed and drained
- 1 can (15 oz.) garbanzo beans or chickpeas, rinsed and drained
- Optional toppings: Sour cream, thinly sliced green onions, shredded cheddar cheese and pickled jalapeno slices

1. In a Dutch oven, saute the onions in oil until tender. Add the brown sugar, chili powder, cumin, espresso powder, cocoa and salt; cook and stir for 1 minute.
2. Stir in tomatoes and beans. Bring to a boil. Reduce heat; cover and simmer for 30 minutes to allow flavors to blend. If desired, serve with sour cream, onions, cheese and jalapeno slices.
1 CUP 272 cal., 6g fat (1g sat. fat), 0 chol., 620mg sod., 45g carb. (14g sugars, 12g fiber), 12g pro.

VIVI
—ET—
MARGOT

11g Pro

FREEZER VEGGIE BURGERS

PROTEIN BOOST
PAGE 320

I try to limit our intake of red meat to once a week, so I'm happy my family likes these burgers. They freeze well so you can make a batch and cook as needed. We like how the outside gets a little crispy.
—*Elaine Solochier, Concord, NC*

PREP: 25 MIN. + FREEZING
BAKE: 30 MIN. • **MAKES:** 6 SERVINGS

- 1 can (16 oz.) kidney beans, rinsed and drained
- ½ cup old-fashioned oats
- 2 Tbsp. ketchup
- ½ cup finely chopped fresh mushrooms
- 1 medium onion, finely chopped
- 1 medium carrot, shredded
- 1 small sweet red pepper, finely chopped
- 2 garlic cloves, minced
- ½ tsp. salt
- ⅛ tsp. white pepper
- 6 hamburger buns, split
- 6 lettuce leaves
- 6 slices tomato

1. Place the beans, oats and ketchup in a food processor; cover and pulse until blended. Transfer to a small bowl; stir in the vegetables, garlic and seasonings. Shape into six 3-in. patties; wrap each in plastic wrap and freeze.
2. To use frozen burgers: Unwrap burgers and place on a baking sheet coated with cooking spray. Bake at 350° for 30 minutes or until heated through, turning once. Serve on buns with lettuce and tomato.
1 BURGER 244 cal., 2g fat (0 sat. fat), 0 chol., 615mg sod., 45g carb. (8g sugars, 7g fiber), 11g pro.

17g Pro

VEGAN TACO SALAD

The best salads are made with ingredients that have different textures and complementary flavors. In this vegan taco salad, you'll love the crunch of the tortilla chips with the sweet, crisp lettuce and meaty crumble mixture.
—Taste of Home *Test Kitchen*

TAKES: 30 MIN. • **MAKES:** 6 SERVINGS

- 1 Tbsp. canola oil
- 1 medium sweet red pepper, chopped
- 1 small onion, chopped
- 3 garlic cloves, minced
- 1 pkg. (12 oz.) frozen vegetarian meat crumbles
- 1½ cups salsa, divided
- 1 Tbsp. chili powder
- 1 tsp. ground cumin
- 8 cups torn romaine
- 1 can (15 oz.) black beans, rinsed and drained
- 1 cup coarsely crushed tortilla chips
- 1 cup frozen corn, thawed
- 2 plum tomatoes, chopped
- 1 medium ripe avocado, peeled and cubed
- ¼ cup chopped fresh cilantro
- ¼ cup vegan ranch salad dressing
- Lime wedges, optional

1. In a large skillet, heat oil over medium heat. Add pepper and onion; cook and stir until tender, 5-7 minutes. Add garlic; cook 1 minute longer. Stir in crumbles, ¾ cup salsa, chili powder and cumin; cook and stir until heated through, 3-5 minutes.
2. In a large bowl, combine romaine, beans, tortilla chips, corn, tomatoes, avocado, cilantro and crumble mixture. Combine remaining salsa and vegan ranch dressing, pour over the salad and toss to coat. If desired, serve with lime wedges.
2 CUPS 354 cal., 15g fat (2g sat. fat), 1mg chol., 807mg sod., 40g carb. (7g sugars, 11g fiber), 17g pro.

20g Pro

RAVIOLI WITH SNAP PEAS & MUSHROOMS

Topped with the toasty texture and flavor of hazelnuts, this pasta makes an easy, earthy weeknight dinner. I serve it with an herb and lettuce salad and white wine.
—Charlene Chambers, Ormond Beach, FL

TAKES: 30 MIN. • **MAKES:** 8 SERVINGS

- 1 pkg. (20 oz.) refrigerated cheese ravioli
- 1 lb. fresh sugar snap peas, trimmed
- 1 Tbsp. butter
- ½ lb. sliced fresh mushrooms
- 3 shallots, finely chopped
- 2 garlic cloves, minced
- 2 cups fat-free evaporated milk
- 8 fresh sage leaves, thinly sliced or 2 tsp. rubbed sage
- 1 tsp. grated lemon zest
- 1 tsp. lemon-pepper seasoning
- ¼ tsp. white pepper
- ¼ cup shredded Parmesan cheese
- ¼ cup hazelnuts, coarsely chopped and toasted

1. In a large saucepan, cook ravioli according to package directions, adding snap peas during the last 3 minutes of cooking; drain.

2. Meanwhile, in a large skillet, heat butter over medium-high heat. Add mushrooms, shallots and garlic; cook and stir until mushrooms are tender. Stir in milk, sage, lemon zest, lemon pepper and white pepper; bring to a boil. Reduce heat; simmer, uncovered, until sauce is slightly thickened, about 2 minutes.

3. Add ravioli and snap peas to sauce; heat through. Sprinkle with cheese and hazelnuts.

NOTE To toast nuts, bake in a shallow pan in a 350°; oven for 5-10 minutes or cook in a skillet over low heat until lightly browned, stirring occasionally.

1 CUP 347 cal., 11g fat (5g sat. fat), 36mg chol., 470mg sod., 44g carb. (11g sugars, 4g fiber), 20g pro.

17g Pro

GRILLED CHICKPEA SALAD SANDWICH

When my mother comes to visit, she enjoys a good old-fashioned chicken salad sandwich. As a vegetarian, I make chickpea salad sandwiches all the time and finally had the guts to make one for her. After some hesitation, she tasted it and was instantly hooked!
—Dannika Stevenson, Akron, OH

TAKES: 30 MIN. • **MAKES:** 4 SERVINGS

- 1 can (16 oz.) chickpeas or garbanzo beans, rinsed and drained
- 1 celery rib, finely chopped
- 2 sweet pickles, finely chopped
- 2 Tbsp. dried cranberries
- 2 Tbsp. finely chopped red onion
- 2 Tbsp. reduced-fat mayonnaise
- 2 tsp. sweet pickle juice
- ½ tsp. minced fresh parsley
- ¼ tsp. salt
- ¼ tsp. pepper
- 4 slices provolone cheese
- 8 slices multigrain bread

In a small bowl, mix first 10 ingredients. Place cheese slices on 4 bread slices; top with chickpea mixture and remaining bread. Preheat panini maker or indoor electric grill. Cook sandwiches, covered, until bread is browned and cheese is melted, 3-5 minutes.

1 SANDWICH 370 cal., 13g fat (4g sat. fat), 18mg chol., 753mg sod., 49g carb. (13g sugars, 9g fiber), 17g pro.

19g Pro

CHEESE MANICOTTI

This is the first meal I ever cooked for my husband, and all these years later he still enjoys my manicotti!
—Joan Hallford, North Richland Hills, TX

PREP: 25 MIN. • **BAKE:** 1 HOUR
MAKES: 7 SERVINGS

- 1 carton (15 oz.) reduced-fat ricotta cheese
- 1 small onion, finely chopped
- 1 large egg, lightly beaten
- 2 Tbsp. minced fresh parsley
- ½ tsp. pepper
- ¼ tsp. salt
- 1 cup shredded part-skim mozzarella cheese, divided
- 1 cup grated Parmesan cheese, divided
- 4 cups marinara sauce
- ½ cup water
- 1 pkg. (8 oz.) manicotti shells
- Additional minced fresh parsley, optional

1. Preheat oven to 350°. In a small bowl, mix the first 6 ingredients; stir in ½ cup mozzarella and ½ cup Parmesan cheese. In another bowl, mix marinara sauce and water; spread ¾ cup sauce onto bottom of a 13x9-in. baking dish coated with cooking spray. Fill uncooked manicotti shells with ricotta mixture; arrange over sauce. Top with remaining sauce.

2. Bake, covered, until pasta is tender, about 50 minutes. Sprinkle with the remaining ½ cup mozzarella and ½ cup Parmesan cheese. Bake, uncovered, until cheese is melted, 10-15 minutes longer. If desired, top with additional parsley.

2 STUFFED MANICOTTI 361 cal., 13g fat (6g sat. fat), 64mg chol., 1124mg sod., 41g carb. (12g sugars, 4g fiber), 19g pro.

25g Pro

ENCHILADA PIE

This impressive, hearty dish is perfect for vegetarians and meat eaters alike.
—Jacqueline Correa, Landing, NJ

PREP: 40 MIN. • **COOK:** 4 HOURS
MAKES: 8 SERVINGS

- 1 pkg. (12 oz.) frozen vegetarian meat crumbles
- 1 cup chopped onion
- ½ cup chopped green pepper
- 2 tsp. canola oil
- 1 can (16 oz.) kidney beans, rinsed and drained
- 1 can (15 oz.) black beans, rinsed and drained
- 1 can (10 oz.) diced tomatoes and green chiles, undrained
- ½ cup water
- 1½ tsp. chili powder
- ½ tsp. ground cumin
- ¼ tsp. pepper
- 6 whole wheat tortillas (8 in.)
- 2 cups shredded reduced-fat cheddar cheese
- Optional toppings: Sour cream, cilantro, lime wedges, salsa

1. Cut three 25x3-in. strips of heavy-duty foil; crisscross so they resemble spokes of a wheel. Place strips on the bottom and up the sides of a 5-qt. slow cooker. Coat strips with cooking spray.
2. In a large saucepan, cook the vegetarian meat crumbles, onion and green pepper in oil until vegetables are tender. Stir in both cans of the beans, tomatoes, water, chili powder, cumin and pepper. Bring to a boil. Reduce heat; simmer, uncovered, for 10 minutes.
3. In prepared slow cooker, layer 1 cup bean mixture, 1 tortilla and ⅓ cup cheese. Repeat layers 5 times. Cover and cook on low until heated through and cheese is melted, 4-5 hours. (To avoid scorching, rotate slow cooker insert a half turn midway through cooking, lifting carefully with oven mitts.)
4. Using foil strips as handles, remove the pie to a platter. Serve with toppings of your choice.
NOTE Vegetarian meat crumbles are a nutritious protein source made from soy. Look for them in the natural foods freezer section.
1 PIECE 367 cal., 11g fat (4g sat. fat), 20mg chol., 818mg sod., 41g carb. (5g sugars, 9g fiber), 25g pro.

NOTES

19g Pro

PRONTO VEGETARIAN PEPPERS

In the summer I love to serve these peppers with salad and a roll. At the end of summer, I freeze them for cold months when produce costs are high. For a hot meal on a cold day, I love to serve them with warm pasta tossed in olive oil.
—Renee Hollobaugh, Altoona, PA

TAKES: 25 MIN. • **MAKES:** 2 SERVINGS

- 2 large sweet red peppers
- 1 cup canned stewed tomatoes
- ⅓ cup instant brown rice
- 2 Tbsp. hot water
- ¾ cup canned kidney beans, rinsed and drained
- ½ cup frozen corn, thawed
- 2 green onions, thinly sliced
- ⅛ tsp. crushed red pepper flakes
- ½ cup shredded part-skim mozzarella cheese
- 1 Tbsp. grated Parmesan cheese

1. Cut peppers in half lengthwise; remove seeds. Place peppers in an ungreased shallow microwave-safe dish. Cover and microwave on high until tender, 3-4 minutes.

2. Combine the tomatoes, rice and water in a small microwave-safe bowl. Cover and microwave on high until rice is tender, 5-6 minutes. Stir in the beans, corn, onions and pepper flakes; spoon into peppers.

3. Sprinkle with mozzarella and Parmesan. Microwave, uncovered, until heated through, 3-4 minutes.

2 STUFFED PEPPER HALVES 341 cal., 7g fat (3g sat. fat), 19mg chol., 556mg sod., 56g carb. (16g sugars, 11g fiber), 19g pro.

17g Pro

SLOW-COOKED LENTIL STEW

This vegetarian stew is perfect when you want to take a break from meat. Adding the cream at the end gives it a smoother texture.
—Michelle Collins, Suffolk, VA

PREP: 45 MIN. • **COOK:** 6 HOURS
MAKES: 8 SERVINGS (2¾ QT. STEW)

- 2 large onions, thinly sliced, divided
- 2 Tbsp. canola oil
- 2 Tbsp. minced fresh gingerroot
- 3 garlic cloves, minced
- 8 plum tomatoes, chopped
- 2 tsp. ground coriander
- 1½ tsp. ground cumin
- ¼ tsp. cayenne pepper
- 3 cups vegetable broth
- 2 cups water
- 2 cups dried lentils, rinsed
- 1 can (4 oz.) chopped green chiles
- ¾ cup heavy whipping cream
- 2 Tbsp. butter
- 1 tsp. cumin seeds
- 6 cups hot cooked basmati or jasmine rice
- Optional: Sliced green onions or minced fresh cilantro

1. In a large skillet, saute half of the onions in oil until tender. Add ginger and garlic; saute for 1 minute. Add the tomatoes, coriander, cumin and cayenne; cook and stir 5 minutes longer.

2. In a 4-or 5-qt. slow cooker, combine the vegetable broth, water, lentils, green chiles, tomato mixture and remaining onion. Cover and cook on low until lentils are tender, 6-8 hours.

3. Just before serving, stir cream into slow cooker. In a small skillet, heat butter over medium heat. Add cumin seeds; cook and stir 1-2 minutes or until golden brown. Add to lentil mixture.

4. To serve, spoon over rice. If desired, sprinkle with green onions or cilantro.

1⅓ CUPS STEW WITH ¾ CUP RICE 499 cal., 16g fat (7g sat. fat), 38mg chol., 448mg sod., 72g carb. (5g sugars, 17g fiber), 17g pro.

POWER BREAKFASTS

17g Pro

SOUTHWEST TORTILLA SCRAMBLE

PROTEIN BOOST
PAGE 320

Here's my version of a deconstructed breakfast burrito that's actually good for you. Go for hefty corn tortillas in this recipe. Flour ones can get lost in the scramble.
—Christine Schenher, Exeter, CA

TAKES: 15 MIN. • **MAKES:** 2 SERVINGS

- 4 large egg whites
- 2 large eggs
- ¼ tsp. pepper
- 2 corn tortillas (6 in.), halved and cut into strips
- ¼ cup chopped fresh spinach
- 2 Tbsp. shredded reduced-fat cheddar cheese
- ¼ cup salsa

1. In a large bowl, whisk egg whites, eggs and pepper. Stir in tortilla strips, spinach and cheese.
2. Heat a large skillet coated with cooking spray over medium heat. Pour in egg mixture; cook and stir until eggs are thickened and no liquid egg remains. Top with salsa.
1 CUP 195 cal., 7g fat (3g sat. fat), 217mg chol., 391mg sod., 16g carb. (2g sugars, 2g fiber), 17g pro.

11g Pro

CINNAMON BLUEBERRY FRENCH TOAST

I like to prep this breakfast in the evening, let it chill, then turn on the slow cooker when we wake up the next morning. It's done just right.
—Angela Lively, Conroe, TX

PREP: 15 MIN. + CHILLING
COOK: 3 HOURS • **MAKES:** 6 SERVINGS

- 3 large eggs
- 2 cups 2% milk
- ¼ cup sugar
- 1 tsp. ground cinnamon
- 1 tsp. vanilla extract
- ¼ tsp. salt
- 9 cups cubed French bread (about 9 oz.)
- 1 cup fresh or frozen blueberries, thawed
- Maple syrup

1. Whisk together the first 6 ingredients. Place half the bread in a greased 5-qt. slow cooker; top with ½ cup blueberries and half the milk mixture. Repeat layers. Refrigerate, covered, for 4 hours or overnight.
2. Cook, covered, on low until a knife inserted in the center comes out clean, 3-4 hours. Serve warm with syrup.
1 CUP 265 cal., 6g fat (2g sat. fat), 100mg chol., 430mg sod., 42g carb. (18g sugars, 2g fiber), 11g pro.

8g Pro

ITALIAN CLOUD EGGS

Drop egg yolks on nests of whipped Italian-seasoned egg whites, then bake in a cast-iron skillet. Dreamy!
—Matthew Hass, Ellison Bay, WI

TAKES: 25 MIN. • **MAKES:** 4 SERVINGS

- 4 large eggs, separated
- ¼ tsp. Italian seasoning
- ⅛ tsp. salt
- ⅛ tsp. pepper
- ¼ cup shredded Parmesan cheese
- 1 Tbsp. minced fresh basil
- 1 Tbsp. finely chopped oil-packed sun-dried tomatoes

1. Preheat oven to 450°. Separate eggs; place whites in a large bowl and yolks in 4 separate small bowls. Beat egg whites, Italian seasoning, salt and pepper until stiff peaks form.

2. In a 9-in. cast-iron skillet generously coated with cooking spray, drop egg white mixture into 4 mounds. With the back of a spoon, create a small well in the center of each mound. Sprinkle with cheese. Bake until light brown, about 5 minutes. Gently slip 1 egg yolk into each mound. Bake until yolks are set, 3-5 minutes longer. Sprinkle with basil and tomatoes. Serve immediately.

1 SERVING 96 cal., 6g fat (2g sat. fat), 190mg chol., 234mg sod., 1g carb. (0 sugars, 0 fiber), 8g pro.

17g Pro

QUINOA BREAKFAST BOWL

This is such a bright and healthy way to enjoy quinoa!
—Karen Kelly, Germantown, MD

TAKES: 30 MIN. • **MAKES:** 1 SERVING

- ⅔ cup water
- ⅓ cup quinoa, rinsed
- ¼ tsp. salt, divided
- ¼ tsp. pepper, divided
- 1 large egg
- ½ cup grape tomatoes, halved
- ¼ cup loosely packed basil leaves
- ½ medium ripe avocado, peeled and sliced
- Balsamic glaze

1. Place water in a small saucepan. Bring to a boil; add quinoa and ⅛ tsp. each salt and pepper. Reduce heat; cover and simmer until tender, 12-15 minutes.

2. Meanwhile, heat a small nonstick skillet over medium-high heat. Break egg into pan; reduce heat to low. Sprinkle with remaining ⅛ tsp. salt and ⅛ tsp. pepper. Cook egg until white is set and yolk begins to thicken, turning once if desired.

3. Fluff quinoa with a fork; place in a serving bowl. Top with tomatoes, basil, avocado and cooked egg. Drizzle with balsamic glaze, or serve glaze on the side.

1 BOWL 411 cal., 19g fat (3g sat. fat), 186mg chol., 674mg sod., 46g carb. (4g sugars, 10g fiber), 17g pro.

11g Pro

HIGH-OCTANE PANCAKES

Fluffy and health-packed, these hotcakes are what we rely on to jump-start frosty winter mornings in Colorado. They keep us satisfied all morning long and are scrumptious!
—Kelly Hanlon, Strasburg, CO

TAKES: 20 MIN. • **MAKES:** 4 PANCAKES

- ⅓ cup plus 1 Tbsp. all-purpose flour
- ¼ cup quick-cooking oats
- 3 Tbsp. toasted wheat germ
- 2 tsp. sugar
- 1¼ tsp. baking powder
- ⅛ tsp. salt
- ⅔ cup fat-free milk
- ¼ cup fat-free plain yogurt
- 1 Tbsp. canola oil

1. In a small bowl, mix the first 6 ingredients. In another bowl, whisk milk, yogurt and oil until blended. Add to flour mixture; stir just until moistened.

2. Lightly coat a nonstick griddle with cooking spray; heat over medium heat. Pour batter by ⅓ cupfuls onto griddle. Cook each pancake until bubbles form on top; flip and cook until second side is golden brown.

FREEZE OPTION Freeze cooled pancakes between layers of waxed paper in an airtight freezer container. To use, place a stack of 2 pancakes on a microwave-safe plate, and microwave on high until heated through, about 1 minute.

2 PANCAKES 281 cal., 9g fat (1g sat. fat), 2mg chol., 450mg sod., 41g carb. (10g sugars, 3g fiber), 11g pro.

21g Pro 5i

GOAT CHEESE & HAM OMELET

As a busy working mom, my breakfast needs to require minimal prep. For this omelet, I often combine the egg mixture beforehand and refrigerate it overnight. Then all I have to do in the morning is heat up my skillet. My favorite part is the goat cheese filling, which gets nice and creamy from the heat of the omelet.
—Lynne Dieterle, Rochester, MI

TAKES: 20 MIN. • **MAKES:** 1 SERVING

- 4 large egg whites
- 2 tsp. water
- ⅛ tsp. pepper
- 1 slice deli ham, finely chopped
- 2 Tbsp. finely chopped green pepper
- 2 Tbsp. finely chopped onion
- 2 Tbsp. crumbled goat cheese
- Minced fresh parsley, optional

1. In a small bowl, whisk egg whites, water and pepper until blended; stir in ham, green pepper and onion. Heat a large skillet coated with cooking spray over medium-high heat. Pour in egg white mixture. Mixture should set immediately at edges. As egg whites set, push cooked portions toward the center, letting uncooked egg flow underneath.

2. When no liquid egg remains, sprinkle goat cheese on 1 side. Fold omelet in half; slide onto a plate. If desired, sprinkle with parsley.

1 OMELET 143 cal., 4g fat (2g sat. fat), 27mg chol., 489mg sod., 5g carb. (3g sugars, 1g fiber), 21g pro.

14g Pro

HUEVOS RANCHEROS WITH TOMATILLO SAUCE

My husband and I visited Cuernavaca, Mexico, a year ago and had huevos rancheros for the first time. My husband loved it so much that he asked me to cook it for him when we got home. This is my version, which is suited to my family's preference for sunny-side up eggs, but poached or scrambled eggs would also be good.
—Cheryl Woodson, Liberty, MO

TAKES: 25 MIN. • **MAKES:** 8 SERVINGS

- 5 tomatillos, husked and halved
- 2 Tbsp. coarsely chopped onion
- 1 to 2 serrano peppers, halved
- 3 garlic cloves, peeled
- 1 tsp. chicken bouillon granules
- 1 can (15 oz.) Southwest or seasoned recipe black beans, undrained
- 8 large eggs
- 1 cup shredded Manchego cheese
- 8 tostada shells, warmed
- ½ cup sour cream
- Optional: Chopped tomato, sliced avocado and minced fresh cilantro

1. Place the tomatillos, onions, peppers, garlic and bouillon in a food processor. Cover and process until finely chopped; set aside. In a small saucepan, mash beans. Cook on low until heated through, stirring occasionally.

2. Meanwhile, in batches, break eggs into a large skillet coated with cooking spray. Cover and cook over low heat for 5-7 minutes or until eggs are set. Sprinkle with cheese.

3. To serve, spread beans over tostada shells; top with eggs, tomatillo sauce and sour cream. Garnish with tomato, avocado and cilantro if desired.

NOTE Wear disposable gloves when cutting hot peppers; the oils can burn skin. Avoid touching your face.

1 SERVING 272 cal., 15g fat (7g sat. fat), 236mg chol., 429mg sod., 18g carb. (2g sugars, 4g fiber), 14g pro.

ALL ABOUT TOMATILLO

Tomatillo, or the Mexican green tomato, is a fruit covered by a thin papery brown husk that is removed before using. Once the husk is removed, a tomatillo resembles a small green tomato in size and shape. It is used in Mexican and Tex-Mex dishes, including guacamole, salsa and sauce. Tomatillos are mild in flavor and offer a hint of lemon and apple, which is enhanced by cooking.

10g Pro

PEACH-STUFFED FRENCH TOAST

With its make-ahead convenience and scrumptious flavor, this recipe is ideal for holiday brunches—and for busy hostesses with a hungry crowd to feed!
—Julie Robinson, Little Chute, WI

PREP: 25 MIN. + CHILLING • **BAKE:** 25 MIN.
MAKES: 10 SERVINGS

- 1 loaf (1 lb.) French bread, cut into 20 slices
- 1 can (15 oz.) sliced peaches in juice, drained and chopped
- ¼ cup chopped pecans
- 4 large eggs
- 4 large egg whites
- 1½ cups fat-free milk
- 3 Tbsp. sugar
- 1¼ tsp. ground cinnamon, divided
- 1 tsp. vanilla extract
- ¼ cup all-purpose flour
- 2 Tbsp. brown sugar
- 2 Tbsp. cold butter
- Maple syrup, optional

1. Arrange half the bread in a 13x9-in. baking dish coated with cooking spray. Top with peaches, pecans and remaining bread.
2. In a small bowl, whisk the eggs, egg whites, milk, sugar, 1 tsp. cinnamon and the vanilla; pour over bread. Cover and refrigerate for 8 hours or overnight.
3. Remove from refrigerator 30 minutes before baking. Bake, uncovered, at 400° for 20 minutes.
4. In a small bowl, combine flour, brown sugar and remaining ¼ tsp. cinnamon; cut in butter until crumbly. Sprinkle over French toast. Bake 5-10 minutes longer or until a knife inserted in the center comes out clean. Serve with syrup if desired.

1 PIECE 267 cal., 8g fat (3g sat. fat), 92mg chol., 368mg sod., 39g carb. (13g sugars, 2g fiber), 10g pro.

NOTES

PROTEIN
BOOST
PAGE 320

12g Pro

PROTEIN WAFFLES

We packed these waffles with protein from eggs, oats, Greek yogurt and even a little vanilla protein powder. They'll power you through the morning.
—Taste of Home *Test Kitchen*

TAKES: 30 MIN. • **MAKES:** 4 WAFFLES

- 3 large eggs, room temperature
- 1 cup old-fashioned oats
- ¾ cup plain whole milk Greek yogurt
- ¼ cup vanilla whey protein powder
- 3 Tbsp. plain oat milk
- 2 Tbsp. honey
- 1¼ tsp. vanilla extract
- ¾ tsp. baking soda
- ¾ tsp. baking powder
- ½ tsp. ground cinnamon
- ¼ tsp. salt
- Optional: Maple syrup and fresh fruit

Preheat waffle maker. Place the first 11 ingredients in a blender; cover and process until smooth. Bake waffles according to maker manufacturer's directions until golden brown. If desired, serve with maple syrup and fresh fruit.

FREEZE OPTION Cool waffles on wire racks. Freeze between layers of waxed paper in an airtight container. Reheat waffles in a toaster on medium setting. Or, microwave each waffle on high until heated through, 30-60 seconds.

1 WAFFLE 250 cal., 10g fat (4g sat. fat), 153mg chol., 591mg sod., 30g carb. (15g sugars, 3g fiber), 12g pro.

8g Pro

MUFFIN-TIN SCRAMBLED EGGS

I made these one year at Christmas as a way to save time, and they were a big hit. I have to make a large batch because my husband and boys can polish them off in a short amount of time. These also freeze very well, if there are any left!
—Jill Darin, Geneseo, IL

PREP: 15 MIN. • **BAKE:** 20 MIN. + STANDING
MAKES: 2 DOZEN

- 24 large eggs
- 1 tsp. salt
- ½ tsp. pepper
- ¼ tsp. garlic powder
- 1 jar (4 oz.) sliced mushrooms, finely chopped
- 1 can (4 oz.) chopped green chiles
- 3 oz. sliced deli ham, finely chopped
- ½ medium onion, finely chopped
- ½ cup shredded cheddar cheese
- Pico de gallo, optional

1. Preheat the oven to 350°. In a large bowl, whisk eggs, salt, pepper and garlic powder until blended. Stir in mushrooms, chiles, ham, onion and cheese. Spoon about ¼ cup mixture into each of 24 greased muffin cups.

2. Bake until eggs are set, 18-20 minutes, rotating pans halfway through baking. Let stand 10 minutes before removing from pans. If desired, serve with pico de gallo.

FREEZE OPTION Freeze cooled baked egg cups in airtight freezer containers. To use, microwave each serving on high for 1¼-1½ minutes or until heated through.

1 EGG CUP 88 cal., 6g fat (2g sat. fat), 190mg chol., 257mg sod., 1g carb. (0 sugars, 0 fiber), 8g pro.

PROTEIN
BOOST
PAGE 320

16g Pro

TROPICAL SMOOTHIE BOWL

This wake-me-up smoothie bowl with fruit, oats and cinnamon helps me start the day feeling satisfied. Sometimes I top it off with granola and berries or cherries.
—Jonelle Dansie, Murray, UT

TAKES: 10 MIN. • **MAKES:** 2 SERVINGS

- 2 Tbsp. frozen orange juice concentrate, thawed
- ¾ cup peeled fresh or frozen mango chunks, thawed
- ¾ cup cubed fresh or frozen pineapple
- ¼ cup quick-cooking oats
- ¼ cup vanilla soy or whey protein powder
- 2 Tbsp. ground flaxseed
- ¼ tsp. ground cinnamon
- ¼ tsp. ground nutmeg
- 1 cup cold water
- Optional toppings: Granola, chopped mango and pineapple

Place orange juice concentrate in a blender. Add fruits, oats, protein powder, flaxseed, seasonings and water. Cover and process until smooth. If desired, garnish with the optional toppings. Serve immediately.

NOTE If desired, 1½ cups fresh or thawed frozen pitted sweet cherries may be substituted for the mango and pineapple. Top with additional cherries and granola.

1¼ CUPS 236 cal., 5g fat (1g sat. fat), 0 chol., 5mg sod., 37g carb. (22g sugars, 7g fiber), 16g pro.

NOTES

13g Pro

PROSCIUTTO EGG PANINI

Change up the usual bacon and egg sandwich by piling on prosciutto instead. It's a breakfast worth waking up for!
—Erin Mylroie, Santa Clara, UT

TAKES: 30 MIN. • **MAKES:** 8 SERVINGS

- 3 large eggs
- 2 large egg whites
- 6 Tbsp. fat-free milk
- 1 green onion, thinly sliced
- 1 Tbsp. Dijon mustard
- 1 Tbsp. maple syrup
- 8 slices sourdough bread
- 8 thin slices prosciutto or deli ham
- ½ cup shredded sharp cheddar cheese
- 8 tsp. butter

1. In a small bowl, whisk eggs, egg whites, milk and onion. Coat a large skillet with cooking spray and place over medium heat. Add egg mixture; cook and stir until completely set.
2. Combine the mustard and syrup; spread over 4 bread slices. Layer with scrambled eggs, prosciutto and cheese; top with remaining bread. Butter the outsides of sandwiches.
3. Cook on a panini maker or indoor grill for 3-4 minutes or until bread is browned and cheese is melted. Cut each sandwich in half to serve.

½ SANDWICH 228 cal., 10g fat (5g sat. fat), 111mg chol., 640mg sod., 21g carb. (3g sugars, 1g fiber), 13g pro.

AGED FOR FLAVOR

Sharp cheddar cheese has been aged longer than regular cheddar. As cheese ages, its flavor becomes more pronounced. Using aged cheese in a recipe can add complexity and rich flavor, even to humble favorites like mac and cheese.

10g Pro

CINNAMON APPLE PANCAKES

My family loves these light and fluffy apple cinnamon pancakes. And, best of all, they're sweet enough to enjoy even without syrup.
—Kim McConnell, Tulsa, OK

TAKES: 25 MIN. • **MAKES:** 6 SERVINGS

- 2 cups whole wheat flour
- 4 tsp. baking powder
- 1 tsp. ground cinnamon
- ½ tsp. salt
- 2 large eggs, room temperature
- 2 cups fat-free milk
- 2 Tbsp. honey
- 1 Tbsp. canola oil
- 1 medium apple, chopped

1. In a bowl, whisk together the first 4 ingredients. In another bowl, whisk together eggs, milk, honey and oil; add to dry ingredients, stirring just until moistened. Stir in apple.

2. Preheat a lightly greased griddle over medium heat. Pour batter by ⅓ cupfuls onto griddle; turn when bubbles form on top. Cook until second side is golden brown.

2 PANCAKES 241 cal., 5g fat (1g sat. fat), 64mg chol., 576mg sod., 42g carb. (12g sugars, 5g fiber), 10g pro.

16g Pro

SAUSAGE & EGG GRITS

I always eat my sausage, grits and eggs together, so I thought it would be fun to mix them up in the same skillet. The resulting breakfast bombshell is loaded with down-home flavor—and it doesn't even use any butter!
—Jeannine Quiller, Raleigh, NC

PREP: 15 MIN. • **COOK:** 20 MIN.
MAKES: 6 SERVINGS

- 4 breakfast turkey sausage links, casings removed
- 1½ cups egg substitute
- 1¼ cups whole milk, divided
- 3 cups water
- ⅛ tsp. salt
- 1 cup quick-cooking grits
- ¾ cup shredded reduced-fat cheddar cheese, divided
- 2 green onions, chopped
- ⅛ tsp. pepper

1. Crumble sausage into a large skillet; cook over medium heat until no longer pink. Remove to paper towels with a slotted spoon. Whisk together egg substitute and ¼ cup milk; add to same skillet. Cook and stir until set; remove from the heat.
2. Meanwhile, in a Dutch oven, bring water, salt and remaining 1 cup milk to a boil. Slowly stir in grits. Reduce heat; cook and stir until thickened, 5-7 minutes.
3. Stir in half the cheese. Add sausage, eggs, green onions and pepper; heat through. Serve in bowls; sprinkle with remaining cheese.

1 CUP 208 cal., 6g fat (3g sat. fat), 25mg chol., 369mg sod., 24g carb. (4g sugars, 1g fiber), 16g pro.

> I was super skeptical making it, but when I took my first bite, I became a believer. Such a good recipe, thanks!
>
> —MIKE, TASTEOFHOME.COM

10g Pro

TURKEY BREAKFAST SAUSAGE

These hearty sausage patties are loaded with flavor but also contain a fraction of the sodium and fat found in commercial breakfast links.
—Judy Culbertson, Dansville, NY

TAKES: 20 MIN. • **MAKES:** 8 SERVINGS

- 1 lb. lean ground turkey
- ¾ tsp. salt
- ½ tsp. rubbed sage
- ½ tsp. pepper
- ¼ tsp. ground ginger

1. Crumble turkey into a large bowl. Add the salt, sage, pepper and ginger; mix lightly but thoroughly. Shape into eight 2-in. patties.
2. In a greased cast-iron or other heavy skillet, cook patties over medium heat until a thermometer reads 165° and juices run clear, 4-6 minutes on each side.

1 PATTY 85 cal., 5g fat (1g sat. fat), 45mg chol., 275mg sod., 0 carb. (0 sugars, 0 fiber), 10g pro.

LOWER-SODIUM BREAKFAST SAUSAGE

Turkey breakfast sausage is naturally leaner than pork patties. But the homemade version gives you an added edge in that it lets you control the sodium. These patties have 25% less sodium than the leading commercially prepared turkey breakfast sausage.

22g Pro

FRENCH OMELET

This cheesy omelet is modeled after one I tasted and loved in a local restaurant. Mine is so hearty and rich-tasting that no one will guess it's lower in fat.
—Bernice Morris, Marshfield, MO

TAKES: 20 MIN. • **MAKES:** 2 SERVINGS

- 2 large eggs
- 4 large egg whites
- ¼ cup fat-free milk
- ⅛ tsp. salt
- ⅛ tsp. pepper
- ¼ cup cubed fully cooked ham
- 1 Tbsp. chopped onion
- 1 Tbsp. chopped green pepper
- ¼ cup shredded reduced-fat cheddar cheese

1. Whisk together first 5 ingredients.
2. Place a 10-in. skillet coated with cooking spray over medium heat. Pour in egg mixture. Mixture should set immediately at edges. As eggs set, push cooked portions toward the center, letting uncooked eggs flow underneath. When eggs are thickened and no liquid egg remains, top 1 half with remaining ingredients. Fold omelet in half. Cut in half to serve.

½ OMELET 186 cal., 9g fat (4g sat. fat), 207mg chol., 648mg sod., 4g carb. (3g sugars, 0 fiber), 22g pro.

10g Pro

PIGS IN A POOL

My kids love sausages and pancakes, but making them for breakfast on a busy weekday is out of the question. My homemade version of pigs in a blanket is a thrifty alternative to the packaged kind, and they freeze like a dream.
—Lisa Dodd, Greenville, SC

PREP: 45 MIN. • **BAKE:** 20 MIN.
MAKES: 4 DOZEN

- 1 lb. reduced-fat bulk pork sausage
- 2 cups all-purpose flour
- ¼ cup sugar
- 1 Tbsp. baking powder
- 1 tsp. salt
- ½ tsp. ground cinnamon
- ¼ tsp. ground nutmeg
- 1 large egg, room temperature, lightly beaten
- 2 cups fat-free milk
- 2 Tbsp. canola oil
- 2 Tbsp. honey
- Maple syrup, optional

1. Preheat oven to 350°. Coat 48 mini muffin cups with cooking spray.
2. Shape sausage into forty-eight ¾-in. balls. Place meatballs on a rack coated with cooking spray in a shallow baking pan. Bake until cooked through, 15-20 minutes. Drain on paper towels.
3. In a large bowl, whisk flour, sugar, baking powder, salt and spices. In another bowl, whisk egg, milk, oil and honey until blended. Add to the flour mixture; stir just until moistened.
4. Place a sausage ball in each mini muffin cup; cover with batter. Bake until lightly browned, 20-25 minutes. Cool 5 minutes before removing from pans to wire racks. Serve warm, with syrup if desired.

FREEZE OPTION Freeze cooled muffins in airtight freezer containers. To use, microwave each muffin on high until heated through, 20-30 seconds.

4 MINI MUFFINS 234 cal., 10g fat (3g sat. fat), 45mg chol., 560mg sod., 26g carb. (9g sugars, 1g fiber), 10g pro.

9g Pro

YOGURT PANCAKES

Get your day off to a great start with these yummy pancakes. Short on time? Make a batch on the weekend!
—Cheryll Baber, Homedale, ID

TAKES: 30 MIN. • **MAKES:** 1 DOZEN

- 2 cups all-purpose flour
- 2 Tbsp. sugar
- 2 tsp. baking powder
- 1 tsp. baking soda
- 2 large eggs, room temperature, lightly beaten
- 2 cups plain yogurt
- ¼ cup water
- Optional: Semisweet chocolate chips, dried cranberries, sliced ripe bananas and coarsely chopped pecans

1. In a small bowl, combine the flour, sugar, baking powder and baking soda. In another bowl, whisk the eggs, yogurt and water. Stir into dry ingredients just until moistened.

2. Pour the batter by ¼ cupfuls onto a hot griddle coated with cooking spray. Sprinkle with optional ingredients if desired. Turn when bubbles form on top; cook until the second side is golden brown.

FREEZE OPTION Arrange cooled pancakes in a single layer on baking sheets. Freeze overnight or until frozen. Transfer to a freezer container. May be frozen for up to 2 months. To use, place pancakes on a microwave-safe plate; microwave on high for 40-50 seconds or until heated through.

2 PANCAKES 242 cal., 5g fat (2g sat. fat), 73mg chol., 432mg sod., 40g carb. (8g sugars, 1g fiber), 9g pro.

MIXING MATTERS

The key to fluffy pancakes is not to overmix the batter, which overworks the gluten in the flour. Use a gentle hand when folding the wet ingredients into the dry ingredients, and mix until just incorporated.

13g Pro

MIXED BERRY FRENCH TOAST BAKE

I just love this recipe! It's perfect for fuss-free holiday breakfasts or laid-back guests. It's scrumptious and so easy to put together the night before.
—Amy Berry, Poland, ME

PREP: 20 MIN. + CHILLING • **BAKE:** 45 MIN.
MAKES: 8 SERVINGS

- 6 large eggs
- 1¾ cups fat-free milk
- 1 tsp. sugar
- 1 tsp. ground cinnamon
- 1 tsp. vanilla extract
- ¼ tsp. salt
- 1 loaf (1 lb.) French bread, cubed
- 1 pkg. (12 oz.) frozen unsweetened mixed berries
- 2 Tbsp. cold butter
- ⅓ cup packed brown sugar
- Optional: Confectioners' sugar and maple syrup

1. Whisk together first 6 ingredients. Place bread cubes in a 13x9-in. or 3-qt. baking dish coated with cooking spray. Pour egg mixture over top. Refrigerate, covered, 8 hours or overnight.
2. Preheat oven to 350°. Remove berries from freezer and French toast mixture from refrigerator and let stand while oven heats. Bake French toast mixture, covered, 30 minutes.
3. In a small bowl, cut butter into brown sugar until crumbly. Top French toast mixture with berries; sprinkle with brown sugar mixture. Bake, uncovered, until a knife inserted in the center comes out clean, 15-20 minutes. If desired, dust with confectioners' sugar and serve with syrup.
1 SERVING 310 cal., 8g fat (3g sat. fat), 148mg chol., 517mg sod., 46g carb. (17g sugars, 3g fiber), 13g pro.

12g Pro

PORTOBELLO MUSHROOMS FLORENTINE

This fun and surprisingly hearty breakfast dish is packed with flavor and richness.
—Sara Morris, Laguna Beach, CA

TAKES: 25 MIN. • **MAKES:** 2 SERVINGS

- 2 large portobello mushrooms, stems removed
- Cooking spray
- ⅛ tsp. garlic salt
- ⅛ tsp. pepper
- ½ tsp. olive oil
- 1 small onion, chopped
- 1 cup fresh baby spinach
- 2 large eggs
- ⅛ tsp. salt
- ¼ cup crumbled goat cheese or feta cheese
- Minced fresh basil, optional

1. Preheat oven to 425°. Spritz the mushrooms with cooking spray; place in a 15x10x1-in. pan stem side up. Sprinkle with garlic salt and pepper. Bake, uncovered, until tender, about 10 minutes.
2. Meanwhile, in a nonstick skillet, heat oil over medium-high heat; saute onion until tender. Stir in spinach until wilted.
3. Whisk together eggs and salt; add to skillet. Cook and stir until eggs are thickened and no liquid egg remains; spoon onto mushrooms. Sprinkle with cheese and, if desired, basil.
1 STUFFED MUSHROOM 170 cal., 10g fat (4g sat. fat), 204mg chol., 428mg sod., 9g carb. (3g sugars, 3g fiber), 12g pro.

10g Pro

SAVORY TOMATO & OLIVE OATMEAL

Who says oatmeal has to be sweet? I love this recipe because it starts my day in a healthy, fulfilling way. The fresh garlic, tomatoes and basil are bright notes in a breakfast that keeps me satisfied until lunch. The oatmeal gives me protein and fiber, and I add a splash of extra virgin olive oil at the end for heart health.
—Roland McAmis Jr., Greeneville, TN

TAKES: 20 MIN. • **MAKES:** 1 SERVING

- 1 cup reduced-sodium chicken broth
- 1 medium tomato, chopped
- ½ cup quick-cooking oats
- 1 garlic clove, minced
- 3 Greek olives, chopped
- 1 Tbsp. chopped fresh basil
- Optional: Additional chopped fresh basil, grated Parmesan cheese, sunny-side up large egg and additional virgin olive oil

In a small saucepan, bring broth to a boil over medium-high heat. Stir in tomato, oats and garlic; reduce heat and simmer 2 minutes. Remove from heat; stir in olives and basil. Add toppings as desired.
1½ CUPS 222 cal., 6g fat (1g sat. fat), 0 chol., 761mg sod., 35g carb. (5g sugars, 5g fiber), 10g pro.

SERVE IT YOUR WAY

You can top savory oatmeal with some diced avocado and crumbled feta cheese, and add some fresh or dried herbs like oregano or parsley to the mixture. Also, feel free to add additional protein, like cooked Italian pork sausage or cooked ground chicken.

31g Pro

POWERHOUSE PROTEIN PARFAITS

Parfaits have marvelous taste and texture, but many are loaded with sugar and leave you peckish for more. Here's my protein-inspired option with yogurt, fruit and nuts.
—Jen Hubin, Minnetonka, MN

TAKES: 15 MIN. • **MAKES:** 4 SERVINGS

- 3 cups fat-free plain Greek yogurt
- ¼ to ⅓ cup honey
- 2 tsp. grated orange zest
- 2 cups Kashi Go Lean Crunch cereal
- 2 cups orange segments
- 2 cups fresh raspberries
- ¼ cup sliced almonds, toasted

In a bowl, mix yogurt, honey and orange zest until blended. Layer half the yogurt mixture, cereal, orange segments and raspberries among 4 parfait glasses. Repeat layers; sprinkle with almonds. Serve immediately.
1 PARFAIT 422 cal., 5g fat (1g sat. fat), 0 chol., 157mg sod., 71g carb. (46g sugars, 12g fiber), 31g pro.

PAGE 320

10g Pro

STRAWBERRY-CARROT SMOOTHIES

My children resist veggies, but they love smoothies. This smoothie packs in lots of good-for-you fruits and veggies. But to my kids, it's just a super delicious breakfast.
—Elisabeth Larsen, Pleasant Grove, UT

TAKES: 5 MIN. • **MAKES:** 5 SERVINGS

- 2 cups reduced-fat plain Greek yogurt
- 1 cup carrot juice
- 1 cup orange juice
- 1 cup frozen pineapple chunks
- 1 cup frozen unsweetened sliced strawberries

Place all ingredients in a blender; cover and process until smooth.
1 CUP 141 cal., 2g fat (1g sat. fat), 5mg chol., 79mg sod., 20g carb. (15g sugars, 1g fiber), 10g pro.

CARROT SMOOTHIE TIPS

Can you taste carrots in smoothies? You can taste the carrots, but they're high in natural sugars and make a delightful complement to other sweet ingredients, such as strawberries.

Do you peel carrots for smoothies? It's up to you! As long as your carrots are washed, you can peel or not peel them according to your preference (and how much time you have).

17g Pro

PROTEIN PANCAKES

Try stirring in cacao nibs, blueberries or chopped pecans to make these pancakes your own. For the best flavor, toast the nuts before adding them to the batter.
—April Preisler, Auburn, CA

TAKES: 25 MIN. • **MAKES:** 4 SERVINGS

- 1 cup almond flour
- 2 tsp. baking powder
- ½ tsp. baking soda
- ¼ tsp. ground cinnamon
- Dash salt
- 1 to 2 Tbsp. protein powder, optional
- 1 large egg, room temperature, lightly beaten
- 1 cup fat-free plain Greek yogurt
- ⅓ cup mashed ripe banana
- 1½ tsp. olive oil

1. In a large bowl, combine flour, baking powder, baking soda, cinnamon and salt. If desired, add protein powder. In a second bowl, combine egg, yogurt, banana and oil; stir into dry ingredients just until moistened.

2. Pour the batter by ¼ cupfuls onto a greased hot griddle. Turn when bubbles form on top; cook until second side is golden brown.

2 PANCAKES 259 cal., 13g fat (1g sat. fat), 47mg chol., 482mg sod., 20g carb. (9g sugars, 3g fiber), 17g pro.

NOTES

8g Pro

APPLE-SAGE SAUSAGE PATTIES

Apple and sausage naturally go together. Add sage, and you've got standout patties. They're freezer-friendly, so make them ahead and grab when needed.
—Scarlett Elrod, Newnan, GA

PREP: 35 MIN. + CHILLING
COOK: 10 MIN./BATCH
MAKES: 16 SERVINGS

- 1 large apple
- 1 large egg, lightly beaten
- ½ cup chopped fresh parsley
- 3 to 4 Tbsp. minced fresh sage
- 2 garlic cloves, minced
- 1¼ tsp. salt
- ½ tsp. pepper
- ½ tsp. crushed red pepper flakes
- 1¼ lbs. lean ground turkey
- 6 tsp. olive oil, divided

1. Peel and coarsely shred apple; place apple shreds in a colander over a plate. Let stand 15 minutes. Squeeze and blot dry with paper towels.

2. In a large bowl, combine egg, parsley, sage, garlic, seasonings and apple. Add turkey; mix lightly but thoroughly. Shape into sixteen 2-in. patties. Place patties on waxed paper-lined baking sheets. Refrigerate patties, covered, 8 hours or overnight.

3. In a large nonstick skillet, heat 2 tsp. oil over medium heat. In batches, cook patties 3-4 minutes on each side or until golden brown and a thermometer reads 165°, adding more oil as needed.

FREEZE OPTION Place uncooked patties on waxed paper-lined baking sheets; wrap and freeze until firm. Remove from pans and transfer to a freezer container; return to freezer. To use, cook frozen patties as directed, increasing time to 4-5 minutes on each side.

1 PATTY 79 cal., 5g fat (1g sat. fat), 36mg chol., 211mg sod., 2g carb. (1g sugars, 0 fiber), 8g pro.

NOTES

11g Pro 5i

STRAWBERRY-LIME QUINOA PARFAITS

When I serve quinoa with strawberries and Key lime pie yogurt, friends scrape the bottoms of their parfait glasses to get every delectable bite.
—Bev Jones, Brunswick, MO

PREP: 10 MIN. • **COOK:** 15 MIN. + CHILLING
MAKES: 4 SERVINGS

- 1 cup water
- ½ cup quinoa, rinsed
- 2 tsp. grated lime zest
- 4 containers (6 oz. each) Key lime pie flavored yogurt
- 2⅔ cups sliced fresh strawberries
- ½ cup flaked coconut

1. In a small saucepan, bring water to a boil. Add quinoa. Reduce heat; simmer, covered, 12-15 minutes or until liquid is absorbed. Remove from heat; fluff with a fork. Stir in lime zest; refrigerate 30 minutes.
2. In 4 parfait glasses, layer ⅓ cup yogurt, ⅓ cup strawberries, ¼ cup quinoa mixture and 1 Tbsp. coconut. Repeat layers.

1 PARFAIT 341 cal., 8g fat (5g sat. fat), 9mg chol., 123mg sod., 60g carb. (43g sugars, 4g fiber), 11g pro.

27g Pro 5i

HASH BROWN BREAKFAST CASSEROLE

This savory, scrumptious recipe uses egg substitute for a dish with lower fat and cholesterol. Serve it with fresh fruit for a morning meal that will keep your family satisfied until lunch!
—Cindy Schneider, Sarasota, FL

PREP: 10 MIN. • **BAKE:** 40 MIN.
MAKES: 4 SERVINGS

- 4 cups frozen shredded hash brown potatoes, thawed
- 1½ cups egg substitute
- 1 cup finely chopped cooked chicken breast
- ½ tsp. garlic powder
- ½ tsp. pepper
- ¾ cup shredded reduced-fat cheddar cheese

1. Preheat oven to 350°. In a large bowl, combine hash browns, egg substitute, chicken, garlic powder and pepper. Transfer the mixture to a greased 8-in. square baking dish; sprinkle with cheese.
2. Bake, uncovered, until a knife inserted in the center comes out clean, 40-45 minutes. Let stand for 5 minutes before serving.

1 PIECE 223 cal., 6g fat (3g sat. fat), 42mg chol., 353mg sod., 16g carb. (2g sugars, 1g fiber), 27g pro.

10g Pro

PUMPKIN PIE OVERNIGHT OATS

Have dessert for breakfast with these pumpkin pie-inspired overnight oats. Simple and easy to make, this recipe creates a hearty breakfast that harnesses all the delicious flavors of fall with warm notes of cinnamon, clove, nutmeg and ginger.
—Molly Allen, Hood River, OR

PREP: 5 MIN. + CHILLING
MAKES: 2 SERVINGS

- 1 cup old-fashioned oats
- 4 Tbsp. packed brown sugar
- 1 tsp. pumpkin pie spice
- ⅔ cup 2% milk
- ½ cup canned pumpkin
- 5 Tbsp. plain Greek yogurt
- 1 tsp. vanilla extract

In a small bowl, whisk together oats, brown sugar and pumpkin pie spice. Stir in milk, pumpkin, yogurt and vanilla until combined. Divide into 2 containers. Cover; refrigerate overnight.

1 SERVING 366 cal., 8g fat (4g sat. fat), 16mg chol., 72mg sod., 65g carb. (36g sugars, 6g fiber), 10g pro.

15g Pro

SAUSAGE-SWEET POTATO HASH & EGGS

When I first began making this dish for breakfast, I served it with fried eggs on top. Now I sometimes make it for supper and serve it without eggs. It's fantastic when I want a dish I can make quickly with minimal cleanup.
—Nancy Murphy, Mount Dora, FL

TAKES: 25 MIN. • **MAKES:** 4 SERVINGS

- ½ lb. Italian turkey sausage links, casings removed
- 2 medium sweet potatoes, peeled and cut into ¼-in. cubes
- 2 medium Granny Smith apples, chopped
- ¼ cup dried cranberries
- ¼ cup chopped pecans
- ¼ tsp. salt
- 4 green onions, sliced
- 4 large eggs

1. In a large skillet coated with cooking spray, cook sausage and sweet potatoes over medium-high heat 8-10 minutes or until sausage is no longer pink, breaking sausage into crumbles.
2. Add apples, cranberries, pecans and salt; cook and stir 4-6 minutes longer or until potatoes are tender. Remove from pan; sprinkle with green onions. Keep warm.
3. Wipe skillet clean and coat with cooking spray; place skillet over medium-high heat. Break eggs, 1 at a time, into pan. Reduce heat to low. Cook to desired doneness, turning after whites are set if desired. Serve with hash.
1 SERVING 338 cal., 14g fat (3g sat. fat), 207mg chol., 465mg sod., 42g carb. (23g sugars, 6g fiber), 15g pro.

5g Pro 5i

LEAN GREEN SMOOTHIE

Kids love the unusual color of this frosty and flavorful smoothie. It's fine-tuned to their liking with bananas, creamy yogurt and spinach.
—Madison Mayberry, Ames, IA

TAKES: 10 MIN. • **MAKES:** 4 SERVINGS

- ¾ cup fat-free milk
- 1½ cups fat-free vanilla yogurt
- 1 cup ice cubes
- 1 cup fresh spinach
- 1 ripe medium banana
- 2 Tbsp. lemon juice

In a blender, combine all ingredients; cover and process for 30 seconds or until smooth. Pour into chilled glasses; serve immediately.
1 CUP 99 cal., 0 fat (0 sat. fat), 4mg chol., 24mg sod., 19g carb. (12g sugars, 1g fiber), 5g pro.

SNACKS, BITES & SWEETS

5g Pro

OATMEAL COOKIE TREATS

These wholesome, budget-friendly treats are great for a meal on the go. *—Angie Provence, Fayetteville, GA*

TAKES: 25 MIN.
MAKES: ABOUT 2½ DOZEN

- 2 large eggs, room temperature
- ¾ cup packed brown sugar
- ½ cup vegetable oil
- ¼ cup evaporated milk
- 1 tsp. vanilla extract
- 2½ cups old-fashioned oats
- ½ cup whole wheat flour
- ½ cup all-purpose flour
- ½ tsp. salt
- ¾ cup raisins
- ½ cup chopped walnuts

In a bowl, combine the first 5 ingredients; mix well. Combine oats, flours and salt; add to brown sugar mixture and mix well. Stir in raisins and walnuts. Drop by rounded tablespoonfuls onto greased baking sheets. Bake at 350° for 12-14 minutes or until set.

2 COOKIES 247 cal., 12g fat (2g sat. fat), 30mg chol., 97mg sod., 32g carb. (16g sugars, 2g fiber), 5g pro.

10g Pro

BANANAS FOSTER FROZEN PROTEIN DESSERT

I love this recipe because it's decadent while still being on the healthy side. It's high in protein too, so it feels like an indulgence while still providing good fuel for the body. *—Liz McLaughlin, Ramona, CA*

PREP: 35 MIN. + FREEZING
MAKES: 12 SERVINGS

- 1 pkg. (12 oz.) cream-filled oval vanilla sandwich cookies
- 1 cup freeze-dried banana slices, optional
- 4 cups (32 oz.) 4% cottage cheese
- 4 medium ripe bananas
- ⅓ cup coconut or regular granulated sugar
- 1 tsp. vanilla extract
- 1 jar (11½ oz.) salted caramel topping, warmed

1. Place the cookies and freeze-dried banana slices in a food processor; pulse until coarse crumbs form. Remove to a bowl. Place cottage cheese, bananas, coconut sugar and vanilla in food processor; process until blended.

2. In an 11x7-in. dish, layer a third each of the cottage cheese mixture, cookie mixture and caramel; repeat layers twice. Cover and freeze 6-8 hours or until firm. Let stand at room temperature for 10 minutes before serving.

1 PIECE 361 cal., 11g fat (4g sat. fat), 23mg chol., 404mg sod., 58g carb. (38g sugars, 1g fiber), 10g pro.

5g Pro

SPICED CARROT CAKE

My mom made this cake for my birthday one year because carrot cake is her favorite. Turns out, it's my favorite too! Now when I make it, I love it with lots of spice. The pumpkin pie spice is a perfect shortcut, but you could use a custom blend of cinnamon, ginger, nutmeg and cloves.
—Jaris Dykas, Knoxville, TN

PREP: 30 MIN. • **BAKE:** 20 MIN. + COOLING
MAKES: 16 SERVINGS

- 3 large eggs, room temperature
- 1 cup packed brown sugar
- ¾ cup fat-free plain yogurt
- ¼ cup canola oil
- 2 tsp. vanilla extract
- 2½ cups all-purpose flour
- 3 tsp. pumpkin pie spice
- 2 tsp. baking soda
- 1 tsp. salt
- 3 cups shredded carrots (about 6 medium)

FROSTING

- ½ cup heavy whipping cream
- 4 oz. reduced-fat cream cheese
- ½ cup confectioners' sugar

1. Preheat oven to 350°. Line bottoms of 2 greased 9-in. round baking pans with parchment; grease paper.

2. Beat first 5 ingredients until well blended. In another bowl, whisk together flour, pie spice, baking soda and salt; stir into egg mixture. Fold in carrots.

3. Transfer to prepared pans. Bake until a toothpick inserted in center comes out clean, 20-25 minutes. Cool in pans 10 minutes before removing to wire racks; remove paper. Cool completely.

4. For frosting, beat cream until soft peaks form. In another bowl, beat cream cheese and confectioners' sugar until smooth; gradually fold in whipped cream.

5. If cakes are domed, trim tops with a serrated knife. Spread frosting between layers and over top of cake. Refrigerate leftovers.

1 PIECE 241 cal., 9g fat (3g sat. fat), 49mg chol., 375mg sod., 36g carb. (19g sugars, 1g fiber), 5g pro.

NOTES

4g Pro

ROSEMARY WALNUTS

My Aunt Mary started making this recipe years ago, and each time we visited her she would have a batch ready for us. The use of cayenne adds an unexpected zing to the savory combo of rosemary and walnuts. When you need a good housewarming or hostess gift, double the batch and save one for yourself.
—Renee D. Ciancio, New Bern, NC

TAKES: 20 MIN. • **MAKES:** 2 CUPS

- 2 cups walnut halves
- Cooking spray
- 2 tsp. dried rosemary, crushed
- ½ tsp. kosher salt
- ¼ to ½ tsp. cayenne pepper

1. Place walnuts in a small bowl. Spritz with cooking spray. Add the seasonings; toss to coat. Place in a single layer on a baking sheet.
2. Bake at 350° for 10 minutes. Serve warm, or cool completely and store in an airtight container.
¼ CUP 166 cal., 17g fat (2g sat. fat), 0 chol., 118mg sod., 4g carb. (1g sugars, 2g fiber), 4g pro.

Excellent! Different from all the sweet nut recipes, and love the kick from the cayenne! Great savory nut recipe that I will definitely make again.

—AMEHART, TASTEOFHOME.COM

3g Pro

GINGER CARDAMOM TEA

I like to add a little spice to my tea, which is why I mix in the ginger and cardamom. Kick up your feet and relax with a steaming mug full of this comforting drink.
—Trisha Kruse, Eagle, ID

TAKES: 25 MIN. • **MAKES:** 4 SERVINGS

- 2 cups water
- 4 tsp. honey
- 1 Tbsp. minced fresh gingerroot
- ½ tsp. ground cardamom
- 6 tea bags
- 1½ cups fat-free milk

1. In a small saucepan, combine water, honey, ginger and cardamom; bring to a boil. Reduce heat; simmer 10 minutes.
2. Pour over tea bags in a 2-cup glass measuring cup. Steep 3-5 minutes according to taste. Strain tea back into saucepan, discarding ginger and tea bags. Stir in milk; heat through.
¾ CUP 55 cal., 0 fat (0 sat. fat), 2mg chol., 39mg sod., 11g carb. (10g sugars, 0 fiber), 3g pro.

14g Pro

OPEN-FACED ROAST BEEF SANDWICHES

Arugula brings the zing to this sandwich. I usually make extras because most people who taste these sandwiches want seconds.
—Mary Price, Youngstown, OH

TAKES: 15 MIN. • **MAKES:** 8 SERVINGS

- 1 lb. sliced deli roast beef
- 8 slices ciabatta bread (½ in. thick)
- 2 cups fresh arugula
- 2 cups torn romaine
- 4 tsp. olive oil
- 1 Tbsp. lemon juice
- 1 Tbsp. white wine vinegar
- 1½ tsp. prepared horseradish

Place roast beef on ciabatta slices. In a large bowl, combine arugula and romaine. In a small bowl, whisk remaining ingredients until blended. Drizzle over greens; toss to coat. Arrange over beef; serve immediately.

1 OPEN-FACED SANDWICH 150 cal., 5g fat (1g sat. fat), 32mg chol., 422mg sod., 14g carb. (1g sugars, 1g fiber), 14g pro.

3g Pro

RAISIN & HUMMUS PITA WEDGES

The best part about this easy hummus appetizer is that you can make your own hummus or, if you don't have time, you can purchase some at the store. It's a year-round food that everyone enjoys.
—Helene Stewart-Rainville, Sackets Harbor, NY

TAKES: 15 MIN. • **MAKES:** 8 SERVINGS

- ¼ cup golden raisins
- 1 Tbsp. chopped dates
- ½ cup boiling water
- 2 whole wheat pita breads (6 in.)
- ⅔ cup hummus
- Snipped fresh dill or dill weed, optional

1. Place raisins and dates in a small bowl. Cover with boiling water; let stand for 5 minutes. Drain well.
2. Cut each pita into 4 wedges. Spread with hummus; top with raisins, dates and, if desired, dill.
1 WEDGE 91 cal., 2g fat (0 sat. fat), 0 chol., 156mg sod., 16g carb. (4g sugars, 3g fiber), 3g pro.

3g Pro

GARLIC PUMPKIN SEEDS

Wondering what to do with all those leftover pumpkin seeds after carving your jack-o'-lantern? Here's the answer.
—Iola Egle, Bella Vista, AR

TAKES: 25 MIN. • **MAKES:** 2 CUPS

- 1 Tbsp. canola oil
- ½ tsp. celery salt
- ½ tsp. garlic powder
- ½ tsp. seasoned salt
- 2 cups fresh pumpkin seeds

1. In a small bowl, combine oil, celery salt, garlic powder and seasoned salt. Add pumpkin seeds to the mixture; toss to coat. Spread a quarter of the seeds in a single layer on a microwave-safe plate. Microwave, uncovered, on high for 1 minute; stir.
2. Microwave 2-3 minutes longer, stirring after each minute, until the seeds are crunchy and lightly browned. Repeat with remaining pumpkin seeds. Serve warm, or cool before storing in an airtight container.
¼ CUP 87 cal., 5g fat (1g sat. fat), 0 chol., 191mg sod., 9g carb. (0 sugars, 1g fiber), 3g pro.

7g Pro 5i

MATCHA CHIA PUDDING

This pudding is quick, easy and super healthy. Combine earthy matcha green tea powder, creamy almond milk and healthy chia seeds for superfood heaven in a little package. Top with tart raspberries and you've got a quick breakfast or perfect midday snack. It is gluten-free, vegan, paleo and whole 30 approved!
—Abra Pappa, New York, NY

PREP: 10 MIN. + CHILLING
MAKES: 4 SERVINGS

- 2 cups unsweetened almond milk
- 3 Tbsp. maple syrup
- 2 Tbsp. matcha (green tea powder)
- ½ cup chia seeds
- ½ cup fresh raspberries

In a large bowl, whisk together almond milk, maple syrup and matcha. Stir in chia seeds. Let mixture sit for 15 minutes, then stir again. Pour into 4 half-pint Mason jars or ramekins. Refrigerate, covered, until thickened, at least 2 hours. Garnish with fresh raspberries.

⅔ CUP 173 cal., 8g fat (1g sat. fat), 0 chol., 90mg sod., 21g carb. (10g sugars, 9g fiber), 7g pro.

MAKE IT YOUR OWN

Give your pudding recipe a spin and use whatever fresh or chopped dried fruits you have on hand—honeydew, pineapple and blueberries are all tasty options. Also consider adding granola, pistachios and dried coconut for more crunch and a satisfying boost of fat, protein or fiber.

These look so good! I'm going to make them soon.

—BRITTNEY109, TASTEOFHOME.COM

6g Pro 5i

FROZEN BERRY & YOGURT POPS

I enjoy these frozen yogurt pops because they double as a healthy snack and a cool, creamy sweet treat.
—Colleen Ludovice, Wauwatosa, WI

PREP: 15 MIN. + FREEZING
MAKES: 10 POPS

- 10 plastic or paper cups (3 oz. each)
- 2¾ cups fat-free honey Greek yogurt
- 1 cup mixed fresh berries
- ¼ cup water
- 2 Tbsp. sugar
- 10 wooden pop sticks

1. Fill each cup with about ¼ cup yogurt. Place berries, water and sugar in a food processor; pulse until berries are finely chopped. Spoon 1½ Tbsp. berry mixture into each cup. Stir gently with a pop stick to swirl.
2. Top cups with foil; insert pop sticks through foil. Freeze until firm.

1 POP 60 cal., 0 fat (0 sat. fat), 0 chol., 28mg sod., 9g carb. (8g sugars, 1g fiber), 6g pro.

FOR FROZEN CLEMENTINE & YOGURT SWIRL POPS Substitute 1 cup seeded clementine segments (about 5 medium) and ¼ cup orange juice for the berries, water and sugar; proceed as directed.

6g Pro

TENDER BISCUITS FOR TWO

These quick and easy rolls are low in fat but not in flavor. They'll dress up any weeknight meal.
—Ane Burke, Bella Vista, AR

TAKES: 30 MIN. • **MAKES:** 2 BISCUITS

- ⅓ cup self-rising flour
- 1 Tbsp. grated Parmesan cheese
- ⅛ tsp. garlic salt
- 3 Tbsp. reduced-fat cream cheese
- 3 Tbsp. fat-free milk
- 1 Tbsp. fat-free plain yogurt

1. In a small bowl, combine the flour, Parmesan cheese and garlic salt. Cut in cream cheese until mixture resembles coarse crumbs. Stir in milk and yogurt just until moistened.
2. Drop by scant ⅓ cupfuls 2 in. apart onto a baking sheet coated with cooking spray. Bake at 400° for 12-15 minutes or until golden brown. Serve warm.

1 BISCUIT 142 cal., 5g fat (4g sat. fat), 18mg chol., 497mg sod., 17g carb. (2g sugars, 0 fiber), 6g pro.

7g Pro

MEXICAN COCOA

The entire family will enjoy this festive drink. Cinnamon sticks give it a great flavor that kids will love.
—Patricia Nieh, Portola Valley, CA

TAKES: 15 MIN. • **MAKES:** 6 SERVINGS

- 4 cups fat-free milk
- 3 cinnamon sticks (3 in.)
- 5 oz. 53% cacao dark baking chocolate, coarsely chopped
- 1 tsp. vanilla extract
- Additional cinnamon sticks, optional

1. In a large saucepan, heat milk and cinnamon sticks over medium heat until bubbles form around sides of pan. Discard cinnamon sticks. Whisk in chocolate until smooth.
2. Remove from the heat; stir in vanilla. Serve in mugs with additional cinnamon sticks if desired.
¾ CUP 177 cal., 9g fat (5g sat. fat), 3mg chol., 85mg sod., 21g carb. (18g sugars, 2g fiber), 7g pro.

9g Pro

SPICED PARTY PEANUTS

These seasoned nuts have just the right blend of spices, sugar and heat to liven up a party. They also make a welcome holiday gift.
—Cynthia DeVol, Pataskala, OH

TAKES: 30 MIN. • **MAKES:** 3 CUPS

- 1 large egg white
- 1 tsp. water
- 3 cups unsalted dry roasted peanuts
- 1 Tbsp. sugar
- 1 tsp. ground cinnamon
- ½ tsp. cayenne pepper
- ¼ tsp. salt
- ¼ tsp. ground cumin
- ¼ tsp. ground coriander

1. In a large bowl, beat the egg white and water until frothy. Stir in peanuts. Combine sugar and spices; add to the peanut mixture, stirring gently to coat.
2. Transfer to an ungreased 15x10x1-in. baking pan. Bake at 325° for 20-25 minutes or until lightly browned, stirring twice. Cool on a wire rack. Store in an airtight container.
¼ CUP 220 cal., 18g fat (3g sat. fat), 0 chol., 56mg sod., 9g carb. (3g sugars, 3g fiber), 9g pro.

6g Pro 5i

HOMEMADE BONE BROTH

This rich broth is worth the effort. Use some in your favorite soup recipes that call for beef stock or broth, then freeze the rest for up to six months.
—Taste of Home *Test Kitchen*

PREP: 1¾ HOURS + COOLING
COOK: 8½ HOURS
MAKES: ABOUT 2½ QT.

- 4 lbs. meaty beef soup bones (beef shanks or short ribs)
- 2 medium onions, quartered
- 3 chopped medium carrots, optional
- 3 chopped celery ribs, optional
- ½ cup warm water (110° to 115°)
- ½ tsp. salt
- 3 bay leaves
- 3 garlic cloves, peeled
- 8 to 10 whole peppercorns
- Cold water

1. Place bones in a large stockpot or Dutch oven; add enough water to cover. Bring to a boil over medium-high heat; reduce heat and simmer 15 minutes. Drain, discarding liquid. Rinse bones; drain.

2. Meanwhile, preheat oven to 450°. In a large roasting pan, roast boiled bones , uncovered, 30 minutes. Add onions and, if desired, carrots and celery. Roast until bones and vegetables are dark brown, 30-45 minutes longer; drain fat.

3. Transfer bones and vegetables to a large stockpot or Dutch oven. Add ½ cup warm water to roasting pan; stir to loosen browned bits. Transfer pan juices to pot. Add salt, bay leaves, garlic, peppercorns and enough cold water just to cover. Slowly bring to a boil; this should take about 30 minutes. Reduce heat; simmer, covered with lid slightly ajar, 8-24 hours, skimming the foam occasionally. If necessary, add water to keep ingredients covered.

4. Remove beef bones; cool. Strain broth through a cheesecloth-lined colander placed over a bowl, discarding vegetables and seasonings. If using immediately, skim fat. Or, refrigerate 8 hours or overnight; remove fat from surface.

1 CUP 30 cal., 0 fat (0 sat. fat), 0 chol., 75mg sod., 0 carb. (0 sugars, 0 fiber), 6g pro.

If you want a clear broth, it's important not to let the mixture boil rapidly. Use the lowest setting you can get while maintaining a gentle bubble.

10g Pro

LIME-MARINATED SHRIMP SALAD

Ceviche is a seafood recipe of raw fish marinated in citrus juice, which cooks the fish without heat. This version starts with cooked shrimp and adds tomatoes, cucumbers and serrano peppers.
—Adan Franco, Milwaukee, WI

PREP: 25 MIN. + CHILLING
MAKES: 10 CUPS

- 1 large white onion, quartered
- 2 to 4 serrano peppers, seeded and coarsely chopped
- 2 medium cucumbers, peeled, quartered and seeds removed
- 2 large tomatoes, cut into chunks
- 2 lbs. peeled and deveined cooked shrimp (26-30 per lb.)
- ¾ cup lime juice
- ½ tsp. salt
- ¼ tsp. pepper
- Tortilla chips or tostada shells

1. Place onion and peppers in a food processor; pulse until finely chopped. Transfer to a large bowl. Place the cucumbers and tomatoes in food processor; pulse until finely chopped. Add to bowl.

2. Place shrimp in food processor; pulse until chopped. Add shrimp, lime juice, salt and pepper to vegetable mixture; toss to coat. Refrigerate until cold. Serve with tortilla chips or tostada shells.

NOTE Wear disposable gloves when cutting hot peppers; the oils can burn skin. Avoid touching your face.

½ CUP 61 cal., 1g fat (0 sat. fat), 69mg chol., 128mg sod., 4g carb. (1g sugars, 1g fiber), 10g pro.

NOTES

> I love that I don't have to deal with raw shrimp in this version of ceviche. It is easy, is fast and tastes fantastic!
>
> —WESOAR, TASTEOFHOME.COM

17g Pro

TERIYAKI BEEF JERKY

Jerky is a portable, chewy snack—and you can make your own with our recipe. The meat has a savory flavor and a bit of heat.
—Taste of Home *Test Kitchen*

PREP: 40 MIN. + MARINATING
BAKE: 3 HOURS + COOLING
MAKES: 8 SERVINGS

- 1 beef flank steak (1½ to 2 lbs.)
- ⅔ cup reduced-sodium soy sauce
- ⅔ cup Worcestershire sauce
- ¼ cup honey
- 3 tsp. coarsely ground pepper
- 2 tsp. onion powder
- 2 tsp. garlic powder
- 1½ tsp. crushed red pepper flakes
- 1 tsp. liquid smoke

1. Trim all visible fat from steak. Freeze, covered, until firm, about 30 minutes. Slice steak along the grain into long ⅛-in.-thick strips.

2. Transfer strips to a large resealable container. In a small bowl, whisk the remaining ingredients; add to beef. Seal container and turn beef to coat. Refrigerate 2 hours or overnight, turning occasionally.

3. Transfer beef and marinade to a large saucepan; bring to a boil. Reduce heat; simmer 5 minutes. Using tongs, remove beef from marinade. Drain on paper towels; pat dry. Discard marinade.

4. Preheat oven to 170°. Arrange beef strips in single layer on wire racks placed on 15x10x1-in. baking pans. Bake in oven until beef becomes dry and leathery, 3-4 hours, rotating pans occasionally. (Or, use a commercial dehydrator or smoker, following manufacturer's directions.)

5. Remove from oven; cool completely. Using paper towels, blot any beads of oil from jerky. Store jerky, covered, in refrigerator or freezer.

1 OZ. COOKED BEEF 132 cal., 6g fat (3g sat. fat), 40mg chol., 139mg sod., 2g carb. (1g sugars, 0 fiber), 17g pro.

DEHYDRATE IN A SMOKER To make in a smoker, omit liquid smoke. Follow Steps 1-3, then proceed with the recipe following the manufacturer's directions for temperature and time. We cooked ours at 170° for 2 hours.

8g Pro

AUNT KAREN'S SHRIMP SALAD

When unexpected company calls during the holidays, this salad is the perfect fit. It's quick to put together, too, leaving you more time to spend with your guests.
—Karen Moore, Jacksonville, FL

PREP: 10 MIN. • **COOK:** 10 MIN. + CHILLING
MAKES: 24 SERVINGS

- 2 lbs. uncooked shrimp (26-30 per lb.), peeled, deveined and halved
- 1 Tbsp. white vinegar
- 1 Tbsp. lemon juice
- 1 Tbsp. plus ⅓ cup mayonnaise, divided
- ½ tsp. garlic salt
- 2 celery ribs, chopped
- 5 hard-boiled large eggs, chopped
- ¼ cup chopped sweet red pepper
- 24 Bibb lettuce leaves or Boston lettuce leaves
- Sliced green onions, optional

1. In a Dutch oven or large saucepan, bring 6 cups water to a boil. Add shrimp; cook, uncovered, until shrimp turn pink, 3-5 minutes. Drain. Transfer to a large bowl. Add vinegar, lemon juice, 1 Tbsp. mayonnaise and the garlic salt; toss to coat. Refrigerate, covered, at least 4 hours or overnight.

2. To serve, stir in remaining ⅓ cup mayonnaise, celery, eggs and red pepper. Serve in lettuce leaves, using about ¼ cup filling for each salad cup. If desired, top with green onions.

1 SALAD CUP 74 cal., 4g fat (1g sat. fat), 85mg chol., 120mg sod., 1g carb. (0 sugars, 0 fiber), 8g pro.

3g Pro 5i

OLD BAY CRISPY KALE CHIPS

Here in East Hampton, New York, harvest time means big bunches of kale from local growers. These crunchy kale chips are delicious, super healthy and easy to make. I make them with seasoning to take the flavor up a notch. For extra zip, add a dash of cayenne pepper.
—Luanne Asta, Hampton Bays, NY

PREP: 10 MIN. • **BAKE:** 25 MIN.
MAKES: 4 SERVINGS

- 1 bunch kale, washed
- 2 Tbsp. olive oil
- 1 to 3 tsp. Old Bay Seasoning
  Sea salt, to taste

1. Preheat oven to 300°. Remove tough stems from kale, and tear leaves into large pieces. Place in a large bowl. Toss with olive oil and seasonings. Arrange the leaves in a single layer on greased baking sheets.

2. Bake, uncovered, 10 minutes and then rotate pans. Continue baking until crisp and just starting to brown, about 15 minutes longer. Let stand at least 5 minutes before serving.

1 SERVING 101 cal., 7g fat (1g sat. fat), 0 chol., 202mg sod., 8g carb. (0 sugars, 2g fiber), 3g pro.

PROTEIN
BOOST
PAGE 320

9g Pro

CILANTRO & LIME CHICKEN WITH SCOOPS

I came up with this recipe when I was preparing for a large party and wanted a healthy Tex-Mex chicken to serve in tortilla chip cups. You can make this party dish ahead of time to free yourself for time-sensitive dishes. Serve the chicken in tortilla cups or in any other savory, crispy cups you like. Enjoy the leftovers over salad greens or wrapped in tender tortillas for burritos.
—Lori C. Terry, Chicago, IL

PREP: 15 MIN. • **COOK:** 3½ HOURS
MAKES: 16 SERVINGS (4 CUPS)

- 1 lb. boneless skinless chicken breasts
- 2 tsp. chili powder
- 2 Tbsp. lime juice
- 1½ cups frozen petite corn, thawed
- 1½ cups chunky salsa
- 1½ cups finely shredded cheddar cheese
- 1 medium sweet red pepper, finely chopped
- 4 green onions, thinly sliced
- Minced fresh cilantro
- Baked tortilla chip scoops

1. Place chicken in a 1½-qt. slow cooker; sprinkle with chili powder and lime juice. Cook, covered, on low 3-4 hours or until tender.
2. Remove chicken; discard cooking juices. Shred chicken with 2 forks; return to slow cooker. Add corn and salsa; cook, covered, on low 30 minutes or until heated through, stirring occasionally.
3. Transfer to a large bowl if desired. Stir in cheese, pepper and green onions. Sprinkle with cilantro; serve with tortilla chip scoops.

¼ CUP CHICKEN MIXTURE 97 cal., 4g fat (2g sat. fat), 26mg chol., 183mg sod., 5g carb. (2g sugars, 1g fiber), 9g pro.

NOTES

8g Pro 5i

FROZEN BANANA TREATS

When we make these treats, my son is in charge of cutting the bananas with a butter knife, pushing in the wooden sticks and rolling the chocolate-covered banana in the granola. It's such fun!
—Aimee Lawrence, Wimberley, TX

PREP: 15 MIN. + FREEZING
MAKES: 8 SERVINGS

- 1½ cups granola without raisins, crushed
- 1 cup semisweet chocolate chips
- ⅓ cup creamy peanut butter
- 8 wooden pop sticks
- 4 large firm bananas, halved widthwise

1. Sprinkle granola onto a large piece of waxed paper; set aside. In a microwave, melt chocolate chips; stir until smooth. Stir in peanut butter until blended.
2. Insert a pop stick into each banana half. Spread with chocolate mixture; roll in granola. Wrap in foil and freeze for 24 hours.
1 SERVING 307 cal., 15g fat (5g sat. fat), 0 chol., 60mg sod., 44g carb. (23g sugars, 7g fiber), 8g pro.

7g Pro

EDAMAME HUMMUS

We love hummus at our house. This recipe is a scrumptious and refreshing twist on an old favorite. It's also a wonderful way to incorporate healthy soy into our diets.
—Marla Clark, Albuquerque, NM

TAKES: 15 MIN. • **MAKES:** 3 CUPS

- 1 pkg. (16 oz.) frozen shelled edamame, thawed
- ½ cup tahini
- ½ cup water
- ⅓ to ½ cup lemon juice
- 2 garlic cloves, minced
- 1 tsp. sea salt
- ¼ cup olive oil
- ¼ cup minced fresh mint
- 2 jalapeno peppers, seeded and chopped, optional
- Assorted fresh vegetables
- Rice crackers

Microwave edamame, covered, on high until tender, 2-3 minutes. Transfer to a food processor; add tahini, water, lemon juice, garlic, salt, oil, mint and, if desired, peppers. Process until smooth, 1-2 minutes. Serve with assorted fresh vegetables and rice crackers.
NOTE Wear disposable gloves when cutting hot peppers; the oils can burn skin. Avoid touching your face.
¼ CUP 166 cal., 13g fat (2g sat. fat), 0 chol., 167mg sod., 6g carb. (1g sugars, 2g fiber), 7g pro.

EDAMAME EXPLAINED

Edamame—soybeans that are harvested early, before the beans become hard—are a popular Asian food. The young beans are parboiled and frozen to retain their freshness. Look for them in the freezer section of grocery and health food stores. Known as a good source of fiber, protein, calcium and vitamin C, edamame are a tasty addition to soups, salads and main dishes. They are also delicious eaten alone as a healthy snack.

10g Pro

OPEN-FACED HAM & APPLE MELTS

As a homework snack or light lunch, these yummy melts mix sweet apple crunch, hearty ham and tangy Dijon flavors wonderfully.
—Sally Maloney, Dallas, GA

TAKES: 15 MIN. • **MAKES:** 4 SERVINGS

- 2 whole wheat English muffins, split
- 2 tsp. Dijon mustard
- 4 slices deli ham
- ½ medium apple, thinly sliced
- 2 slices reduced-fat Swiss cheese, halved

1. Place English muffin halves cut sides up on a baking sheet. Broil 4-6 in. from the heat for 2-3 minutes or until golden brown.
2. Spread with mustard. Top with ham, apple slices and cheese. Broil 3-4 minutes longer, until cheese is melted.
1 MUFFIN HALF 130 cal., 3g fat (1g sat. fat), 14mg chol., 429mg sod., 17g carb. (5g sugars, 3g fiber), 10g pro.

9g Pro

ZIPPY SHRIMP SKEWERS

These flavorful skewers deliver a mouthwatering kick with minimal effort. Fix them for your next party and watch them disappear.
—Jalayne Luckett, Marion, IL

PREP: 10 MIN. + MARINATING
GRILL: 5 MIN. • **MAKES:** 6 SERVINGS

- 2 Tbsp. brown sugar
- 2 tsp. cider vinegar
- 1½ tsp. canola oil
- 1 tsp. chili powder
- ½ tsp. salt
- ½ tsp. paprika
- ¼ tsp. hot pepper sauce
- ¾ lb. uncooked shrimp (31-40 per pound), peeled and deveined

1. In a large shallow dish, combine the first 7 ingredients; add shrimp. Turn to coat; cover and refrigerate for 2-4 hours.
2. Drain and discard marinade. Thread shrimp onto 6 metal or soaked wooden skewers. Grill, uncovered, on a lightly oiled rack over medium heat or broil 4 in. from the heat until shrimp turn pink, 2-3 minutes on each side.
1 SKEWER 57 cal., 1g fat (0 sat. fat), 84mg chol., 199mg sod., 2g carb. (2g sugars, 0 fiber), 9g pro.

11g Pro 5i

PROTEIN ICE CREAM

You'd never know this vanilla ice cream contains 10 grams of protein. Coconut milk creates a creamy base, while maple syrup and vanilla extract give it a subtly sweet flavor.
—Taste of Home *Test Kitchen*

PREP: 15 MIN. + FREEZING • **MAKES:** 1 QT.

- 1 can (13½ oz.) coconut milk
- 1½ cups whey protein powder (vanilla or chocolate)
- ⅓ cup maple syrup
- 1 tsp. vanilla extract
- ¼ tsp. salt
- ¼ cup miniature semisweet chocolate chips, optional

1. Place coconut milk, protein powder, maple syrup, vanilla extract and salt in a food processor or blender; puree until smooth. If desired, stir in mini chocolate chips.
2. Transfer mixture to 9x5-in. loaf pan. Freeze until firm, 3-4 hours. Let stand at room temperature for 15 minutes before serving.
½ CUP165 cal., 8g fat (8g sat. fat), 8mg chol., 122mg sod., 12g carb. (10g sugars, 0 fiber), 11g pro.

STAUB
STAUB

5g Pro

BUFFALO-STYLE CHICKEN CHILI DIP

Longing for that Buffalo wing flavor without the bones? This do-ahead dip freezes well in individual containers, so you can pull one out when you want to spread a little cheer.
—Brenda Calandrillo, Mahwah, NJ

PREP: 30 MIN. • **COOK:** 30 MIN.
MAKES: 11 CUPS

- 3 celery ribs, finely chopped
- 1 large onion, chopped
- 1 large carrot, finely chopped
- 5 garlic cloves, minced
- 2 Tbsp. butter
- 2 lbs. ground chicken
- 1 Tbsp. olive oil
- 2 cups chicken broth
- 1 can (16 oz.) kidney beans, rinsed and drained
- 1 can (15 oz.) cannellini beans, rinsed and drained
- 1 can (15 oz.) crushed tomatoes
- 1 can (15 oz.) tomato sauce
- 1 can (6 oz.) tomato paste
- ¼ cup Louisiana-style hot sauce
- 3 tsp. smoked paprika
- 1 bay leaf
- ¾ tsp. salt
- ¼ tsp. pepper
- Crumbled blue cheese, optional
- Celery stalks and tortilla chips

1. In a Dutch oven, saute the celery, onion, carrot and garlic in butter until tender. Remove and set aside. In the same pan, cook chicken in oil until meat is no longer pink; drain.
2. Stir in the broth, beans, tomatoes, tomato sauce, tomato paste, hot sauce, paprika, bay leaf, salt, pepper and vegetable mixture. Bring to a boil; reduce heat. Simmer, uncovered, for 12-15 minutes or until slightly thickened. Discard bay leaf.
3. Transfer desired amount of dip into serving dish; if desired, sprinkle with blue cheese. Serve with celery and chips. Cool remaining dip; transfer to freezer containers. Cover and freeze for up to 3 months.
4. To use frozen dip: Thaw dip in the refrigerator. Place in a saucepan; heat through. If desired, sprinkle with blue cheese. Serve with celery and chips.
¼ CUP 64 cal., 3g fat (1g sat. fat), 15mg chol., 192mg sod., 6g carb. (1g sugars, 1g fiber), 5g pro.

NOTES

INDEX

✓ INDICATES A GLP-1/POWER-PACKED RECIPE

G

H

I

P. 12

J

K

L

M

P. 108

T

P. 42

V

W

Y

Z